THE CAPTURED IMAGINATION

Drawings by Joan Miró from the Fundació Joan Miró, Barcelona

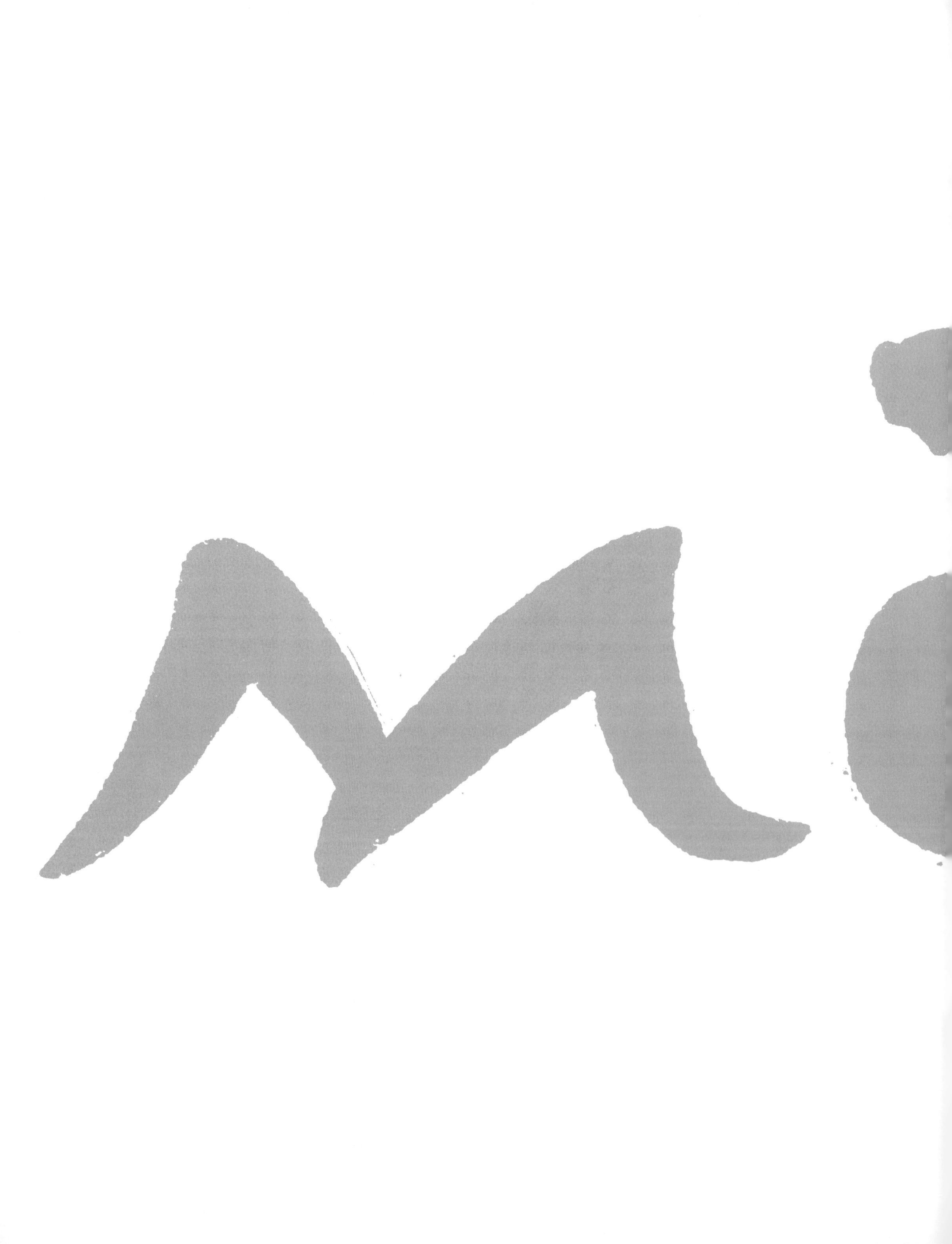

THE CAPTURED IMAGINATION

Drawings by Joan Miró
from the Fundació Joan Miró, Barcelona

Margit Rowell

The American Federation of Arts
Distributed by the
University of Pennsylvania Press

Exhibition Itinerary

Philadelphia Museum of Art Philadelphia, Pennsylvania	October 4–November 29, 1987
Fort Worth Art Museum Fort Worth, Texas	December 13, 1987–February 14, 1988
San Francisco Museum of Modern Art San Francisco, California	March 5–May 1, 1988

This catalogue has been published in conjunction with the exhibition, *The Captured Imagination: Drawings by Joan Miró from the Fundació Joan Miró, Barcelona,* which was organized by the American Federation of Arts.

The exhibition and publication have been made possible through the generous support of the National Endowment for the Arts and the National Patrons of the American Federation of Arts.

The catalogue has additionally been supported by The J.M. Kaplan Fund and the DeWitt Wallace Fund through the AFA's Revolving Fund for Publications.

International transportation provided by Iberia Airlines.

The American Federation of Arts is a national non-profit, educational organization, founded in 1909 to broaden the knowledge and appreciation of the arts of the past and present. Its primary activities are organizing exhibitions and film programs, which travel throughout the United States and abroad, and fostering a better understanding among nations by the international exchange of art.

Edited by Letitia Burns O'Connor, Perpetua Press
Designed by Dana Levy, Perpetua Press, Los Angeles
Composition by Continental Typographics, Chatsworth, CA
Printed by Dai Nippon Printing Company, Tokyo

AFA Exhibition No. 85–6

©1987 by The American Federation of Arts
Published by The American Federation of Arts
41 East 65th Street, New York, New York 10021
LCC: 87–070555
ISBN: 0–917418–82–4 (paperback)
ISBN: 0–8122–8086–5 (cloth bound)

Clothbound edition distributed by the University of Pennsylvania Press,
Blockley Hall, 418 Service Drive, Philadelphia, PA 19104

Contents

Acknowledgments

T*he Captured Imagination: Drawings by Joan Miró from the Fundació Joan Miró, Barcelona* has been organized by the American Federation of Arts in collaboration with the Fundació Joan Miró and under the curatorial supervision of Margit Rowell, Curator at the Musée National d'Art Moderne and recently appointed Director of Exhibitions for the Fundació Joan Miró. There has never before been an exhibition in this country devoted to this important artist's drawings, and it was for this reason that Ms. Rowell proposed the project as a valuable undertaking for the AFA.

There are many to whom the AFA is deeply indebted for the development and fruition of this exhibition and its accompanying publication. We wish to thank Mrs. Rosa Maria Malet, Director of the Fundació Joan Miró, who has generously made available the vast and relatively unseen resources of the collection. Mrs. Malet graciously assisted the AFA with all aspects of the exhibition and wrote the preface to this catalogue.

To Margit Rowell, guest curator and author of this catalogue, goes our deep appreciation for her keen curatorial vision and poetic insight into the drawings the artist has described as his "intimate documents."

We are also extremely grateful to Anne d'Harnoncourt, Ann Percy, and Suzanne Wells of the Philadelphia Museum of Art; E.A. Carmean of the Fort Worth Art Museum; and John R. Lane and Graham Beal of the San Francisco Museum of Modern Art for their early and enthusiastic support of the exhibition, which enabled us to organize such an excellent tour.

For their painstaking attention to the manuscript and the technical preparation of the catalogue, and for its elegant design, I would like to thank Letitia Burns O'Connor and Dana Levy of Perpetua Press in Los Angeles.

The AFA's work on this exhibition was initiated by my distinguished predecessor, Wilder Green, who deserves special credit for his commitment to a project of such importance. I would also like to thank Jane S. Tai, Associate Director for Exhibitions, and Jeffery Pavelka, former Director of the Exhibition Program, for their guidance of the project; Amy V. McEwen who as Exhibition Coordinator was fully involved in all aspects of the exhibition, its tour, and the catalogue production; Michaelyn Mitchell and James Stave who have also participated in the organization of the exhibition and the catalogue; Albina De Meio, Registrar, and Guillermo Alonso, Associate Registrar, for their assistance in bringing the exhibition from Barcelona and attending to its circulation around the country; and Sandra Gilbert, Public Information and Promotion Director, for her important efforts on behalf of the exhibition.

We would like to express our gratitude to the National Endowment for the Arts for their generous support of the exhibition. The catalogue has also been supported by The J.M. Kaplan Fund and the DeWitt Wallace Fund through the AFA's Revolving Fund for Publications.

Special gratitude is also extended to Iberia Airlines, which has provided the international transportation for this exhibition.

Finally, I would like to thank the National Patrons of the AFA, under the direction of Margot Linton and Joan Majeune, who have designated the project as the National Patron Exhibition of 1987.

MYRNA SMOOT
Director
The American Federation of Arts

Preface

The Fundació Joan Miró is pleased to have collaborated with the American Federation of Arts on the organization of an exhibition selected from one of the most striking features of its permanent collection, its collection of drawings, thus making them available to the American public for the first time. This collection of about five thousand pieces contains drawings done by Joan Miró throughout the course of his life, as well as prints and various notes. With the exception of the earliest representational drawings—landscapes or academic subjects, which were done from life—most of these drawings constitute the first, critical steps of the artist toward the final realization of a work. It would be a presumption, therefore, to ascribe a value to this material beyond that which it had for the artist himself, namely, as an instrument serving in function much like a paintbrush or palette.

These preliminary studies of most of his paintings furnish proof that reflection, rather than spontaneous impulse, informed Joan Miró's work, and that the end result stemmed from an intricate process of speculation.

I recall a remark Miró made after he donated his drawings to the Fundació. With a curious mixture of timidity and impishness, he exclaimed, "I've been left naked." His phrasing could not have been more explicit. The artist had just presented to the public eye material that had been previously undisclosed, which allows us to trace the creative process behind each of his paintings, to discern the pentimenti, and to grasp his concerns.

Contrary to what Miró could suppose, the collection of drawings has added, if it is possible, an even greater note of seduction to his work. If, in the past, the spectator shared in the magic of Miró's imagination, now, after these drawings have been made available to the public, he also participates in the alchemy that lay hidden behind it.

If this group of drawings indeed constitutes one of the most notable features of the Fundació's permanent collection, its donation by the artist himself leaves an important legacy that allows the scholar and spectator a fuller grasp of the breadth and significance of Miró's work. The Fundació's collection includes 180 paintings on various surfaces, 150 sculptures, and nine textiles, as well as the entire collection of his graphic work.

During its twelve years of existence, the Fundació Joan Miró has made use of this material to organize, both on site and elsewhere, exhibitions and activities promoting the study and dissemination of the work of its founder. In keeping with Miró's express wishes, the Fundació has also carried out an active exhibition program, which has earned it the distinction of being one of the most important centers for contemporary art in Spain today.

At the time when Joan Miró wanted to provide his native city with a center which, under his patronage, would carry out the activities outlined above, the political climate was unfavorable to any sort of enterprise that might challenge the imposed order. It was necessary, therefore, to find a legal solution that would assure the center's autonomy and complete liberty of action. The most feasible solution was to make the proposed center a private foundation, and so the Fundació Joan Miró opened its doors to the public in June, 1975.

The Fundació Joan Miró has a unique landmark to house its permanent collection and activities: a building designed especially for this purpose by the Catalan architect, Josef Lluis Sert. In designing the Fundacio's site, Sert, an intimate friend of Miró with a thorough understanding of his work and of the ideal conditions for its viewing, took two factors into special consideration: lighting and a spatial arrangement permitting fluid circulation. The even, diffuse lighting of the rooms is achieved through the use of skylights in the shape of quarter-cylinders which define, from the exterior, the characteristic outline of the building. The spatial arrangement is organized around a central courtyard, a concept adopted from the compluvium of the Roman house and medieval cloister, which has survived as one of the native elements of popular Mediterranean architecture, a style which had a very decisive influence on Sert.

Although the works of Joan Miró belonging to the Fundació are loaned to other institutions with fair regularity, the collection of drawings has seldom been exhibited outside of Sert's building. It is, therefore, a very special occasion for the Fundació to agree to loan a significant portion of its collection of drawings. Several factors influenced this decision. The first of these was the much-deserved prestige that the American Federation of Arts enjoys. The second factor was the prominent place that Miró occupies in both public and private collections throughout the United States, which suggests that the American public would appreciate this relevant material completing the panorama of Joan Miró's work. Finally, it struck us as particularly appropriate that Margit Rowell, a sound connoisseur of Miró and author of various studies on the artist, should be the curator responsible for handling the exhibition.

We wish to thank the Philadelphia Museum of Art, the Fort Worth Art Museum, and the San Francisco Museum of Modern Art for supporting this project of the American Federation of Arts, thus allowing this important exhibition of the Fundació Joan Miró to be shown in the United States.

ROSA MARIA MALET
Director of the Fundació Joan Miró

Introduction

The Captured Imagination

"The drawings I sometimes do before doing certain paintings are intimate *documents so to speak. They help me arrive at a complete formal divestiture and thus attain the* true expression of the spirit. *Once the paintings are finished, I destroy these drawings or else hold on to them to use as a springboard for other works."*[1]

The drawings in the collection of the Fundació Joan Miró in Barcelona were in Miró's possession until 1976. The existence of these "intimate documents" of the artist's image-making process was virtually unknown up to that time.[2] Miró did not consider himself a draftsman; he used drawing essentially as a medium through which to capture an inner vision and explore pictorial and sculptural ideas. These studies, once discovered, transformed his public image, forcing a reassessment of his proverbial identity as a truly childlike and completely spontaneous artist.

It had always been assumed that Miró was a painter who found his images and techniques directly on the canvas. These studies show that this evaluation was not entirely accurate. Miró's paintings were frequently an enlargement and development of a visual idea first captured on a tiny scrap of paper—the back of an envelope, a torn newspaper, invitations, bills, cigarette packages, boarding passes, metro tickets—or in one of the notebooks that he filled with sketches, particularly during the early years.

These drawings show the first elusive and momentary vision which, in a sense, took him by surprise. It was, of course, this effect of immediacy that Miró sought to create in his finished works (paintings, sculpture, prints). However, the paradox, as Miró came to understand it, was that to transmit that moment of revelation or discovery required an intense concentration and discipline. Although methodical rigor was part of Miró's character and temperament, the state of innocence and amazement he sought to

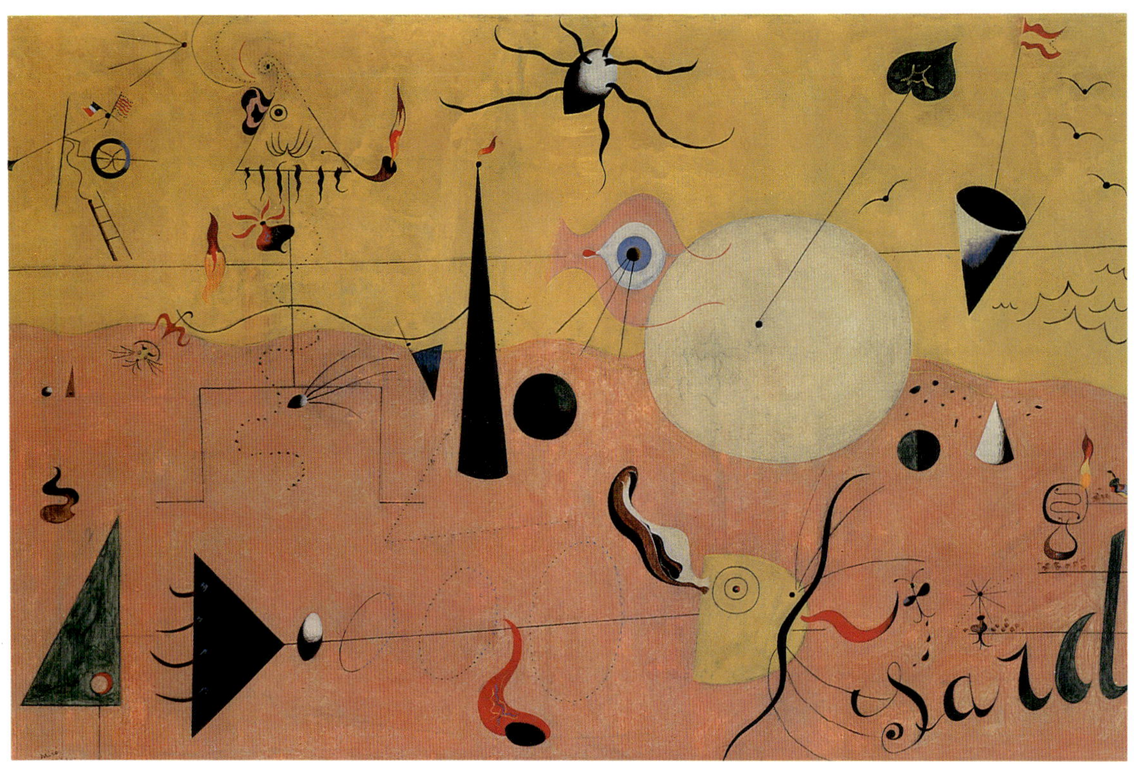

Figure A. Joan Miró. *The Hunter (Catalan Landscape)*, 1923–24

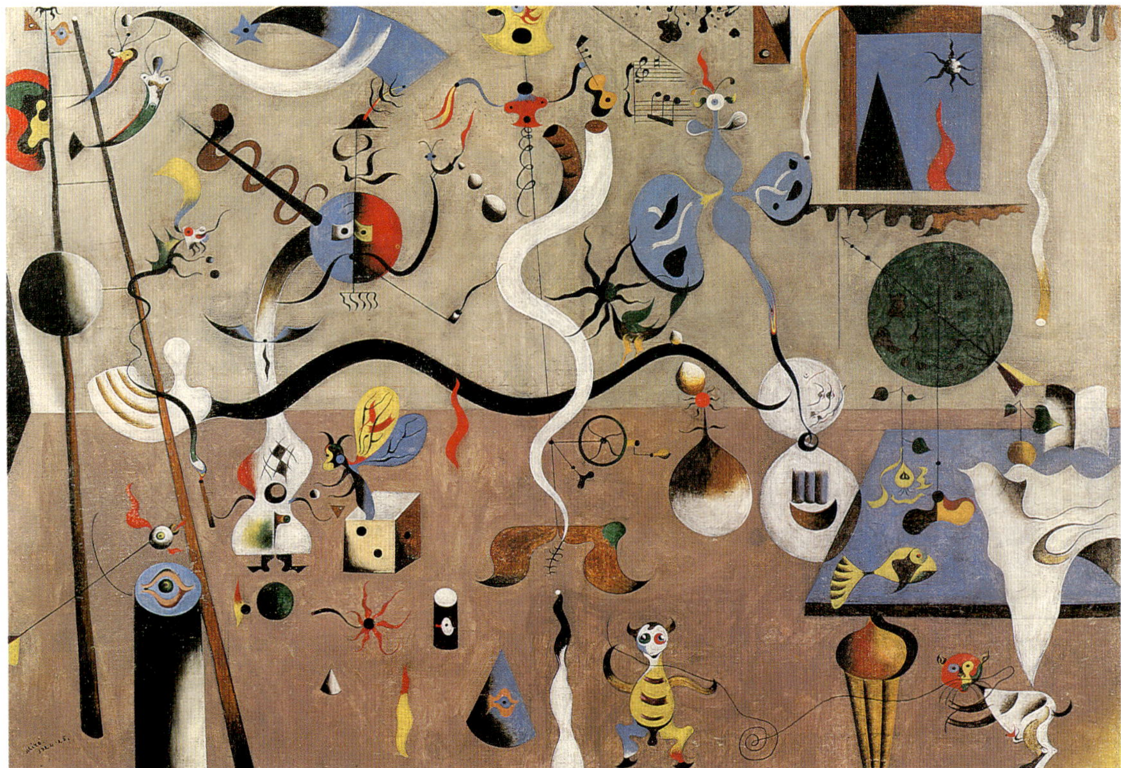

Figure C. Joan Miró. *Carnival of Harlequin,* 1924–25

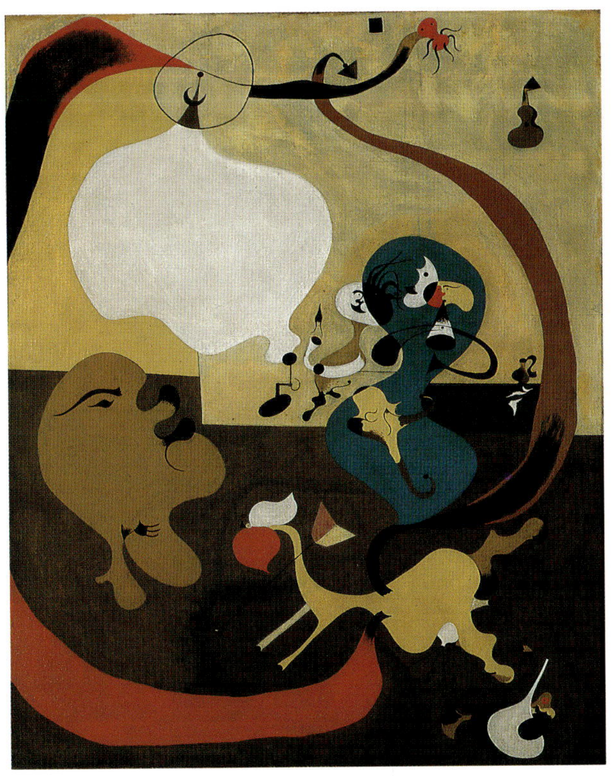

Figure E. Joan Miró. *Dutch Interior II*, Summer 1928

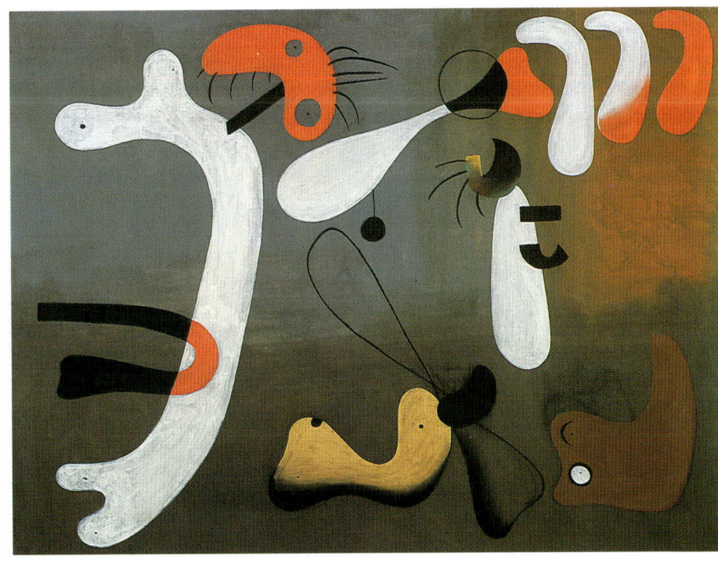

Figure F. Joan Miró. *Painting*, 1933

express would nonetheless be difficult to infinitely repeat, revitalize, and sustain. Miró continuously searched for catalysts to surprise and trigger his imagination. These drawings are a testimony of his constantly renewed quest for a fresh and spontaneous vision and are, therefore, particularly valuable to understanding his process and objectives.

Early Drawings, 1901–20

The first group of sketches included here [cat. nos. 1–19] are childhood drawings (1901–08) and figure studies (1912–20), all done in Barcelona. Miró's earliest drawings, like most children's drawings, show a microscopic attention to detail and a complete disregard for academic conventions.

In a brief autobiographical essay of 1957, Miró wrote about this period: "To escape from the daily drudgery, I took drawing lessons after the regular school day was over.... That class was like a religious ceremony for me; I washed my hands carefully before touching the paper and pencils. The implements were like sacred objects, and I worked as though I were performing a religious rite. This state of mind has persisted, even more pronounced. I was unable to copy a human face from a reproduction, however, I drew the leaves of trees with loving care."[3] Already Miró's commitment to drawing and painting, as an escape from his daily existence and a communion with the world of nature, are reflected in his earliest experiences.

During this period, Miró filled small sketchbooks with studies of familiar farmhouses, churches, or trees. It is, however, his studies of isolated objects drawn from nature that show, in the obsessive attention to detail, his emerging artistic personality. These objects or still lives, although inspired by a model, are completely transformed by Miró's subjectivity, becoming emblematic motifs that denote his intensely personalized (and indeed childlike) relationship to the world around him.

Miró's drawings between 1912 and 1915 show the influence of the formal training he took at that time. He has said that he had great difficulty in rendering the shapes of objects until one of his early instructors taught him to draw from touch. But whereas the edges and contours of objects he clasped in his hands with his eyes closed were real to him, the academic conventions of shading and crosshatching were not, and by 1917 he had turned these devices for rendering volume toward other ends. In the studies of nudes from 1917–19, which are constructions of curved and broken lines, crosshatching or shading was used to underscore the taut rhythmic articulations of his figures. At times he even used crosshatching as decorative patterning. These early works anticipate Miró's manner of disregarding accepted conventions to arrive at a personal understanding of expressive form.

Studies for Paintings, the 1920s

Miró's most intense period of experimentation began in Paris around 1923. His direct contacts with the Dada movement, and later with the Surrealists, were crucial to his subsequent orientation and development. The poets and painters who gravitated around Miró's apartment on the rue Blomet (Robert Desnos, Tristan Tzara, Benjamin Péret, and his neighbor André Masson) encouraged a kind of creative freedom he had never known. They authorized not only incongruous images drawn from the broadest pictorial and nonpictorial references (from completely banal events to trance- or dream-inspired images; from found objects to all manifestations of accident or chance or even verbal images), but also the complete restructuring of poetic and pictorial syntax. More precisely, they used and abused myriad syntactic devices for dismantling and recasting given reality: fragmentation, collage, assemblage; inverted syntax, citation, and paraphrase.

More importantly, the Dada poets and painters made no distinction between painting and poetry, and this indistinction became central to the direction Miró's art would take. A poetic reality—unstructured, irrational, emotional—was the reality Miró sought to express. The experience of poetry provided him with a shock of recognition: it not only acted as a liberating force but proposed structures and models for his own impulses and images. In the summer of 1924, Miró wrote to Michel Leiris from his farm in Montroig:

> I am working furiously; you and all my other writer friends have given me much help and improved my understanding of many things. I think about our conversation, when you told me how you started with a word and watched to see where it would take you. I have done a series of small things on wood, in which I take off from some form in the wood. Using an artificial thing as a point of departure like this, I feel is parallel to what writers can obtain by starting with an arbitrary sound: the R.R. from the song of a cricket, for example, or the isolated sound of a consonant or vowel, any sound, be it nasal or labial. This can create a surprising metaphysical state in you poets, even when you use the sound of vowels or consonants that have no meaning at all.
>
> In leafing through my notebook I have also noticed the extremely disturbing quality of the dissociated drawings I sometimes do—meant for canvases I am preparing and on which I jot down a number of remarks: names of colors or simply the monosyllabic *yes* when I feel that an idea should be carried out. I intend to do all these drawings. In other drawings, of objects that fly around on a flat surface, I write isolated letters. I agree with Breton that there is something extremely disturbing about a page of writing.[4]

Thus, whereas between 1919 and 1923

Miró had painted images of the family farm at Montroig with an almost Persian miniaturist precision, the drawings from the period 1923–27 [cat. nos. 20–56] show attempts to translate many of the same motifs into a loose metaphoric sign language. There is no color in these drawings. Likewise, in some paintings from 1924, such as *Portrait of Mme K* (Collection Mrs. René Gaffé, France), Miró used little color. He had discovered that, even on canvas, a monochromatic skeletal structure was enigmatic, evocative, and expressive of itself. He describes this realization in his letter to Michel Leiris:

> More or less total destruction of everything I left behind last summer and which [I] thought I would pick up again. Still too real! I am moving away from all pictorial conventions (that poison). In spreading out my canvases I have noticed that the ones that have been painted touch the spirit less directly than the ones that are simply drawn (or that use a minimum of color); the intromission of exciting materials (colors), however stripped of pictorial meaning, *shakes up* your blood and the exhalted sensation that *claws* at the soul is ruined. You already know the pictorial process: 1. Pure line. 2. Pure colors. 3. Nuances, the charm and music of colors. Final stage of degeneration.[5]

Miró later described this period as one in which many of his initial images were inspired by hallucinations brought on by hunger. Although it is historically true that this was a financially difficult period for Miró, in the context of the rue Blomet his hallucinations seem a kind of exercise that, once experienced, he attempted to repeat and control in order to sharpen his imaginary powers, bring on extreme states of receptivity (or, even, innocence), and provoke unprecedented images. Indeed Miró's hunger-inspired trances may be compared to Robert Desnos' experiments with hypnotism, during which he found some of his most brilliant poetic images. For these men, such techniques were crucial for bypassing the rational patterns, acquired conventions, and conscious images of a normal awakened state.

Miró also understood that the inchoate notations of a visual idea did not necessarily make a successful painting. Even though his initial vision may have been based on a mysterious impulse, he subsequently thought it through in pictorial terms, and attempted to reenact the same spontaneity on the canvas. In reference to this period, he would say, "I made preliminary sketches of the general layout of the painting so that I'd know just where everything was going to go. Then after having thought about it for a long time, I started painting and making changes as I went along."[6]

Starting in 1928–29, Miró developed his ideas in more rigorously pictorial terms, both as concerns drawing and color. Whereas his paintings from 1924–27 were inspired by poetic discourse (sometimes even inspired by literary sources),[7] in 1928 he felt the need to address himself to more purely plastic problems. He began to look toward classical painting for inspiration: Miró drew on Jan Steen's *The Dancing Lesson of the Cat* [Fig. D] for *Dutch Interior II* [Cat. nos. 61–63]; the English painter Constable suggested the *Portrait of a Lady in 1820* [cat. nos. 67–71]; Raphael's *La Fornarina* inspired a painting by the same name [cat. nos. 79–83]. Although this development initially appears incongruous, it is not far removed from the Dada poets' practice of citation, paraphrase, even homonymic verse, in which, while retaining the precise syntactical structure of a familiar phrase, they displaced or transformed verbal constituents or content, thereby creating new but not altogether unfamiliar images.

Miró's search for new references in classical forms of painting probably expressed his desire to move away from the loose poetic idiom, which had become almost too natural and predictable; through its systematic development, he was no longer taken off guard by what he found. He was, furthermore, loath to be identified with the Surrealists or labeled as a "literary painter." But his new approach may also be partly attributed to his move to

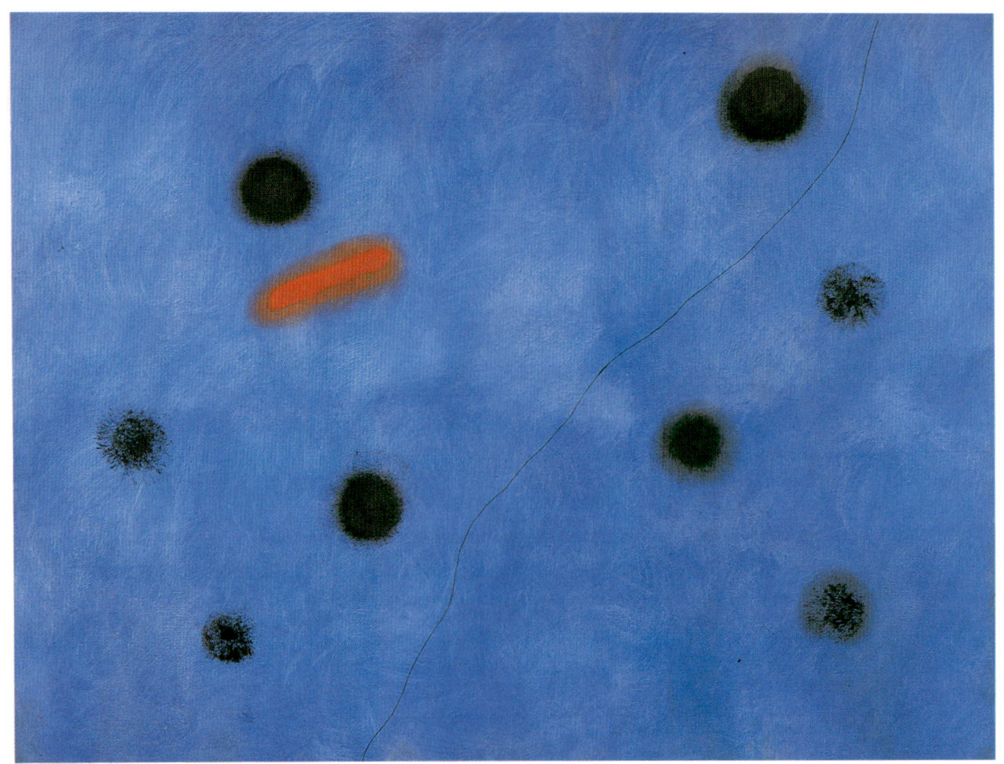

Figure J. Joan Miró. *Blue I*, March 1961

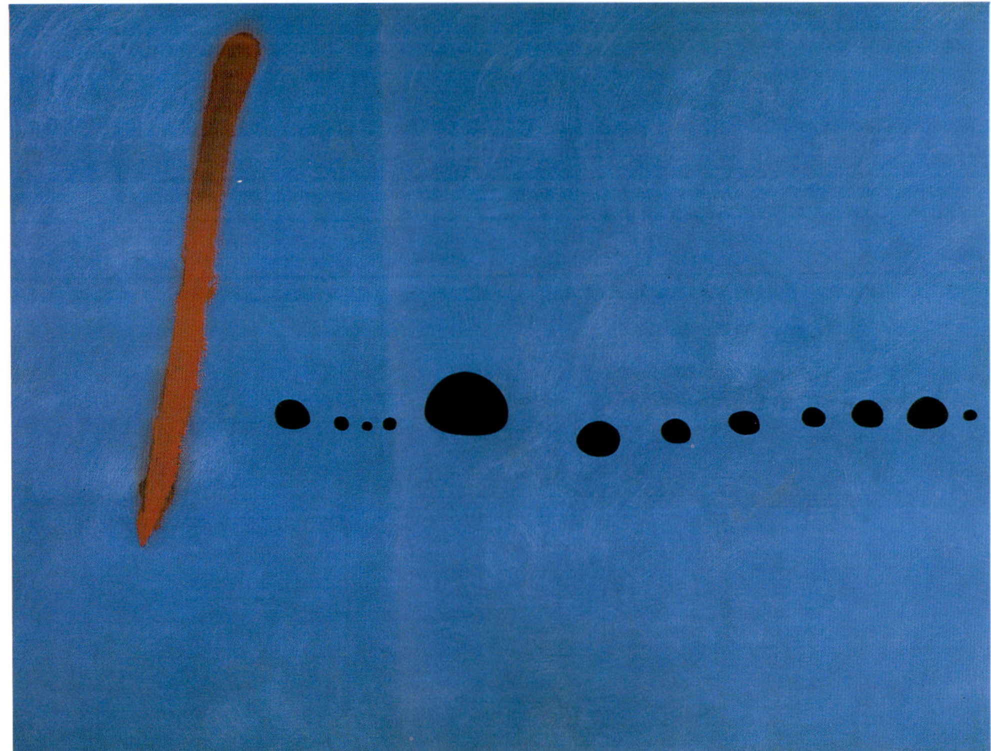

Figure K. Joan Miró. *Blue II*, March 1961

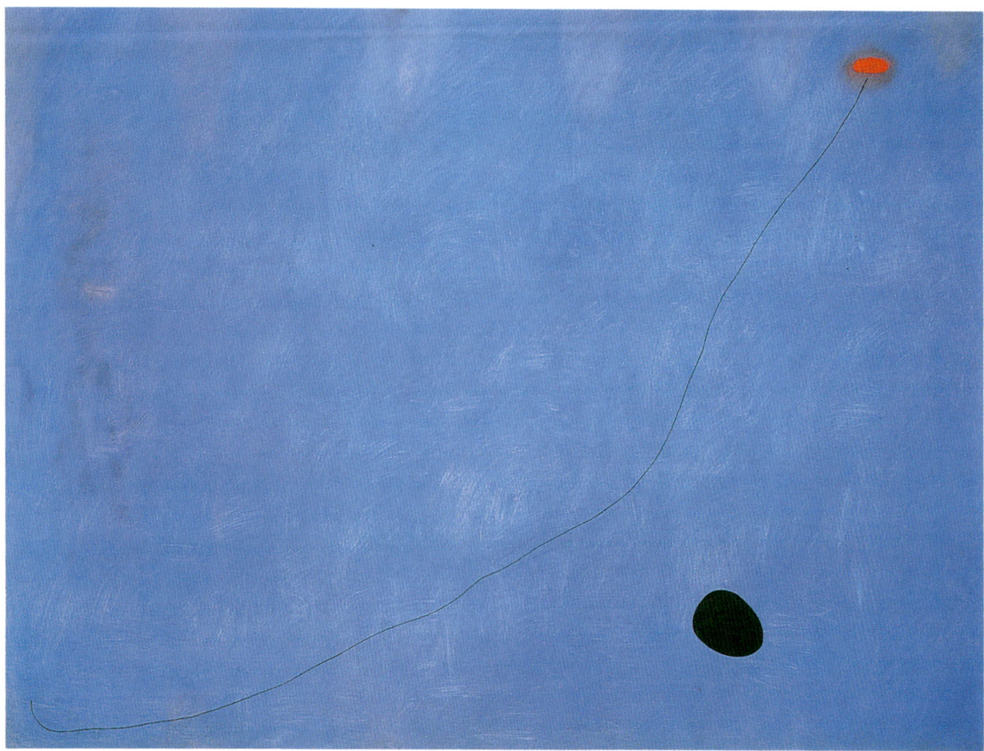

Figure L. Joan Miró. *Blue III*, March 1961

the rue Tourlaque in 1927, where he saw fewer poets but developed closer friendships with Jean Arp, Max Ernst, and René Magritte. The former's use of flat color, simplified spatial divisions, and unified organic shapes, and the latter's allusions to more traditional representation and more academic techniques surely influenced Miró's orientation toward more classical subjects, flatter color, and more tightly articulated compositional schemes.

Collages and Studies, the 1930s–1940s

Miro always maintained that he drew his inspiration from contact with the real world. But his focus on reality changed constantly, as he looked for ever-new challenges to keep his spontaneity alive. The different forms of reality that inspired his work could be found in the objects of nature, in the dislocated images of poetry, in classical paintings seen in museums or reproduced on postcards, even in printed illustrations in advertisements of utilitarian objects. (Such newspaper illustrations inspired the preliminary drawings [cat. nos. 72–78] for the painting *Queen Louise of Prussia* of 1929.) The explicit forms and content of all these referents were filtered through Miró's subjectivity into personalized shapes and images entirely divested of their initial visual functions.

A series of large collages from 1933 [cat. nos. 84–89] shows an extraordinary reserve of images and a unique and idiosyncratic manner of transforming them into a personal vocabulary. These collages, which provided the basic shapes and compositional schemes for a group of major paintings of that same year, are based initially on the Dada and Surrealist invention of the "found object." The newsprint images used in these works (of siphon bottles, golf club treads, flatware, tennis racquets, meat cleavers) are small and commonplace. Cut out and scattered in seemingly random patterns on large sheets of white paper, their choice and arrangement reflect decisions based purely on an immediate and out-of-context appeal. Miró's attraction to these newsprint reproductions may have been partially inspired by his friendship with Max Ernst; their isolation, displacement, and seemingly random distribution evoke the poetic and pictorial processes of Tzara and Arp. However, in the final paintings derived from these collages, only the spatial relationships between the motifs and their curved cutout silhouettes would be maintained. "In 1933," he later said, "I used to tear newspapers into rough shapes and paste them on cardboard. Day after day I would accumulate such shapes. After the collages were finished they served me as points of departure for paintings. I did not copy the collages. I merely let them suggest shapes to me."[8]

Whereas the process of selection, destruction of content, and transformation into entirely different forms and effects indeed derived from Miró's Dada experience, the paintings, which generally show a controlled distribution of homogeneous, brightly colored, anonymous shapes on a dark ground, obey more formalist considerations. Indeed, these paintings seem among the most abstract of Miró's career, both in their spatial composition and motifs. It was precisely at this time that Miró was invited to join the Paris-based "Abstraction-Création" group, to which his reply was the following: "Have you ever heard of anything more stupid than 'abstraction-abstraction'? And they ask me into their deserted house, as if the marks I put on a canvas did not correspond to a concrete representation of my mind, did not possess a profound reality, were not a part of the real itself!...I cannot understand—and consider it an insult—being placed in the category of 'abstract' painters."[9]

The fluid organic shapes that Miró's scissors discovered in the collage process would be translated into the mythological personages of the "Minotaur" series [cat. nos. 90–95] later that same year.[10] The bonelike articulation of these elongated amoebic shapes endowed with symbolic sexual attributes appears to echo Picasso's "Bather" series from the late 1920s to early 1930s. However, the explicitly cosmic context, open space, and transparent silhouettes, as well as our knowledge of the sources of these forms in the collages, identify them with Miró's private vision and iconography. These same shapes, moreover, will be found in his later sculptures of assembled objects or his solar and lunar birds from the mid forties to early fifties.

Wartime Studies, 1937–42

The total contrast between the loose floating images from the early 1930s and the 1937 studies of nudes [cat. nos. 96–99] is easy to explain. Starting in 1936, Miró lived in exile in Paris. This estrangement from the devastating events of the Spanish Civil War provoked, in his words, a need to come to terms with his immediate reality. It was in this climate and context that he painted the famous *Still Life with Old Shoe* (1937, Museum of Modern Art, New York) and his own *Self-portrait* (1937–38, Museum of Modern Art, New York), both done directly from a model. He attended life drawing classes at the Académie de la Grande Chaumière in order to confront the human figure. But the academic disciplines with which he tried to sublimate his anxiety did not assuage his inner upheaval. These drawings of nudes–brutally distorted and traced with an unsteady line–clearly reflect Miró's subjective frame of mind more than the studio models who presumably inspired them.

When Miró moved to Normandy in 1939, he found a refuge in nature and a peace of mind, which freed his inspiration and his drawing style. His famous series of gouaches, the "Constellations," which he began in Normandy and finished in Palma, express a deliberate withdrawal from the political reality of the ongoing Spanish war and World War II. In fact, he would say that "the night, music, and the stars"[11] became his pictorial referents. These gouaches reveal a cosmic vision animated by mythical figures, animals, stars, and comets, translated into linear or emblematic forms. These elements would come to constitute his mature stylistic repertory.

Studies for Sculptures, 1945–56

Upon his return in 1940 to Spain and to the familiar reality of Montroig, Miró began to think of making sculpture, based on an analogous iconography and executed according to the assemblage process. His crudely drawn sketches for three-dimensional figures [cat. nos. 104–111] evoke a sense of volume through the sparest linear indications, without shading or color. The shapes are inspired by the forms of nature and sometimes by real objects he found on walks in the countryside and could clasp in his hands. Again, the found object that generates new images is the process shaping these works.

In a book of working notes that Miró kept during 1941–42, he wrote: "when sculpting, start from the objects I collect, just as I make use of stains on paper and imperfections in canvases—do this here in the country in a way that is really alive, in touch with the elements of nature. ...make a cast of these objects and work on it like Gonzalez does until the object as such no longer exists but becomes a sculpture....it is in sculpture that I will create a truly phantasmagoric world of living monsters....may my sculptures be confused with elements of nature, trees, rocks, roots, mountains, plants, flowers....with only rare exceptions it would be a great mistake to cast my sculptures in metal; that would be the work of a sculptor, a *specialist*, and I must avoid that."[12]

Miró chose to execute many of his early sculptures in ceramic [figs. G, H, I] because the muted patinas of natural pigments and materials were important to him. He also favored the somewhat rustic execution that he could achieve through working the clay with his own hands, and the complete unpredictability of what would occur during the firing process. Some of the bronze casts he made later, in the 1960s (despite his observation that metal was perhaps not his ideal medium), show an attempt to reproduce a similar rough finish, and suggest the effects of natural materials and a natural coalescence of forms.

The 1960s and 1970s

During the 1950s Miró did few drawings or paintings. He made sculpture, worked on lithographs, and executed a number of commissioned ceramic walls, activities that corresponded to his desire to gain a broader audience for his work. But in 1960, after moving into a large and spacious studio in Mallorca, he began to think seriously again about painting, this time on a monumental scale that, for lack of space, he had never before been able to undertake. Characteristically, the preliminary ideas for these paintings, many of which as finished works measured about seven by twelve feet, were made on tiny bits of torn paper measuring less than three by four inches. Despite the fact that Miró's vision was conceived for a grand scale, when the artist actually confronted the vast emptiness of his canvas, he must have realized that the approach and concentration it required were radically different. The extremely reductive motifs found in these paintings—whether a broad slash, a tenuous meandering line, or a series of dots—appear to culminate all his earlier oeuvre. They are the distillation of a lifetime's activity devoted to the same landscape motifs, the same manual operations, the same mental and physical discipline. Although it is tempting once again to evoke the notion of abstraction, it is more apt to describe these paintings in terms of physical and metaphysical landscapes.

As he grew older, Miró's mental and manual discipline was more and more focused on this kind of reductive statement that contained a whole universe of meaning. His description of preparing the three blue paintings of 1961 [figs. J, K, L], the first of a series of large triptychs he painted during the 1960s, is eloquent of his state of mind.

> The very last works are the three large blue canvases. They took me a long time. Not to paint, but to think them through. It took an enormous effort on my part, a very great inner tension to reach the emptiness I wanted. The preliminary stage was intellectual.... It was like preparing the celebration of a religious rite or entering a monastery. Do you know how Japanese archers prepare for competitions? They begin by getting themselves into the right state, exhaling, inhaling, exhaling. It was the same thing for me. I knew that I had everything to lose. One weakness, one mistake, and everything would collapse.
>
> I began by drawing them in charcoal, very precisely. (I always start work very early in the morning.) In the afternoon, I would simply look at what I had drawn. For the rest of the day, I would prepare myself internally. And finally, I began to paint: first the background, all blue, but it was not simply a matter of applying color like a house painter: all the movements of the brush, the wrist, the breathing of the hand—all these things played a role. 'Perfecting' the background put me in the right state to go on with the rest. This struggle exhausted me. I have not painted anything since. These canvases are the culmination of everything I have tried to do up to then.[13]

Miró had made at least eight tiny sketches for this triptych over a period of about six months (including those illustrated here) [cat. nos. 112–114] before he touched the canvas. In this instance, it is clear that the risks involved in realizing a project were equally shared between formulating the first ideas and executing the final paintings. Thus, the spontaneity of Miró's art, particularly in his most empty and abstract works, derived from an inner vision and a rigorous discipline, which he maintained throughout the gestation process. The initial act of discovery, the image seen in his mind's eye, was seized on paper in a few seconds. Once he approached the canvas, this vision or immediate irruptive image dictated the basic structure and emotion, which directed and controlled its execution.

Paradoxically, Miró considered himself primarily a colorist: "Talented as concerns color but with forms a complete failure. Cannot tell the difference between a straight line and a curve."[14] Yet, it was the visionary images seen first in his drawings, where they are captured with a swift cursory line, that essentially define the singularity of Miró's art. Although the color in his paintings is vivid, vibrant, and personal, it is the figures that give meaning to the ground, the drawing that gives meaning to his color. A single dot, a curve, a flourish, or straight line invest a saturated chromatic field with infinite poetic resonance and meaning.

As Miró repeatedly said, "the marks I put on a canvas...correspond to a concrete representation of my mind, ... possess a profound reality, ...[are] a part of the real itself."[15] It is clear that Miró's every line, gesture, or dot, or even a colorfield, evoked natural phenomena: the sun, rain, snow, night, the stars, for example. Furthermore, Miró invested his more typical or figurative motifs (a woman, bird, or snail, for example) with a mythical or cosmic content. Thus, the immediate reality that triggered Miró's imagination was translated or sublimated into more universal statements of meaning.

Miró's figurative themes presumably required fewer preliminary drawings. The paintings of women and birds surrounded by cosmic motifs were generally simpler in compositional terms, and he seemed to prefer to project them directly on the canvas in order to retain a rough spontaneity and freshness in their rendering. Although at diverse moments of his career he produced many drawings on these subjects, these may be understood as warming-up exercises, or even as finished works, rather than preliminary studies. This view is suggested by the fact that he did not keep them, and few remained in his personal collection.

In 1924, Miró wrote to Michel

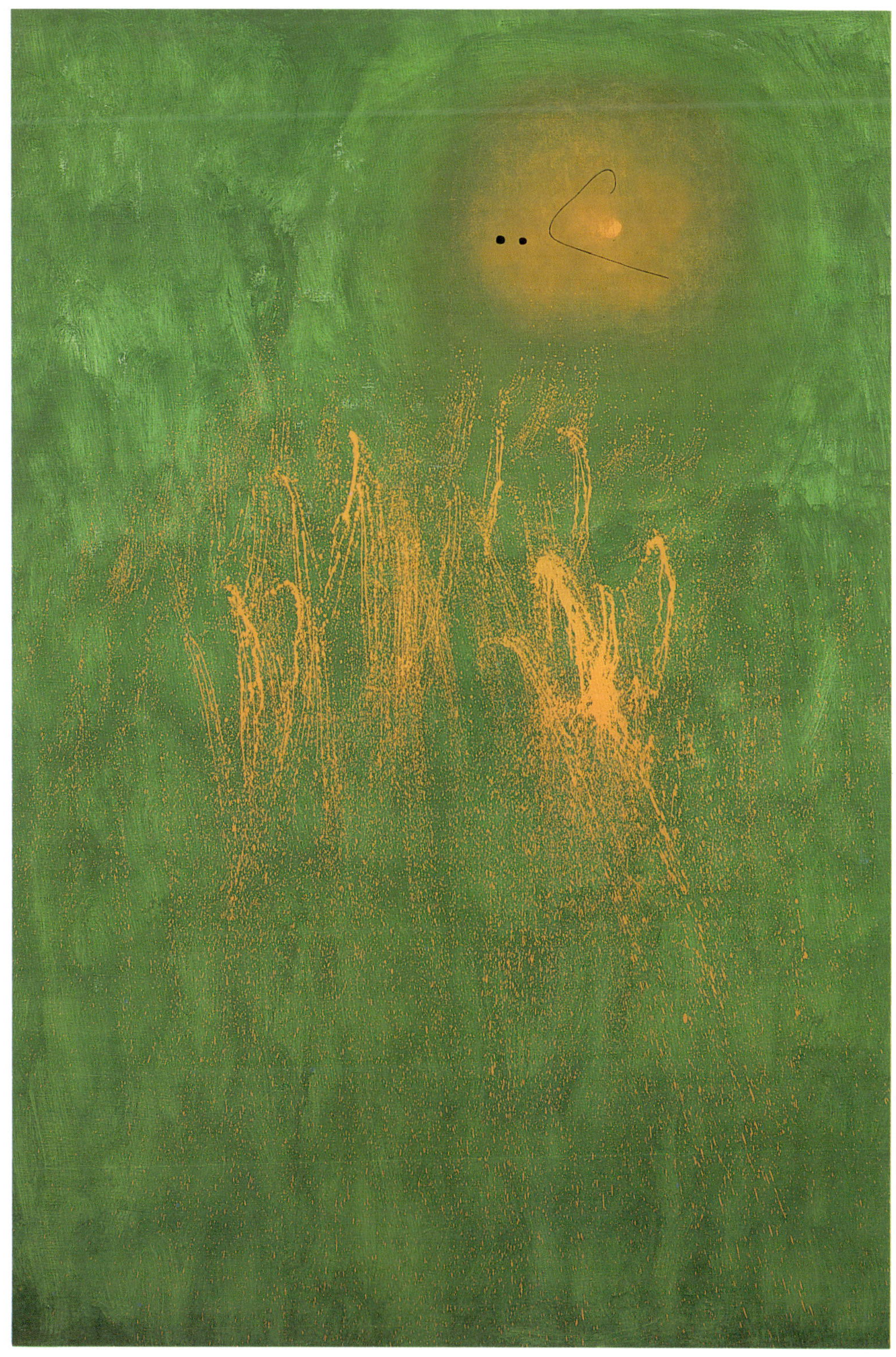

Figure M. Joan Miró. *Hair Pursued by Two Planets*, 1968

Leiris from his farm in Montroig: "I hope that my latest works will amaze you a little."[16] Even today, over sixty years later, Miró's art does not cease to amaze us by the innocence and transcendence of the vision portrayed. Whereas the paintings show the more complete expression of the poet-painter—suggesting the mental and manual disciplines he invoked to keep his spontaneity alive—the drawings are quite different. They show the artist in an act of self-discovery and are indeed a "true expression of the spirit."[17]

Notes

1. Letter from Miró to Pierre Matisse, March 7, 1937. All Miró quotes are from M. Rowell, ed., *Joan Miró: Selected Writings and Interviews*, G.K. Hall & Co., Boston, 1986. This quote, p. 148.

2. The studies in Miró's own collection first came to public attention in 1976, when a part of them were published in G. Picon, ed., *Joan Miró: Carnets catalans*, Albert Skira, Geneva, 1976.

3. M. Rowell, ed., op. cit. Letter from Miró to Jacques Dupin, October 9, 1957, p. 44.

4. Ibid. Letter from Miró to Michel Leiris, August 10, 1924, p. 86.

5. Ibid.

6. Ibid. Interview with Lluis Permanyer, 1978, p. 291.

7. See R. Krauss and M. Rowell, *Joan Miró: Magnetic Fields*, The Solomon R. Guggenheim Museum, New York, 1972.

8. M. Rowell, ed., op. cit. Interview with James Johnson Sweeney, 1948, p. 209.

9. Ibid. Interview with Georges Duthuit, 1937, pp. 150–51. The term "abstraction-abstraction" was a lapsus on Miró's part.

10. Published in the Surrealist magazine, *Minotaure*, in 1933.

11. M. Rowell, ed., op. cit. Interview with James Johnson Sweeney, 1948, p. 209.

12. Ibid. Working notes, p. 175.

13. Ibid. Interview with Rosamond Bernier, 1961, pp. 258–59.

14. Ibid. Letter from Miró to Michel Leiris, September 25, 1929, p. 110.

15. See note 9 above.

16. M. Rowell, ed., op. cit. Letter from Miró to Michel Leiris, October 31, 1924, p. 87.

17. See epigraph, p. 11, and fn. 1 above.

Checklist of the Exhibition

Early Drawings, 1901–20

1. *Flower Pot with Flowers*, 1901
   Pencil on paper
   21.1 x 12 cm., 8⁵⁄₁₆ x 4¾ in.
   FM 20
2. *The Pedicure*, 1901
   Pencil, watercolor, and gouache on paper
   11.6 x 17.7 cm., 4⅝ x 6¹¹⁄₁₆ in.
   FM 22
3. *Flower Pot with Flowers*, 1906
   India ink and colored pencil on paper
   49.7 x 32.5 cm., 19⁹⁄₁₆ x 12¹³⁄₁₆ in.
   FM 42
4. *Pinecone*, 1907
   Pastel and charcoal on paper
   31 x 23.5 cm., 12³⁄₁₆ x 9¼ in.
   FM 110
5. Project for a piece of jewelry, ca. 1908
   Pencil and charcoal on paper
   48.5 x 63.2 cm., 19⅛ x 24⅞ in.
   FM 246
6. *Three Heads*, ca. 1912
   Charcoal on paper
   43.8 x 63.2 cm., 17¼ x 24⅞ in.
   FM 145
7. *Male Figure Study*, 1915
   Pencil and pastel on brown paper
   18.9 x 12.5 cm., 7⁷⁄₁₆ x 4¹⁵⁄₁₆ in.
   FM 241
8. *Male Figure Study*, 1915
   Pencil and pastel on brown paper
   18.9 x 12.5 cm. 7⁷⁄₁₆ x 4¹⁵⁄₁₆ in.
   FM 242
9. *Standing Female Nude*, 1917
   Pencil on paper
   21.2 x 15.2 cm., 7⁷⁄₁₆ x 4¹⁵⁄₁₆ in.
   FM 249
10. *Spanish Dancer*, 1917
    Pencil on paper
    19.4 x 13.6 cm., 7⅝ x 5⅜ in.
    FM 257
11. *Female Nude Leaning Forward*, 1917
    Pencil on paper
    21.1 x 15.1 cm., 8⁵⁄₁₆ x 5⁵⁄₁₆ in.
    FM 259
12. *Seated Male Nude*, 1917
    Pencil on paper
    19.3 x 16.5 cm., 7⅝ x 6½ in.
    FM 261
13. *Woman with Arms Spread*, 1917
    Pencil on paper
    19.4 x 13.6 cm., 7⅝ x 5⅜ in.
    FM 254
14. *Woman Holding Her Chin*, 1917
    Pencil on paper
    19.4 x 13.6 cm., 7⅝ x 5⅜ in.
    FM 252
15. *Male Figure Study*, ca. 1917
    Pencil on paper
    31.2 x 21.6 cm., 12⁵⁄₁₆ x 8½ in.
    FM 405
16. *Seated Female Nude*, 1917
    Pencil on paper
    31.3 x 21.5 cm., 12⁵⁄₁₆ x 8⁷⁄₁₆ in.
    FM 417
17. *Standing Female Nude*, 1918
    Pencil on paper
    26.4 x 20.3 cm., 10⅜ x 8 in.
    FM 264
18. *Male Figure Study*, 1919
    Pencil on paper
    23.2 x 15 cm., 9⅛ x 5⅞ in.
    FM 509
19. *Male Figure Study*, 1920
    Pencil on paper
    15 x 23.2 cm., 5⅞ x 9⅛ in.
    FM 514

Studies for Paintings, the 1920s

20. Study for *Pastoral*, ca. 1923
    Charcoal and pencil on paper
    15.1 x 23 cm., 6 x 9⅛ in.
    FM 4352
    Fairly exact study for painting dated 1923–24. Collection Stefan T. Edlis, Chicago (Dupin, 83)
21. Study for *The Hunter (Catalan Landscape)*, ca. 1923
    Pencil on paper
    14 x 20.5 cm., 5½ x 8⅛ in.
    FM 528
    Inscribed upper center in dotted letters: "Toulouse-Rabat," referring to flight route over Montroig; and lower right in Catalan: "small dog/fire/grill/frying pan"
    Early study for painting dated 1923–24 (Figure A). Collection The Museum of Modern Art, New York. (Dupin, 84)
22. Study for *The Hunter (Catalan Landscape)*, ca. 1923
    Pencil on paper
    7.8 x 11.5 cm., 3¹⁄₁₆ x 4½ in.
    FM 525
23. Study for *The Hunter (Catalan Landscape)*, ca. 1923
    Pencil on paper
    8.5 x 11 cm., 3⅜ x 4⁵⁄₁₆ in.
    FM 674
    Inscribed upper center in Catalan: "Attention: side of canvas is damaged"; and on left: "empty/sex"; on right of center: "white/green/sardine"
24. Study for *The Hunter (Catalan Landscape)*, ca. 1923
    Pencil and ink on paper
    15 x 21.5 cm., 5¹⁵⁄₁₆ x 8¼ in.
    FM 526
25. Study for *Automaton*, ca. 1924
    Pencil on paper
    7.8 x 13.7 cm., 3¹⁄₁₆ x 5⅜ in.
    FM 4347
    Study for larger drawing dated 7 November 1924. Collection Morton G. Neumann Estate (Dupin, p. 148)

26. Study for *Head of a Smoker*, ca. 1924
Pencil and colored pencil on paper
9.5 x 17.5 cm., 3¾ x 6⅞ in.
FM 4348
Inscribed center: "Jou" (for "journal"); stamp on right: "For the brave, nothing is impossible"
Study for painting dated 1924. Collection Musée d'Ixelles, Brussels (Dupin, 96).

27. Study for *The Gas Lamp*, ca. 1924
Pencil and colored crayon on paper
16.7 x 19.3 cm., 6 9/16 x 7⅝ in.
FM 555
Study for painting, 1925. Ex-collection M. Cuttoli, Paris (Dupin, 88)

28. Study for *The Family*, ca. 1924
Pencil on paper
19.2 x 16.7 cm., 7 9/16 x 6 9/16 in.
FM 672
Inscribed lower left in French: "1. very luminous like a cat's eyes/ 2. id. like a star; very mysterious"; upper right: "The Family"; lower right: 3. like a tree/ 4. like an onion"
Study for large drawing dated 1924. Collection The Museum of Modern Art, New York (Dupin, p. 206)

29. Study for *The Family*, ca. 1924
Pencil on paper
5.6 x 7 cm., 2 3/16 x 2¾ in.
FM 673
Study for large drawing dated 1924. Collection The Museum of Modern Art, New York (Dupin, p. 206)

30. Study for *The Spanish Dancer*, ca. 1924
Pencil on paper
20.5 x 13.5 cm., 8 1/16 x 5 5/16 in.
FM 4478
Inscribed in Catalan with list of colors
Study for painting, 1924. Collection Mrs. René Gaffé, France (Dupin, 87)

31. Study for *The Spanish Dancer*, ca. 1924
Pencil on paper
12 x 7.3 cm., 4¾ x 2⅞ in.
FM 4477
Study for painting, 1924. Collection Mrs. René Gaffé, France (Dupin, 87)

32. Study for *The Spanish Dancer*, ca. 1924
Pencil and white gouache on paper
26.3 x 20.5 cm., 10⅜ x 8 1/16 in.
FM 4480B
Inscribed in Catalan with colors, numbers
Study for painting, 1924. Collection Mrs. René Gaffé, France (Dupin, 87)

Figure B. Magazine cover used as a source for *The Spanish Dancer*, ca. 1924
See description in list of figure illustrations, page 30.

33. Study for *Carnival of Harlequin*, ca. 1924
Pencil on paper
26.8 x 20.5 cm., 10 9/16 x 8 1/16 in.
FM 4362
Inscribed in French clockwise from upper left to lower left: "In background the Seine and the Eiffel Tower/monocle/eye/balloon/umbrella/ or light bulb?/light bulb/gloves, naked arm/ white of a statue/crocodile/dog with butterfly wings/ flower bed with grass and small flowers/ boxing gloves"
Early study for painting, dated on painting 1924-25. Collection The Albright-Knox Art Gallery, Buffalo (Figure C) (Dupin, 101)

34. Study for *Carnival of Harlequin*, ca. 1924
Pencil on paper
26.8 x 20.5 cm., 10 9/16 x 8 1/16 in.
FM 4363
Inscribed idem in French clockwise from upper left to lower left: "frog's head/Harlequin/ rooster's head/Harlequin's carnival/blue/white"
Early study for painting, dated 1924–25. Collection The Albright-Knox Art Gallery, Buffalo (Dupin, 101)

35. Study for *Carnival of Harlequin*, ca. 1924
Pencil and colored crayon on paper
16.7 x 19.3 cm., 6 9/16 x 7½ in.
FM 669
More advanced study for *Carnival of Harlequin*.

36. Study for *Head of a Catalan Peasant*, ca. 1925
Pencil on paper
26.8 x 20.5 cm., 10 9/16 x 8 1/16 in.
FM 671B
Inscribed on right half in Catalan: top: "very blue sky"; on left: "for sky, see Italian Primitives/ horizon"; on face: "ocher green/ very warm colors"; below: "yellow"

37. Study for *Head of a Catalan Peasant*, ca. 1925
Pencil and colored crayon on paper
19.3 x 16.7 cm., 7½ x 6 9/16 in.
FM 670
Study for painting dated 1925. Private collection (Dupin, 101)

38. Study for *Head of a Catalan Peasant*, ca. 1925
Pencil on paper
7 x 5.7 cm., 2¾ x 2¼ in.
FM 639
Inscribed in French with title.

39-43. Five pages from a notebook, ca. 1925–26
Pencil on paper
18.6 x 14.9 cm., 7 5/16 x 5⅞ in.
FM 744–787
Notebook includes drawings for paintings from the period 1925–27

44. Study for "*Et les seins mouraient*," ca. 1927
Pencil on paper
14.1 x 18.6 cm., 5 9/16 x 7 5/16 in.
FM 7098
Inscribed in French with title.
Studies for the frontispiece of Benjamin Peret's book by same title (Marseille, 1929). Frontispiece dated 1927 on plate.

45. Study for "*Et les seins mouraient*," ca. 1927
Pencil on paper
14.1 x 18.6 cm., 5 9/16 x 7 5/16 in.
FM 7099
Inscribed in French with title.
Studies for the frontispiece of Benjamin Peret's book by same title (Marseille, 1929). Frontispiece dated 1927 on plate.

46. Study for "*Et les seins mouraient*," ca. 1927
Pencil on paper
18.6 x 14 cm., 7 5/16 x 5 9/16 in.
FM 7100
Inscribed in French with title.
Studies for the frontispiece of Benjamin Peret's book by same title (Marseille, 1929). Frontispiece dated 1927 on plate.

47. Study for *Landscape*, ca. 1927
Pencil on paper
21.2 x 27.5 cm., 8⅜ x 10³⁄₁₆ in.
FM 789
Study for painting dated 1927. Collection The Australian National Gallery, Canberra (Dupin, 180)

48. Study for *Landscape*, ca. 1927
Pencil on paper
21.2 x 27.5 cm., 8⅜ x 10³⁄₁₆ in.
FM 790
Study for painting dated 1927. Collection The Australian National Gallery, Canberra (Dupin, 180)

49. Study for *Landscape, The Hare*, 1927
Pencil on paper
21.2 x 27.4 cm., 8⅜ x 10⅝ in.
FM 675
Study for painting dated 1927. Collection The Solomon R. Guggenheim Museum, New York (Dupin, 184)

50. Study for *Landscape, The Snake*, 1927
Pencil on paper
21.2 x 27.4 cm., 8⅜ x 10⅝ in.
FM 676
Study for painting dated 1927. Private collection, Paris (Dupin, 183)

51. Study for *The Circus Horse*, 1927
Pencil on paper
27 x 20.3 cm., 10⅝ x 8 in.
FM 686
Study for painting, 1927. Private collection, Paris (Dupin, 212)

52. Study for *The Circus Horse*, 1927
Pencil on paper
27 x 20.3 cm., 10⅝ x 8 in.
FM 687
Study for painting, 1927. Private collection, Paris (Dupin, 211)

53. Drawing, ca. 1927
Pencil on paper
15.5 x 21.5 cm., 6⅛ x 8⁷⁄₁₆ in.
FM 530

54. Drawing, ca. 1927
Pencil on paper
15.5 x 21.5 cm., 6⅛ x 8⁷⁄₁₆ in.
FM 531

55. Study for *Painting on White Ground, The Dog*, 1927
Pencil on paper
20.3 x 27 cm., 8 x 10⅝ in.
FM 693
Study for painting, 1927. Ex-collection Tériade, Paris (Dupin, 227)

56. Study for *Painting on White Ground*, 1927
Pencil on paper
20.3 x 27 cm., 8 x 10⅝ in.
FM 694
Study for painting, 1927. Collection H.C. Bechtler, Zurich (Dupin, 231)

57. Drawing, ca. 1928
Pencil on paper
15.8 x 21.5 cm., 6¼ x 8⁷⁄₁₆ in.
FM 529
Study for series of larger drawings on theme, "The Lovers," dated 1928. Collection Stefan T. Edlis, Chicago (See also Dupin, p.186)

58. Study for *Still Life with Gas Lamp*, 1928
Pencil on paper
21.2 x 27.3 cm., 8⅜ x 10¾ in.
FM 803
Study for painting, 1928. Ex-collection Mrs. Marcel Duchamp, Paris (Dupin, 283)

59. Study for *Still Life with Gas Lamp*, 1928
Pencil on paper
21.2 x 27.3 cm., 8⅜ x 10¹³⁄₁₆ in.
FM 805–809
Collage incorporating four smaller studies. Inscribed lower left: "chick-pea"; upper right.: "bean"

60. Study for *Still Life with Gas Lamp*, 1928
Carbon pencil on paper
50 x 60 cm., 19¹¹⁄₁₆ x 13⅝ in.
FM 810

61. Study for *Dutch Interior II*, 1928
Pencil on paper
21.9 x 16.8 cm., 8⅝ x 6⅝ in.
FM 798

62. Study for *Dutch Interior II*, 1928
Pencil on paper
21.9 x 16.8 cm., 8⅝ x 6⅝ in.
FM 799

63. Study for *Dutch Interior II*, 1928
Pencil on paper
61.5 x 47.5 cm., 24³⁄₁₆ x 18¹¹⁄₁₆ in.
FM 802

Figure D. Postcard of *The Dancing Lesson of the Cat*, 17th-century painting by Jan Steen Inspiration for *Dutch Interior II*, 1928 (Figure E). See description of Figures D and Figure E in list of figure illustrations.

64. Study for *The Potato,* 1928
Pencil on paper, 18 x 13.6 cm., 7⅟₁₆ x 5⅜ in.
FM 793
Study for painting, 1928. Private collection, New York (Dupin, 237)

65. Study for *Dutch Interior III*, 1928
Pencil on paper
21.8 x 16.8 cm., 8⁹⁄₁₆ x 6⅝ in.
FM 794
Study for painting, 1928. Collection Mrs. Wolfgang Schoenberg, New York (Dupin, 236)

66. Study for *Dutch Interior III*, 1928
Charcoal on paper
61.5 x 47.2 cm., 24³⁄₁₆ x 18⁹⁄₁₆ in.
FM 796

67. Study for *Portrait of a Lady in 1820*, 1929
Pencil on paper
21.8 x 16.8 cm., 8⁹⁄₁₆ x 6⅝ in.
FM 960
Study for painting, 1929. Collection unknown (Dupin, 240)

68. Study for *Portrait of a Lady in 1820*, 1929
Pencil on paper
16.8 x 19.6 cm., 6⅝ x 7³⁄₁₆ in.
FM 962
Study for painting, 1929. Collection unknown (Dupin, 240)

69. Study for *Portrait of a Lady in 1820*, 1929
Pencil on paper
21.8 x 16.8 cm., 8⁹⁄₁₆ x 6⅝ in.
FM 964
Study for painting, 1929.

70. Study for *Portrait of a Lady in 1820*, 1929
Pencil on paper
21.8 x 16.8 cm., 8⁹⁄₁₆ x 6⅝ in.
FM 965
Inscribed in French upper left: "It's thin"
Study for painting, 1929.

71. Study for *Portrait of a Lady in 1820*, 1929
Pencil on paper
21.8 x 16.8 cm., 8⁹⁄₁₆ x 6⅝ in.
FM 963

72. Study for *Queen Louise of Prussia*, 1929
Pencil on newspaper
20.5 x 20.5 cm., 8¹⁄₁₆ x 8¹⁄₁₆ in.
FM 943
Study for painting, 1929. Collection Meadows Museum, Southern Methodist University, Dallas (Dupin, 241)

73. Study for *Queen Louise of Prussia*, 1929
Pencil on cardboard (subway ticket)
5.8 x 3 cm., 2⁵⁄₁₆ x 1¹³⁄₁₆ in.
FM 944
Study for painting, 1929. Collection Meadows Museum, Southern Methodist University, Dallas (Dupin, 241)

74. Study for *Queen Louise of Prussia*, 1929
Pencil on paper
13.6 x 21.1 cm., 5⅜ x 8⁵⁄₁₆ in.
FM 945

75. Study for *Queen Louise of Prussia*, 1929
Pencil on paper
13.6 x 21.1cm., 5⅜ x 8⁵⁄₁₆ in.
FM 946

76. Study for *Queen Louise of Prussia*, 1929
Pencil on paper
13.6 x 21.1 cm., 5⅜ x 8⁵⁄₁₆ in.
FM 947

77. Study for *Queen Louise of Prussia*, 1929
Pencil on paper
13.6 x 21.1 cm., 5⅜ x 8⁵⁄₁₆ in.
FM 957
Inscribed in French on right: "very concentrated/pure spirit/not painting!/But *very rich* in color/fine texture/very well painted"

78. Study for *Queen Louise of Prussia*, 1929
Charcoal and pencil on paper
48.5 x 62.5 cm., 19¼ x 23⅞ in.
FM 958

79. Study for *La Fornarina*, 1929
Pencil on paper
16.1 x 10.5 cm., 6⁵⁄₁₆ x 4⅛ in.
FM 968
Study for painting, 1929, inspired by Raphael's *La Fornarina*. Collection unknown (Dupin, 242)

80. Study for *La Fornarina*, 1929
Pencil on paper
15.9 x 10.2 cm., 6¼ x 4¹⁄₁₆ in.
FM 967
Study for painting, 1929, inspired by Raphael's *La Fornarina*. Collection unknown (Dupin, 242)

81. Study for *La Fornarina*, 1929
Ink and pencil on paper
22 x 16.9 cm., 8¹⁄₁₆ x 6⅝ in.
FM 970
Inscribed in French: "Too many references to earlier things/still too realistic"

82. Study for *La Fornarina*, 1929
Pencil on paper
22 x 16.9 cm., 8¹⁄₁₆ x 6⅝ in.
FM 969

83. Study for *La Fornarina*, 1929
Charcoal on paper
64.1 x 49.3 cm., 25¼ x 19⁷⁄₁₆ in.
FM 971

Series of Preparatory Collages for Paintings, 1933

84. Collage, 26 January 1933
Cardboard and fragments of newspaper illustrations on white paper
47.1 x 63.1 cm., 18⁹⁄₁₆ x 24¹³⁄₁₆ in.
FM 1289
Study for unidentified painting, 1933. (Perhaps, Dupin, 331?)

85. Collage, 28 January 1933
Fragments of newspaper illustrations on white paper
47.5 x 62.8 cm., 18¹⁄₁₆ x 24¾ in.
FM 1291
Study for *Painting*, 1933 (Figure F)
Philadelphia Museum of Art, A.E. Gallatin Collection (Dupin, 335)

86. Collage, 1 February 1933
Fragments of newspaper illustrations on white paper
47.1 x 63.1 cm., 18⁹⁄₁₆ x 24¹³⁄₁₆ in.
FM 1294
Study for *Painting*, 1933. Collection unknown (Dupin, 332)

87. Collage, 2 February 1933
Fragments of newspaper illustrations on white paper
47 x 63 cm., 18½ x 24¹³⁄₁₆ in.
FM 1295

88. Collage, 6 February 1933
Fragments of newspaper illustrations on white paper
47.1 x 63.1 cm., 18⁹⁄₁₆ x 24¹³⁄₁₆ in.
FM 1298
Study for *Painting*, 1933. Collection unknown (Dupin, 337)

89. Collage, 10 February 1933
Fragments of newspaper illustrations on white paper
47 x 63 cm., 18½ x 24¹³⁄₁₆ in.
FM 1304
Study for *Painting*, 1933. Collection Wadsworth Atheneum, Hartford (Dupin, 344)

Legend of the Minotaur, 1933

Drawings from a series prepared for the publication *Minotaure*, (Paris), no. 3–4, 12 December 1933. Most of the drawings illustrated here were not published in this issue.

90. Study, 23 August 1933
Pencil on paper
23.7 x 15.8 cm., 9⁵⁄₁₆ x 6¼ in.
FM 1311

91. Study, 8 September 1933
Pencil on paper
15.8 x 23.7 cm., 6¼ x 9⁵⁄₁₆ in.
FM 1307

92. Study, 26 September 1933
Pencil on paper
15.8 x 23.7 cm., 6¼ x 9⁵⁄₁₆ in.
FM 1309

93. Study, 28 September 1933
Pencil on paper
15.8 x 23.7 cm., 6¼ x 9⁵⁄₁₆ in.
FM 1310

94. Study, 28 August 1933
Pencil on paper
15.8 x 23.7 cm., 6¼ x 9⁵⁄₁₆ in.
FM 1312

95. Study, 25 September 1933
Pencil on paper
15.8 x 23.7 cm., 6¼ x 9⁵⁄₁₆ in.
FM 1316

Wartime Studies (1937–42)

Life drawings done at the Académie de la Grande Chaumière, Paris, 1937

96. *Standing Nude*, 1937
Pencil on paper
27 x 20.8 cm., 10⅝ x 8³⁄₁₆ in.
FM 1525

97. *Standing Nude*, 1937
Pencil on paper
33.7 x 25.8 cm., 13¼ x 10³⁄₁₆ in.
FM 1527

98. *Standing Nude*, 1937
Pencil on paper
33.7 x 25.8 cm., 13¼ x 10³⁄₁₆ in.
FM 1606

99. *Kneeling Female Nude*, 1937
Pencil on paper
26 x 33.8 cm., 10¼ x 13⁵⁄₁₆ in.
FM 1528

100. Eight studies, March 1942
Pencil on torn newspaper
Irregular: 4.5–8.2 x 32.7–33.6 cm., 1¾–3¼ x 12⅞–13¼ in.
FM 1869–1876
Drawings on the Barcelona newspaper, *La Vanguardia* (5 March 1942), announcing the bombing of parts of Paris. Miró had by this time returned to Spain.

101. *Self-Portrait*, 14 March 1942
Pencil on newspaper
25 x 25 cm., 9⅞ x 9⅞ in.
FM 1842
Drawing on a 1937 issue of *La Vanguardia*, saved from Paris, concerning Civil War in northern Spain.

102. Study, 2 June 1942
Pencil on paper
15 x 22 cm., 5¹⁵⁄₁₆ x 8¹¹⁄₁₆ in.
FM 1845

103. Study, 2 June 1942
Pencil on paper
22 x 15 cm., 8¹¹⁄₁₆ x 5¹⁵⁄₁₆ in.
FM 1846
These two studies from June 1942 show a return to earlier motifs and a loose linear style, which would characterize Miró's production in the 1940s.

Studies for Sculptures, 1945–56

104. Project for a sculpture, 28 July 1945
Pencil on tan cardboard
75 x 52.5 cm., 29½ x 20¹¹⁄₁₆ in.
FM 3742

105. Study for *Project for a Monument*, 15 August 1951
Pencil on paper
23.2 x 19.3 cm., 9⅛ x 7⅝ in.
FM 3722
Study for sculpture, 1954 (Figure G) made of stone, bone, metal, porcelain hook. Collection Fundació Joan Miró, Barcelona

106. Study for *Project for a Monument*, 16 August 1951
Pencil on paper
23 x 19.9 cm., 9¹⁄₁₆ x 7¹³⁄₁₆ in.
FM 3720
Inscribed in Catalan on left: "Bronze/unique piece."
Study for sculpture, 1954 (Figure H) made of cement, bronze, copper, porcelain hook. Collection Fundació Joan Miró, Barcelona

107. Study for *Project for a Monument*, 17 August 1951
Pencil on paper
23.4 x 19.5 cm., 9³⁄₁₆ x 7¹¹⁄₁₆ in.
FM 3723
Study for sculpture, 1954 (Figure I) made of cement, iron, leather, wood. Collection Fundació Joan Miró, Barcelona

108. Study for ceramic sculpture, ca. 1956
Ink on cardboard
Irregular: 10 x 8.3 cm., 3¹⁵⁄₁₆ x 3¼ in.
FM 2367

109. Study for ceramic sculpture, ca. 1956
Ink on cardboard
Irregular: 7.2 x 8.3 cm., 2¹³⁄₁₆ x 3¼ in.
FM 2369
Inscribed in French and Catalan clockwise from top to lower left: "Montroig/in the spirit of projects for a monument/bottle/ make stone shapes solid"

110. Study for ceramic sculpture, ca. 1956
Ink on cardboard
Irregular: 9.8 x 8.7 cm., 3⅞ x 3⁷⁄₁₆ in.
FM 2372
Inscribed in Catalan: "object/cuttle-bone/on studio table"

111. Study for ceramic sculpture, ca. 1956
Ink on paper
Irregular: 10.8 x 13 cm., 4¼ x 5⅛ in.
FM 2375
Inscribed in Catalan: "rounded" or "turned" (not clearly legible). It is difficult to identify these four studies, ca. 1956, with precise pieces. However, certain motifs and the assemblage process are typical of Miró's ceramics of 1956.

1960s

112. Study for *Blue I*, 27 February 1960
Ink, blue and red pencil on paper
7.2 x 9.6 cm., 2¹³⁄₁₆ x 3¾ in.
FM 2446
Study for painting, March 1961, (Figure J). Collection Hubert de Givenchy, Paris (Dupin, 969)

113. Study for *Blue II*, 6 May 1960
Ballpoint pen, blue and red pencil on paper
10.0 x 13.3 cm., 4 x 5¼ in.
FM 2444
Study for painting, March 1961 (Figure K). Collection Musée National d'Art Moderne, Centre Georges Pompidou, Paris
(Dupin, 970)

114. Study for *Blue III*, 6 May 1960
Ballpoint pen and blue pencil on paper
9.4 x 13.3 cm., 3¹¹⁄₁₆ x 5¼ in.
FM 2445
Study for painting, March 1961 (Figure L). Collection Pierre Matisse Gallery, New York
(Dupin, 971)

115. Study for *Mural Painting for a Temple I*, 6 September 1960
Ink on paper
7.4 x 7.5 cm., 2¹⁵⁄₁₆ x 3 in.
FM 4621
Inscribed in French: "orange"
Study for painting, May 1962. Collection Adrien Maeght, Paris

116. Study for *Mural Painting for a Temple II*, 6 September 1960
Ink on paper
6.6 x 7.9 cm., 2⅝ x 3⅛ in.
FM 4622
Inscribed in French: "green"
Study for painting, May 1962. Collection Adrien Maeght, Paris

117. Study for *Mural Painting for a Temple III*, 6 September 1960
Ink on paper
6.6 x 7.9 cm., 2⅝ x 3⅛ in.
FM 4623
Inscribed in French: "red"
Study for painting, May 1962. Collection Adrien Maeght, Paris

118. Drawing, 15 April 1961
Ink on paper
10 x 15.2 cm., 3¹⁵⁄₁₆ x 6 in.
FM 2337

119. Drawing, 15 April 1961
Ink on paper
10 x 15.2 cm., 3¹⁵⁄₁₆ x 6 in.
FM 2338

120. Drawing, 15 April 1961
Ink on paper
10 x 15.2 cm., 3¹⁵⁄₁₆ x 6 in.
FM 2339

121. Drawing, 23 September 1966
Ballpoint pen and colored crayon on paper
15.2 x 19.5 cm., 6 x 7¹¹⁄₁₆ in.
FM 2924

122. *The Fall of the Bird before Fate*, 11 February, 1967
Ballpoint pen and colored crayon on paper
15.2 x 20.7 cm., 6 x 8⅛ in.
FM 4551
Inscribed in French with title and date.

123. *Bird in the Night*, 21 October 1967
Ballpoint pen and colored crayons on paper
15.2 x 19.6 cm., 6 x 7¹¹⁄₁₆ in.
FM 4562
Inscribed in French with title and date.

124. Study, 23 September 1967
Ballpoint pen and colored crayon on paper
20.7 x 15 cm., 8⅛ x 5¹⁵⁄₁₆ in.
FM 2763
Inscribed in Catalan lower left: "with the fingers"
Related to painting, *Flight of the Migratory Bird*, 1968. Private collection, Paris.

125. *The Hand in Infinity*, 28 December 1967
Ballpoint pen, blue and red pencil on paper
15.6 x 19.5 cm., 6⅛ x 7¹¹⁄₁₆ in.
FM 2078
Inscribed in French with title and date.

126. *The Star of Hope Rises II*, 25 March 1968
Ballpoint pen, green and yellow pencil on paper
15.7 x 21.5 cm., 6³⁄₁₆ x 8⁷⁄₁₆ in.
FM 2068
Inscribed in French with title and date.

127. Studies for *Drop of Water on the Rose-colored Snow*, 20 September 1966
Pencil, ballpoint pen, and colored crayon on paper
15.3 x 19.5 cm., 6⅛ x 7¹¹⁄₁₆ in.
FM 3427
Inscribed in French: "Drop of water on the snow on a starry night/ Hair in space on a starry night"; dated.
Study for painting, 18 February 1968. Private collection, USA.

128. Studies for *Hair Pursued by Two Planets*, 22 September/19 October 1966
Pencil, ballpoint pen, and colored crayon on paper
15.3 x 19.5 cm., 6⅛ x 7¹¹⁄₁₆ in.
FM 3428
Inscribed in Catalan: "Pass the brush all over the forms, directly, with black. Add green and yellow freely over a preliminary coat of white"; dated twice; lower right: "do not sign"
Study for painting, 18 March 1968 (Figure M). Collection Pierre Matisse Gallery, New York.

129. Studies for painting, 7 February 1967
Pencil, ballpoint pen, and colored crayon on paper
15.3 x 19.5 cm., 6⅛ x 7¹¹⁄₁₆ in.
FM 3429
Inscribed in Catalan: "gray halo well defined; put on coat of white before putting on the color"; dated. These studies are related to those for *Hair Pursued by Two Planets*, above.

1970s

Since Dupin's catalogue raisonné of Miró stops in 1960, it is difficult to attribute the following studies to specific paintings.

130. Studies, ca. 1971
Ballpoint pen and colored pencils on paper
21 x 26.8 cm., 8¼ x 10¾ in.
FM 2492
Inscribed in Catalan: "Small canvases with little dots in different colors/black accents with the fingers/moisten with turpentine"

131. Studies, 25 January 1971
Ballpoint pen and colored pencils on paper
21 x 26.8 cm., 8¼ x 10¾ in.
FM 2493
Inscribed in Catalan: "3 medium-sized canvases/ moisten first with turpentine/follow with a black accent/think of Mark Tobey"; dated.

132. Study for *Red Accent*, 1 September 1972
Ballpoint pen and colored crayons on torn newspaper

4.6 x 14.5 cm., 1 13/16 x 5 11/16 in.
FM 3261
Inscribed with initials for colors; on right in Catalan: "very dry white brush", title and date.

133. *Bird I*, 7 November 1972
Black and blue pencils on paper
19.8 x 15.5 cm., 7 13/16 x 6 1/8 in.
FM 3207
Inscribed in French with title and date; lower left in Catalan: "larger than 120" [Note: *120* indicates a standard canvas size, approximately 78 x 52 in.]

134. *Landscape*, 10 December 1972
Ballpoint pen and colored pencils on paper
15.5 x 19.8 cm., 6 1/8 x 7 13/16 in.
FM 3273
Inscribed in French with title and date; lower left in Catalan: "larger than 120"

135. *Landscape*, 1973
Ballpoint pen, yellow and green colored pencils on paper
8 x 12.5 cm., 3 1/8 x 4 15/16 in.
FM 2060

136. *Landscape: Homage to Urgell*, 25 December 1972
Ballpoint pen and colored pencils on paper
8.2 x 11.5 cm., 3 1/4 x 4 3/4 in.
FM 3263
Inscribed in French with title and date.

137. *Person in Front of the Moon*, 13 March 1972
Ballpoint pen on paper
8 x 12.5 cm., 3 1/8 x 4 15/16 in.
FM 3252
Inscribed in French with title and date, initials indicating colors, and "2 x 2," indicating size in meters.

138. *Woman in the Night*, 31 October 1972
Ballpoint pen and colored crayons on paper
19.8 x 15.6 cm., 7 13/16 x 6 1/8 in.
FM 3253
Inscribed in French with title and date.

139. *Landscape II*, 10 January 1973
Ballpoint pen and colored pencils on paper
19.8 x 15 cm., 7 13/16 x 5 15/16 in.
FM 2107
Inscribed in French with title and date.

140. Studies for *Sign I, II, III*, 30 March 1973
Ballpoint pen and colored pencils on paper
15.5 x 19.8 cm., 6 1/8 x 7 13/16 in.
FM 2126
Inscribed in French with title and date.

141. Studies for *Sign I, II, III*, 30 March 1973
Ballpoint pen and colored pencils on paper
15.5 x 19.8 cm., 6 1/8 x 7 13/16 in.
FM 2127
Inscribed in French with title and date.

142. Study for *The Hope of the Condemned Man*, 10 January 1973
Ballpoint pen and colored pencils on paper
15.5 x 19.8 cm., 6 1/8 x 7 13/16 in.
FM 2117
Study for painting, 1974. Collection Fundació Joan Miró, Barcelona.

143. Study for *The Hope of the Condemned Man*, 10 January 1973
Ballpoint pen and colored pencils on paper
15.5 x 19.8 cm., 6 1/8 x 7 13/16 in.
FM 2118
Study for painting, 1974. Collection Fundació Joan Miró, Barcelona.

144. Study for *The Hope of the Condemned Man*, 10 January 1973
Ballpoint pen and colored pencils on paper
15.5 x 19.8 cm., 6 1/8 x 7 13/16 in.
FM 2119
Study for painting, 1974. Collection Fundació Joan Miró, Barcelona.

145. *Hand Flying Off Toward Hope*, n.d.
Ballpoint pen and colored crayons on paper
21 x 29.6 cm., 8 1/4 x 11 5/8 in.
FM 2105
Inscribed in French with title.

146. Studies for a series, ca. 1973
Ink and colored crayons on paper
21 x 27 cm., 8 1/4 x 10 5/8 in.
FM 1921
Inscribed in Catalan: "Do the colors with pencil/the moon in solid gray/the lines should be very precise, and loose, like I did in Levallois/all the signs should be very direct"

147. Study, ca. 1973
Collage, ink, and colored crayons on paper
30 x 21.2 cm., 12 x 8 1/2 in.
FM 1927
Study related to same series.

148. Study, ca. 1973
Ballpoint pen and colored pencil on paper
27 x 21.2 cm., 10 5/8 x 8 1/2 in.
FM 1925

149. *The Crucified Prisoner*, 10 February 1974
Ballpoint pen and colored pencils on paper
21 x 14 cm., 8 1/4 x 5 1/2 in.
FM 2043
Inscribed in French with title and date.

List of Figure Illustrations

Figure A
Joan Miró
The Hunter (Catalan Landscape), 1923–24
Oil on canvas
64.8 x 100.3 cm., $25\frac{1}{2}$ x $39\frac{1}{2}$ in.
Collection The Museum of Modern Art, New York. Purchase.

Figure B
Magazine cover that inspired *The Spanish Dancer*, ca. 1924
Printed on paper
28.5 cm. x 20.7 cm., $11\frac{1}{4}$ x $8\frac{1}{8}$ in.
FM 4479
Study for painting, 1924. Collection Mrs. René Gaffé, France (Dupin, 87)

Figure C
Joan Miró
Carnival of Harlequin, 1924–25
Oil on canvas
66 x 93 cm., 26 x $36\frac{5}{8}$ in.
Collection Albright-Knox Art Gallery, Buffalo, New York. Room of Contemporary Art Fund, 1940

Figure D
Postcard of the painting by Jan Steen, *The Dancing Lesson of the Cat*, 17th century
Printed on cardboard
14 x 8.9 cm., $5\frac{1}{2}$ x $3\frac{1}{2}$ in.
FM 3142
Inspiration for painting *Dutch Interior II*, 1928 (Figure E). Peggy Guggenheim Collection, Venice (Dupin, 235)

Figure E
Joan Miró
Dutch Interior II, Summer 1928
Oil on canvas
92.1 x 73 cm., $36\frac{5}{16}$ x $28\frac{13}{16}$ in.
Peggy Guggenheim Collection, Venice; Solomon R. Guggenheim Foundation, New York
Photo: Carmelo Guadagno

Figure F
Joan Miró
Painting, 1933
Oil on canvas
130.8 x 163.2 cm., $51\frac{3}{8}$ x $64\frac{1}{4}$ in.
Philadelphia Museum of Art, A.E. Gallatin Collection

Figure G
Joan Miró
Project for a Monument, 1954
Stone, bone, metal, porcelain hook
45 x 26 x 16 cm., 18 x $10\frac{1}{4}$ x $6\frac{5}{8}$ in.
FM 7245
Collection Fundació Joan Miró, Barcelona

Figure H
Joan Miró
Project for a Monument, 1954
Cement, bronze, copper, porcelain hook
53 x 13 x 13 cm., 21 x $5\frac{1}{4}$ x $5\frac{1}{4}$ in.
FM 7246
Collection Fundació Joan Miró, Barcelona

Figure I
Project for a Monument: Personnage, 1954
Bronze, wood
34.5 x 39.5 x 15 cm., $13\frac{7}{8}$ x $15\frac{7}{8}$ x 6 in.
FM 7264
Collection Fundació Joan Miró, Barcelona

Figure J
Joan Miró
Blue I, March 1961
Oil on canvas
270 x 355 cm, $106\frac{1}{4}$ x $139\frac{3}{4}$ in.
Collection Hubert de Givenchy, Paris

Figure K
Joan Miró
Blue II, March 1961
Oil on canvas
270 x 355 cm., $106\frac{1}{4}$ x $139\frac{3}{4}$ in.
Collection Musée National d'Art Moderne, Centre Georges Pompidou, Paris

Figure L
Joan Miró
Blue III, March 1961
Oil on canvas
270 x 355 cm., $106\frac{1}{4}$ x $139\frac{3}{4}$ in.
Collection Pierre Matisse Gallery, New York

Figure M
Joan Miró
Hair Pursued by Two Planets, 1968
Oil on canvas
195.5 x 130.2 cm., $76\frac{7}{8}$ x $51\frac{1}{4}$ in.
Collection Pierre Matisse Gallery, New York

Early Drawings, 1901-20

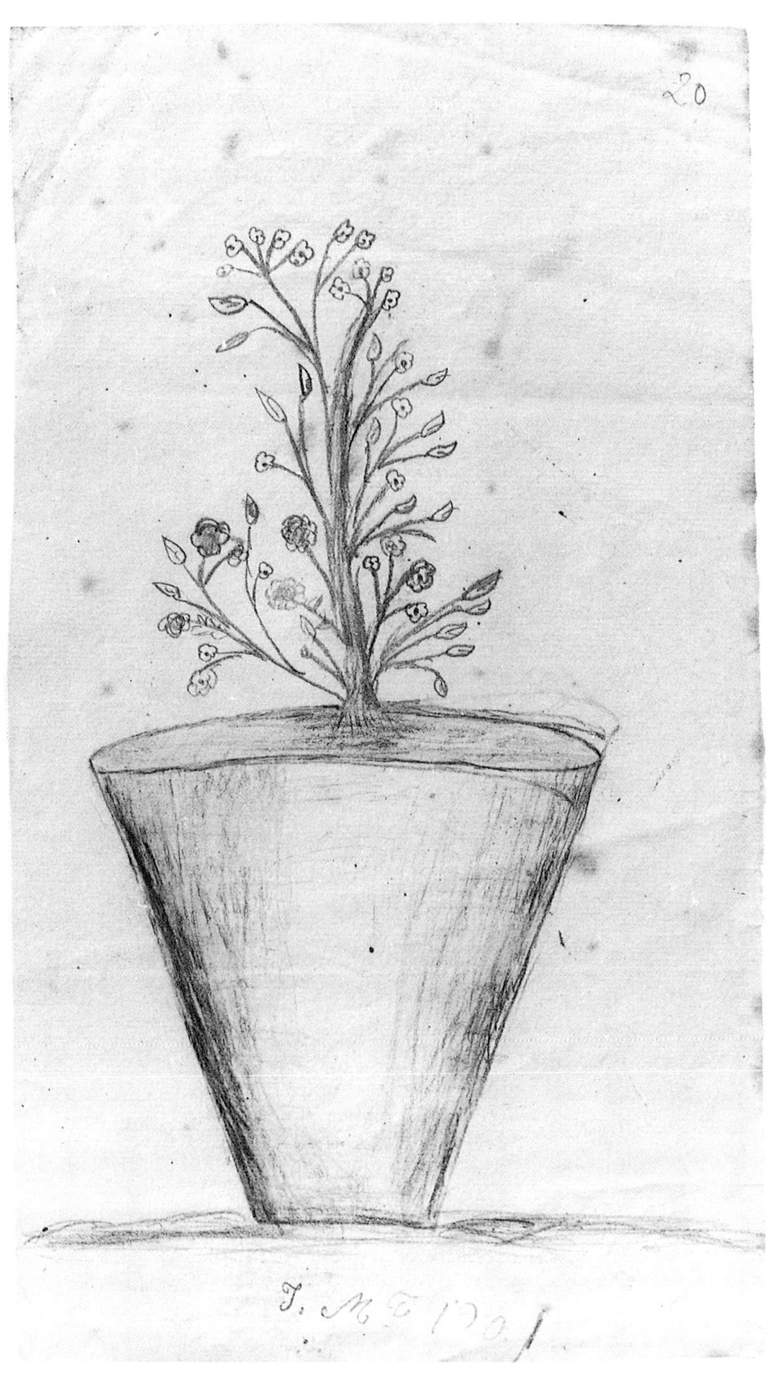

1. *Flower Pot with Flowers*, 1901

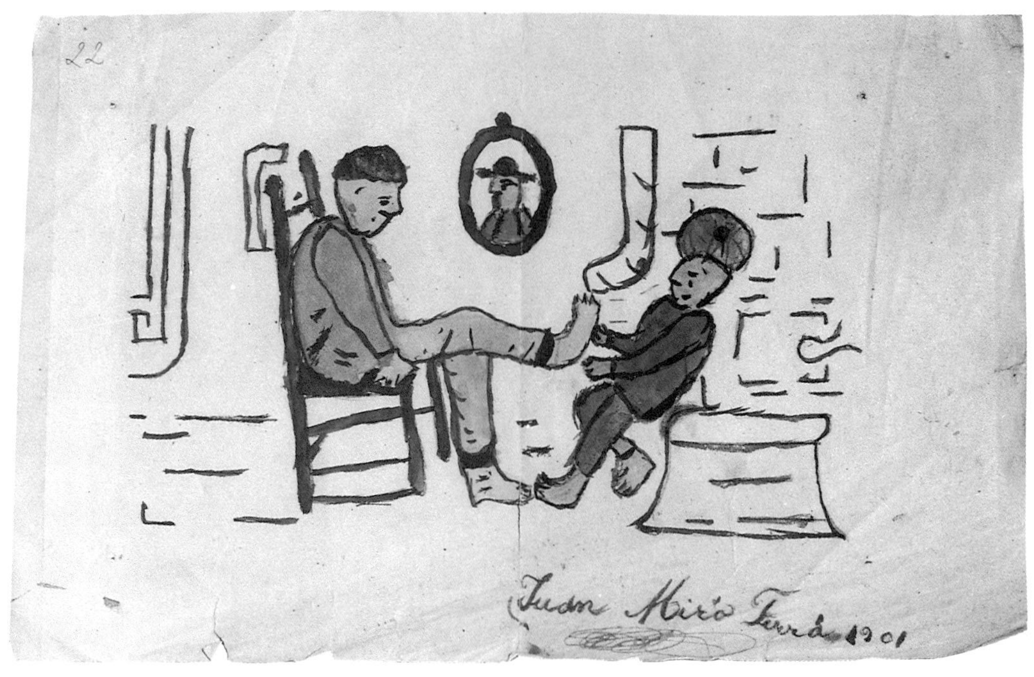
2. *The Pedicure*, 1901

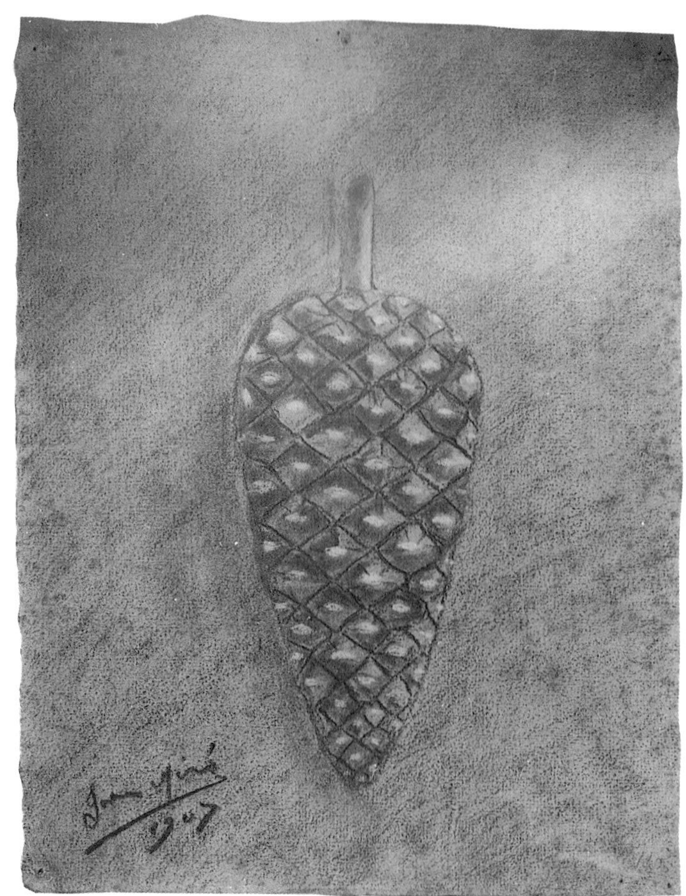
4. *Pinecone*, 1907

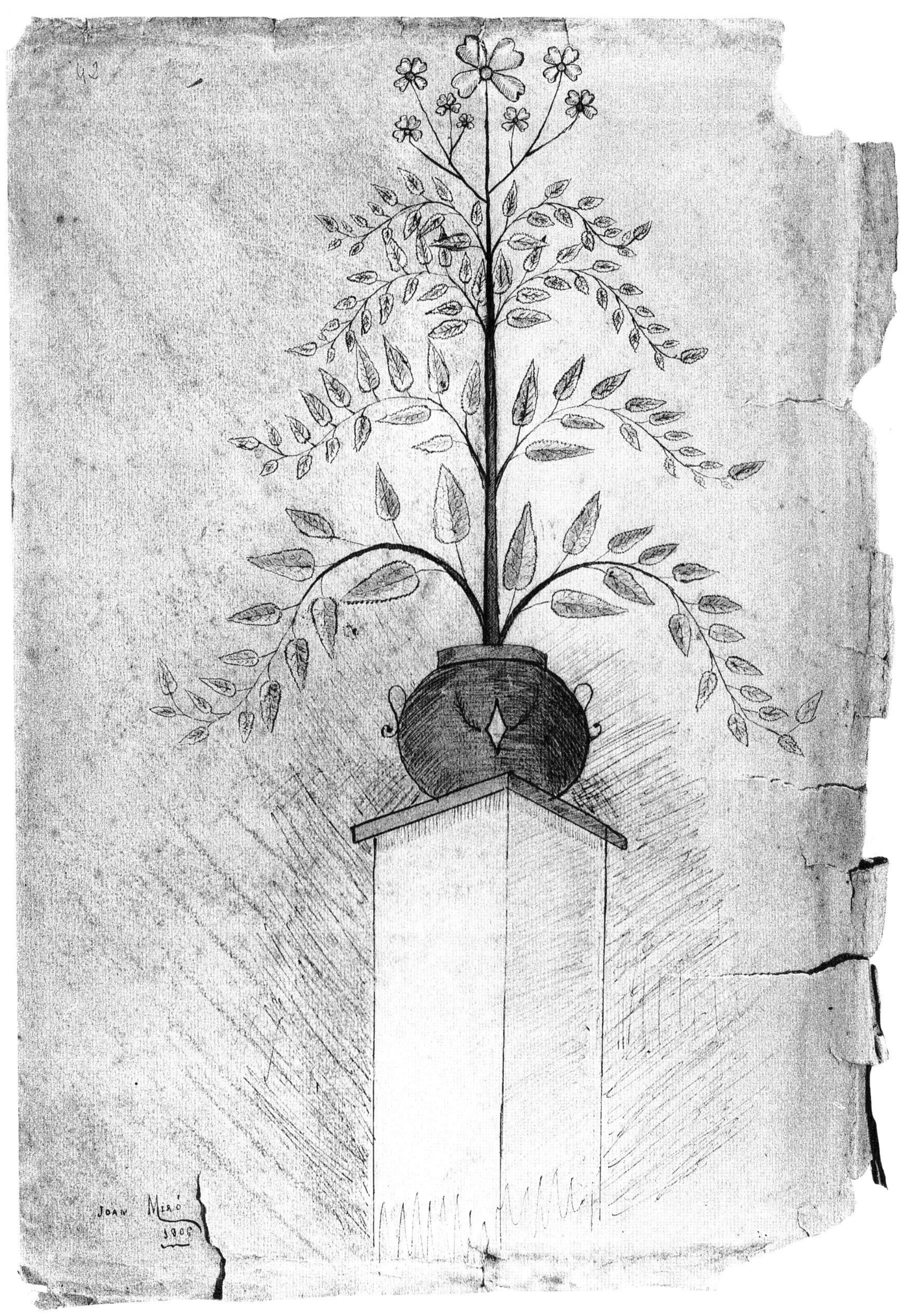

3. *Flower Pot with Flowers*, 1906

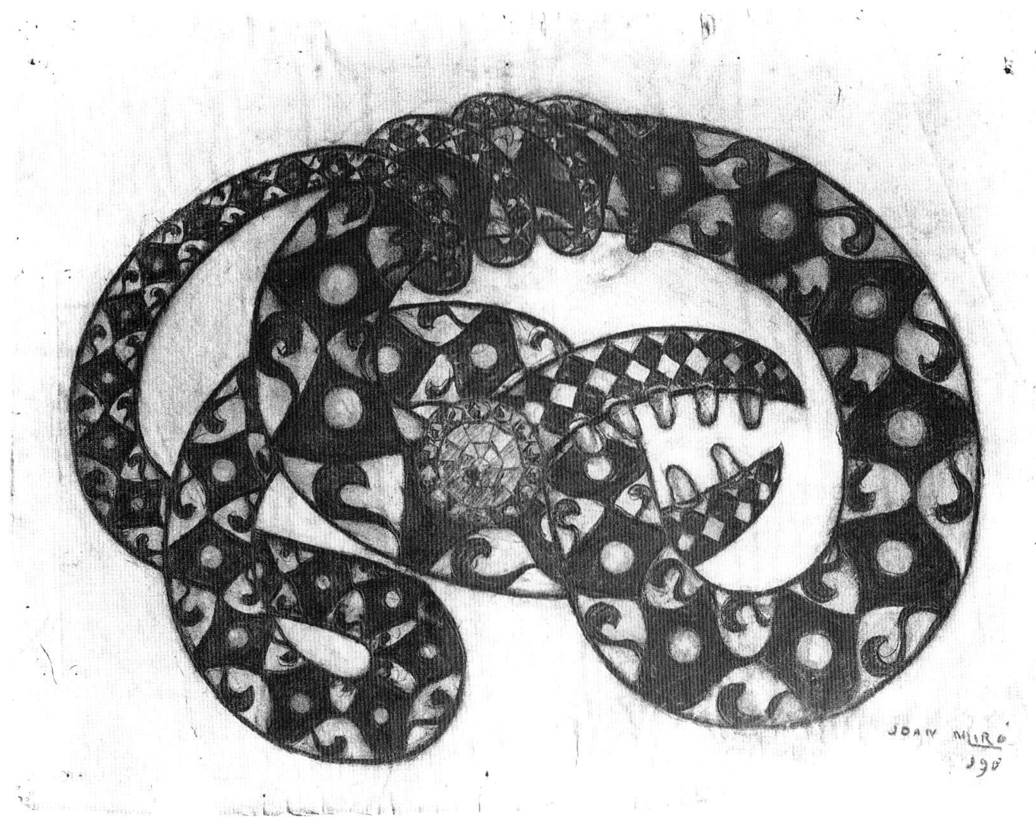

5. Project for a piece of jewelry, ca. 1908

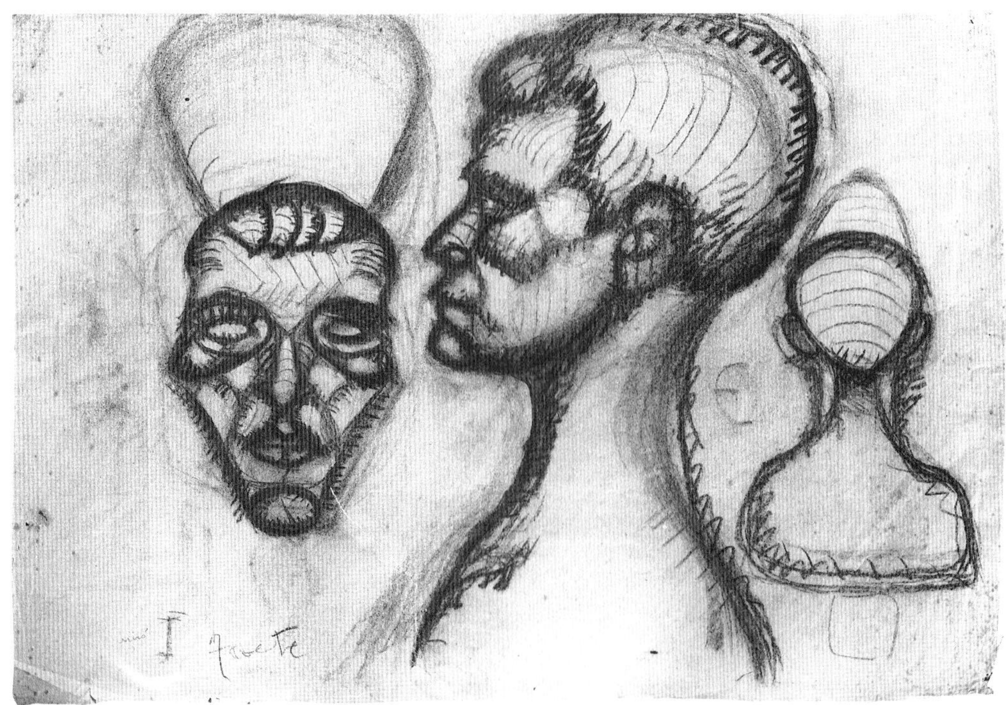
6. *Three Heads*, ca. 1912

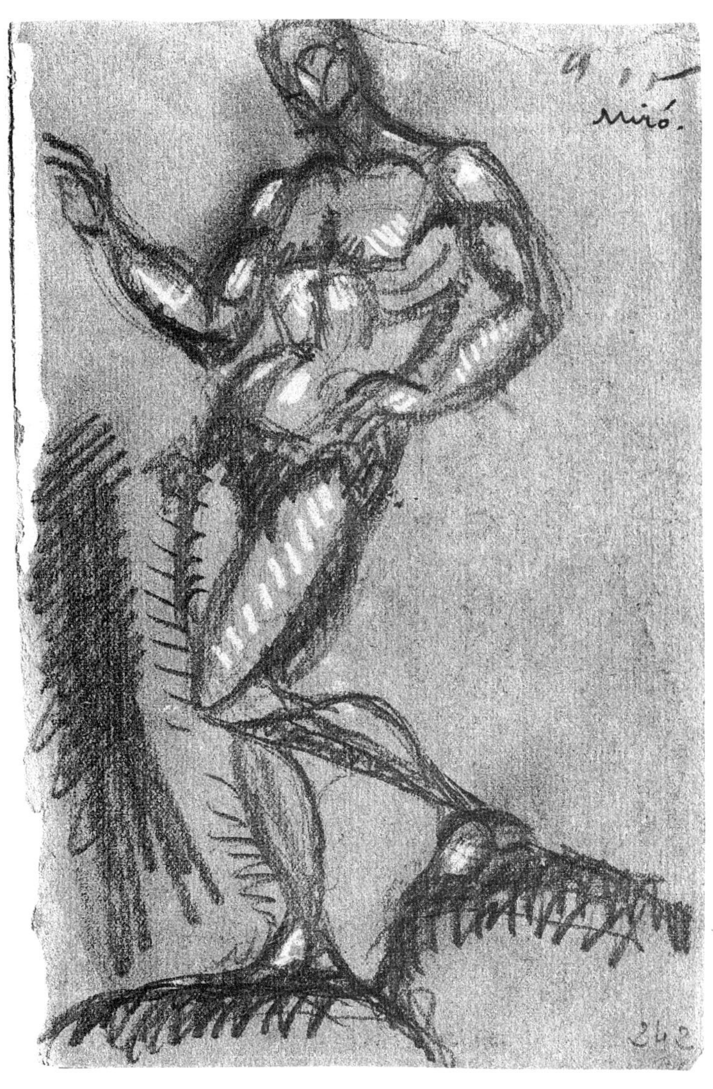

7. *Male Figure Study*, 1915

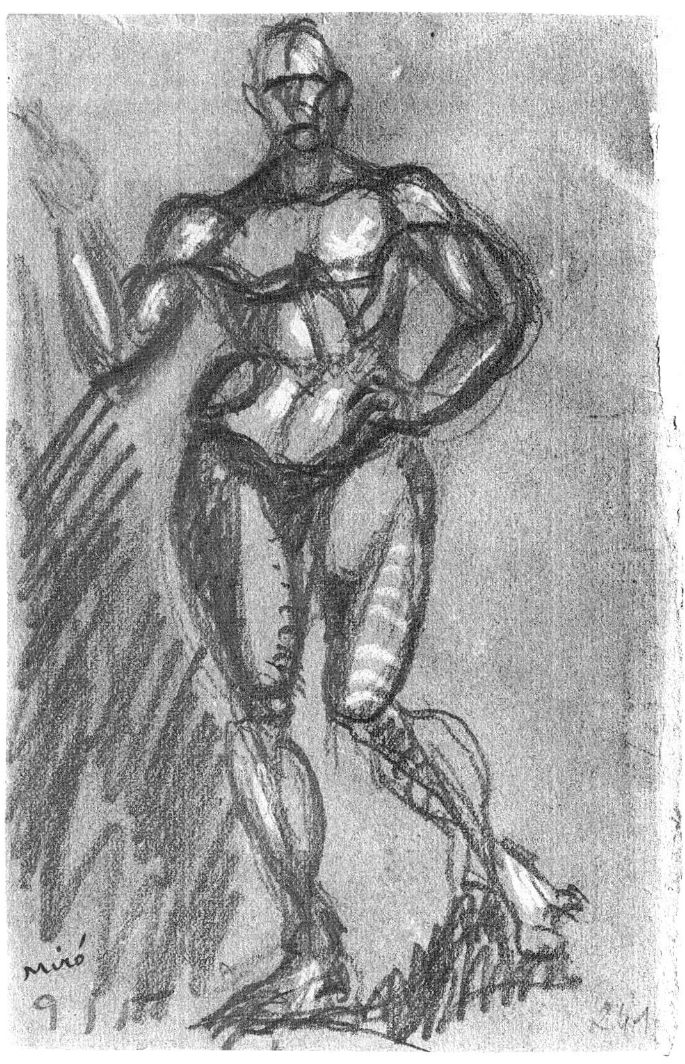

8. *Male Figure Study*, 1915

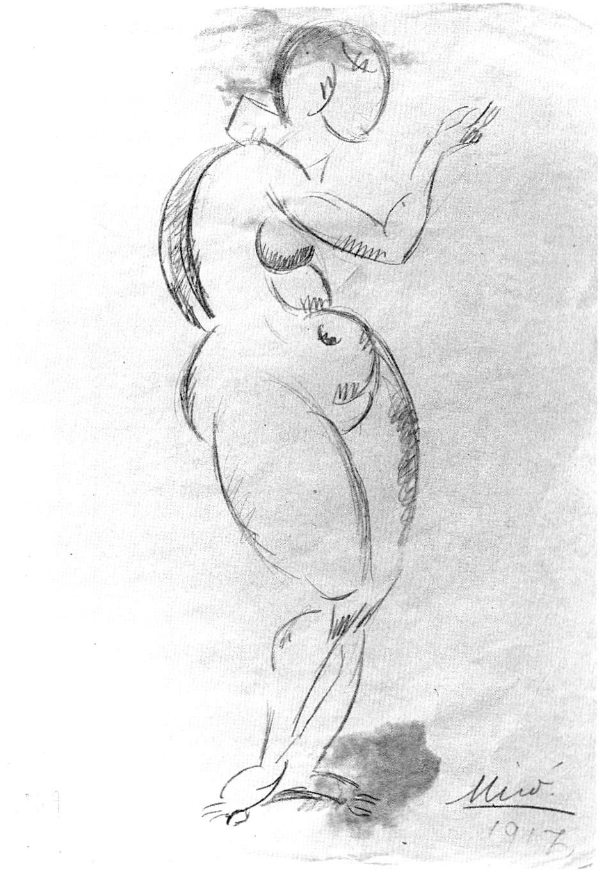

9. *Standing Female Nude*, 1917

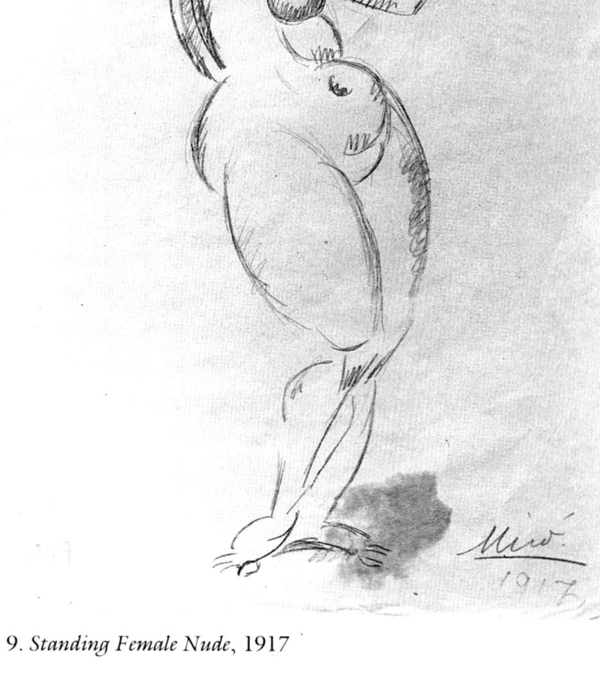

10. *Spanish Dancer*, 1917

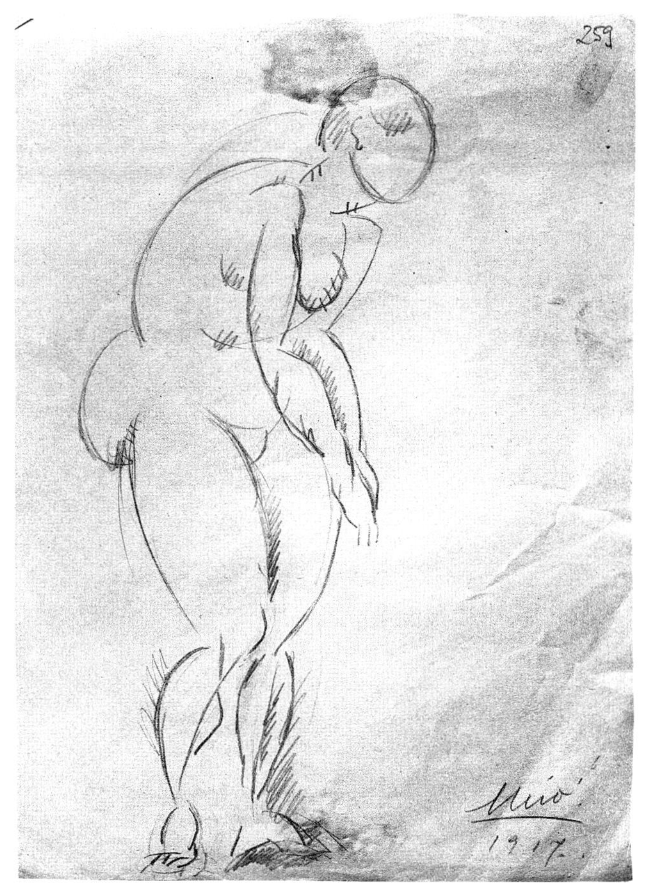

11. *Female Nude Leaning Forward*, 1917

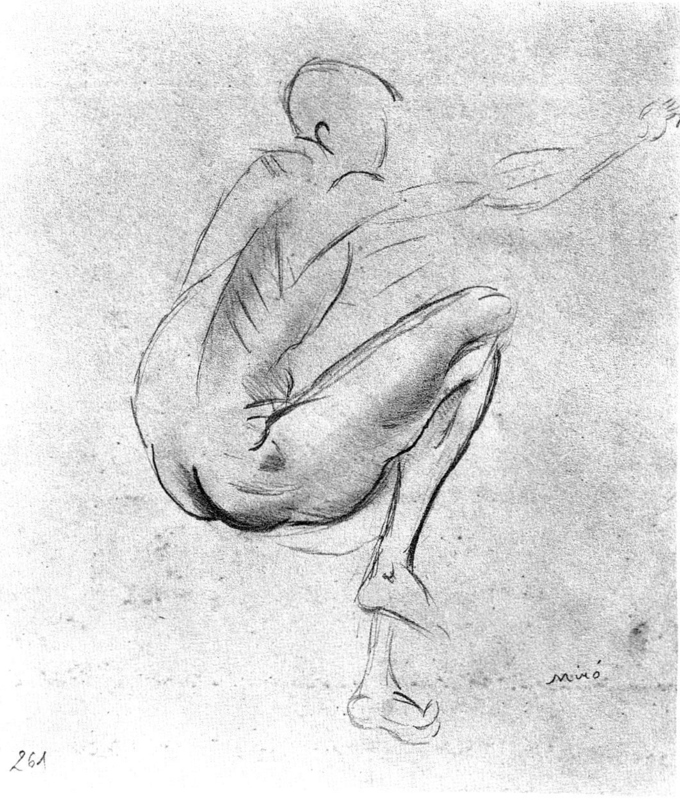

12. *Seated Male Nude*, 1917

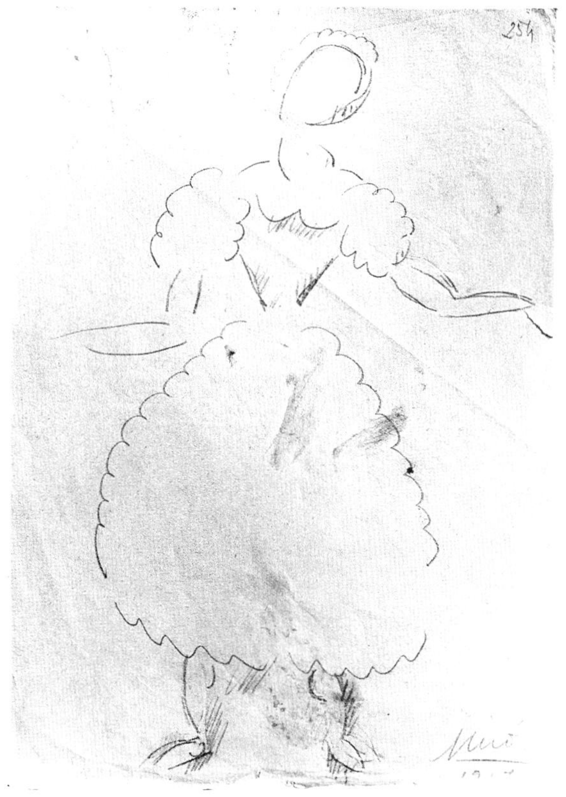

13. *Woman with Arms Spread*, 1917

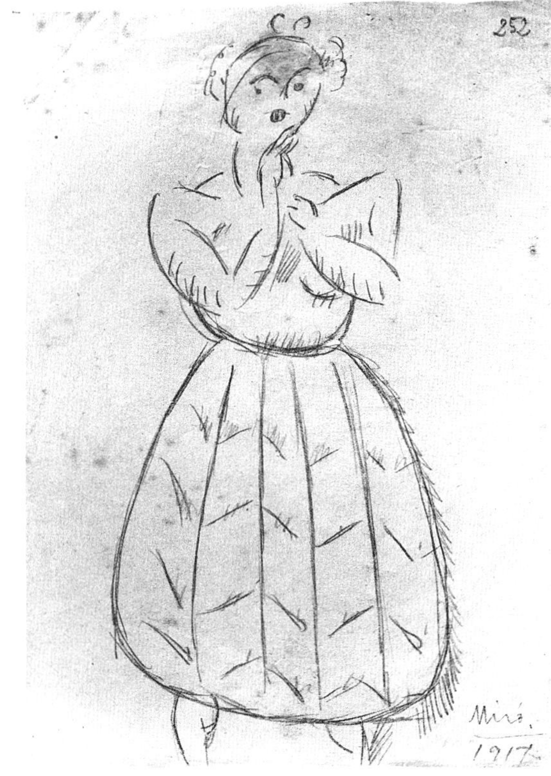

14. *Woman Holding Her Chin*, 1917

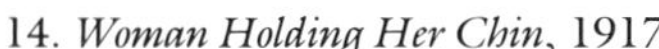

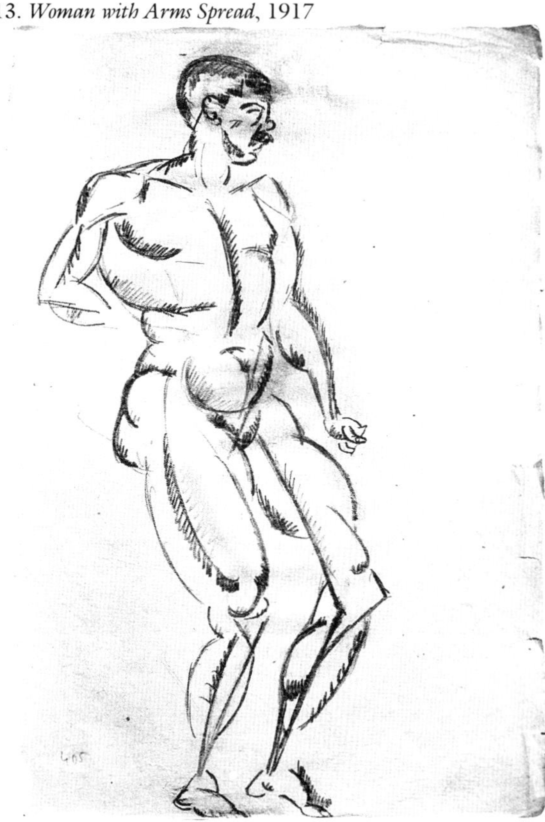

15. *Male Figure Study*, ca. 1917

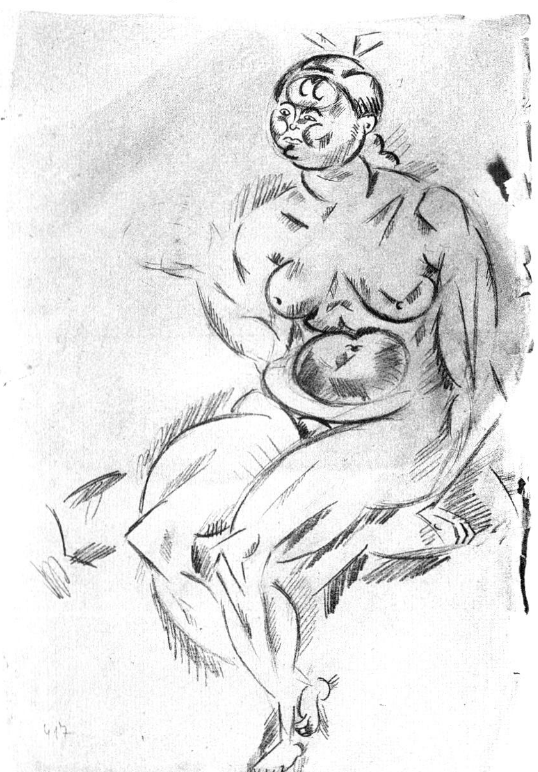

16. *Seated Female Nude*, 1917

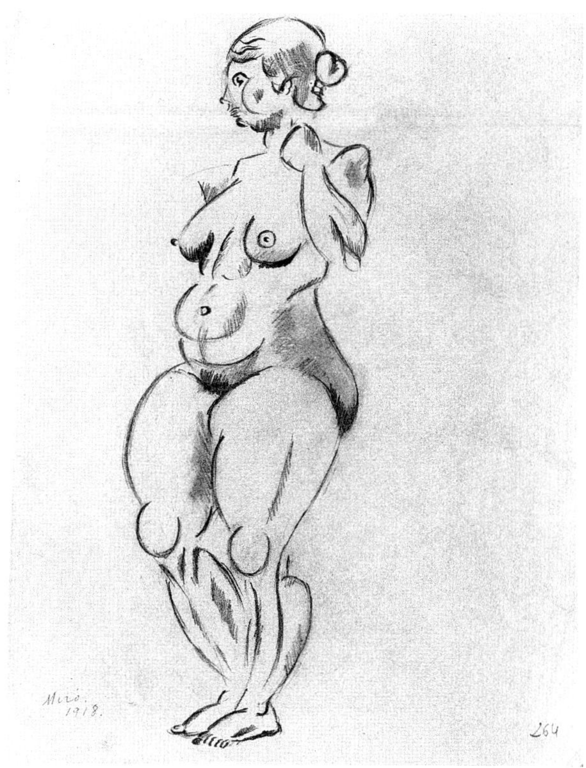

17. *Standing Female Nude*, 1918

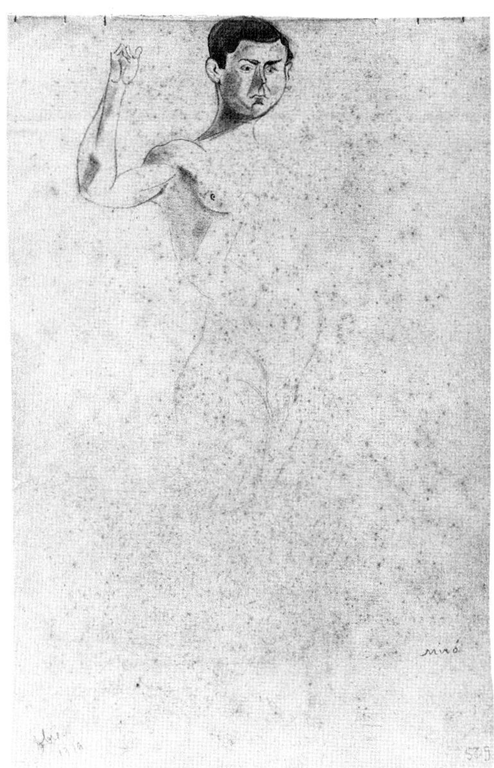

18. *Male Figure Study*, 1919

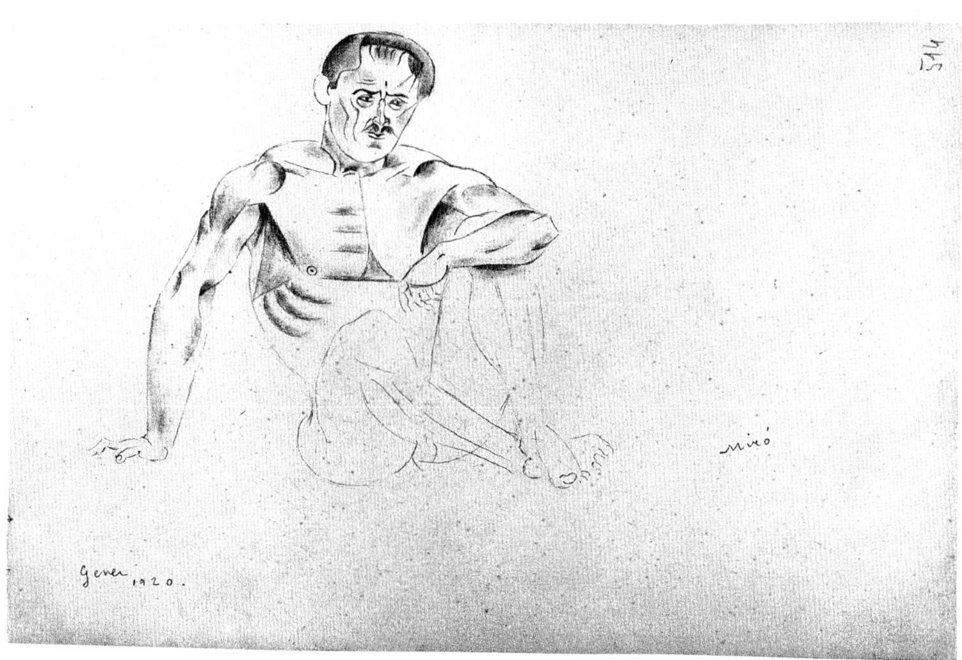

19. *Male Figure Study*, 1920

Studies for Paintings, the 1920s

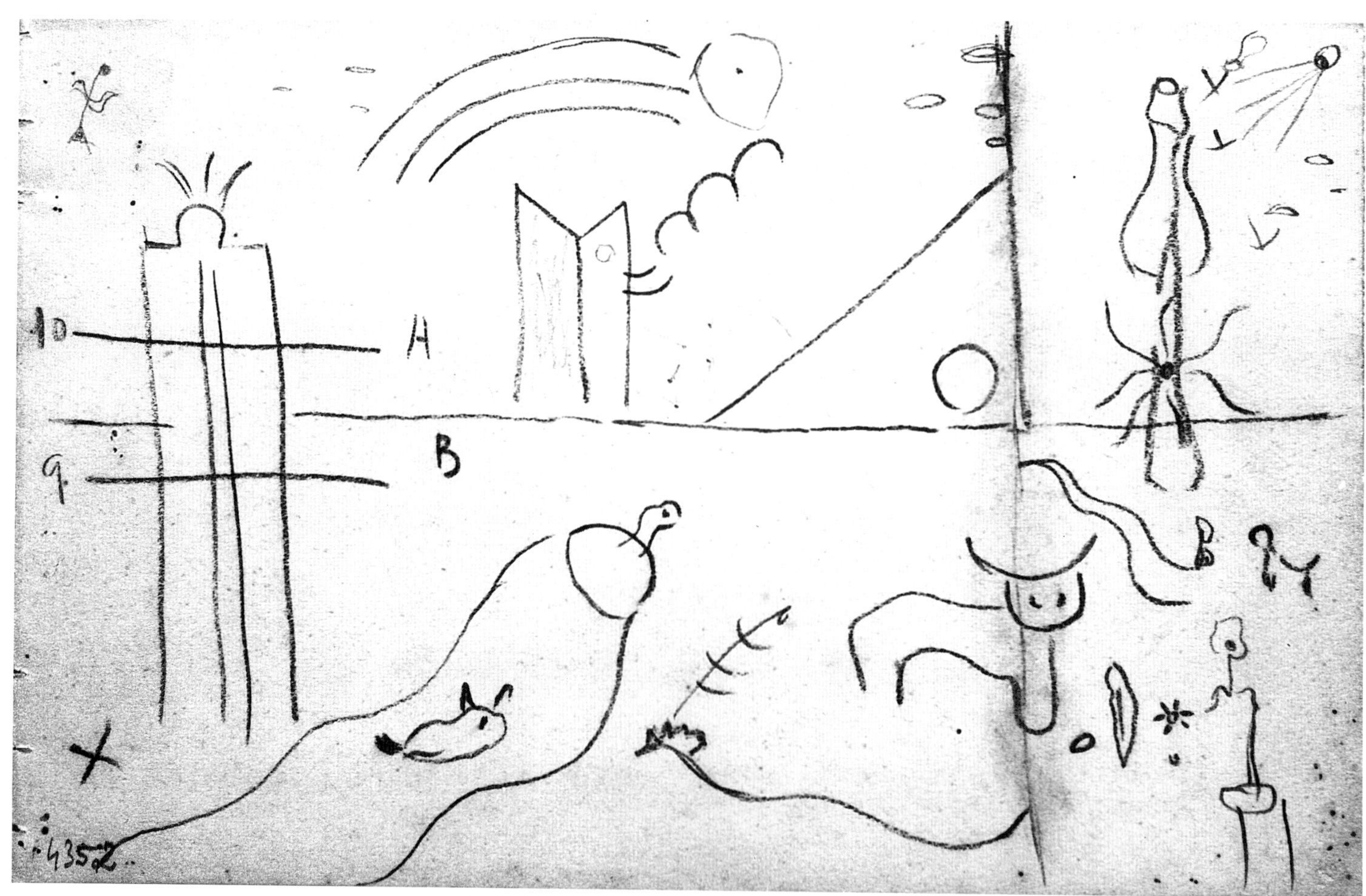

20. Study for *Pastoral*, ca. 1923

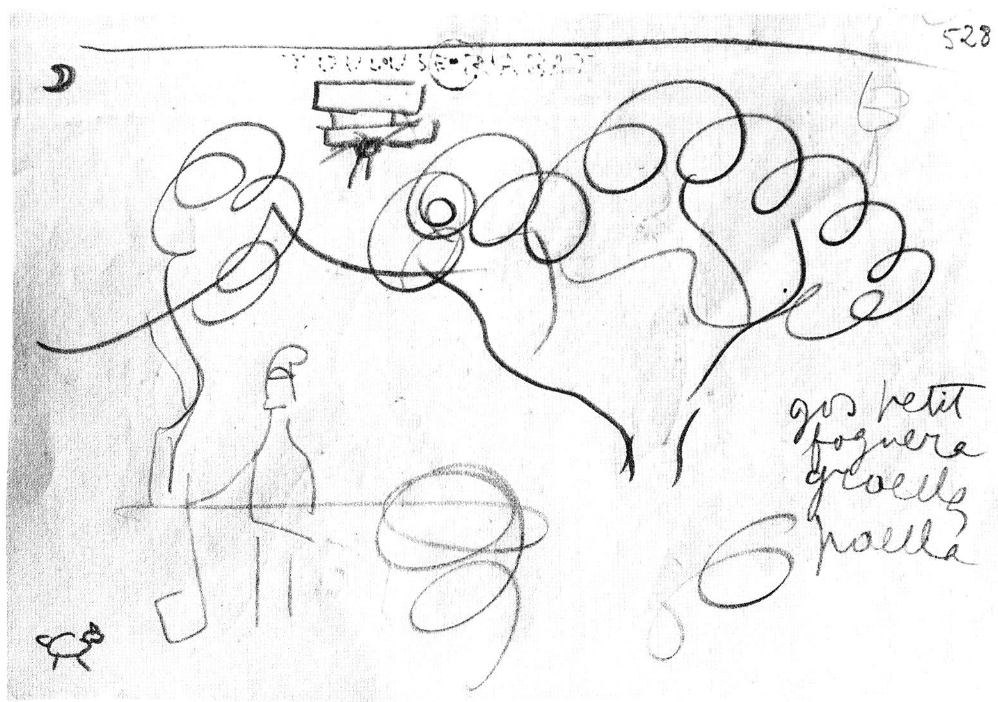

21. Study for *The Hunter (Catalan Landscape)*, ca. 1923

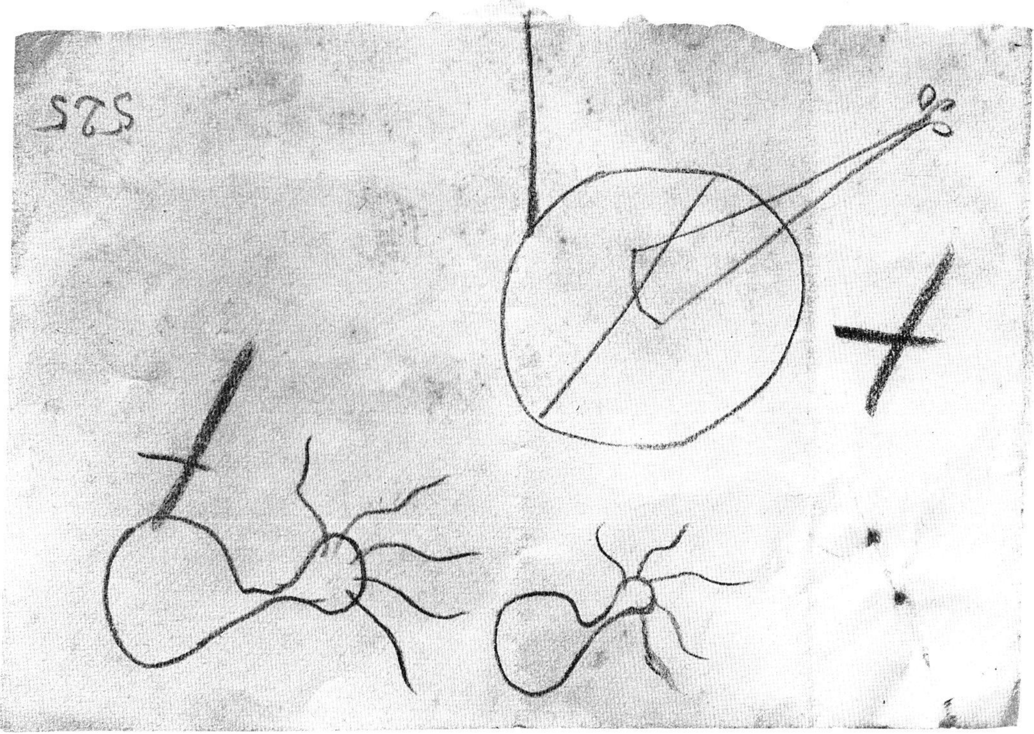

22. Study for *The Hunter (Catalan Landscape)*, ca. 1923

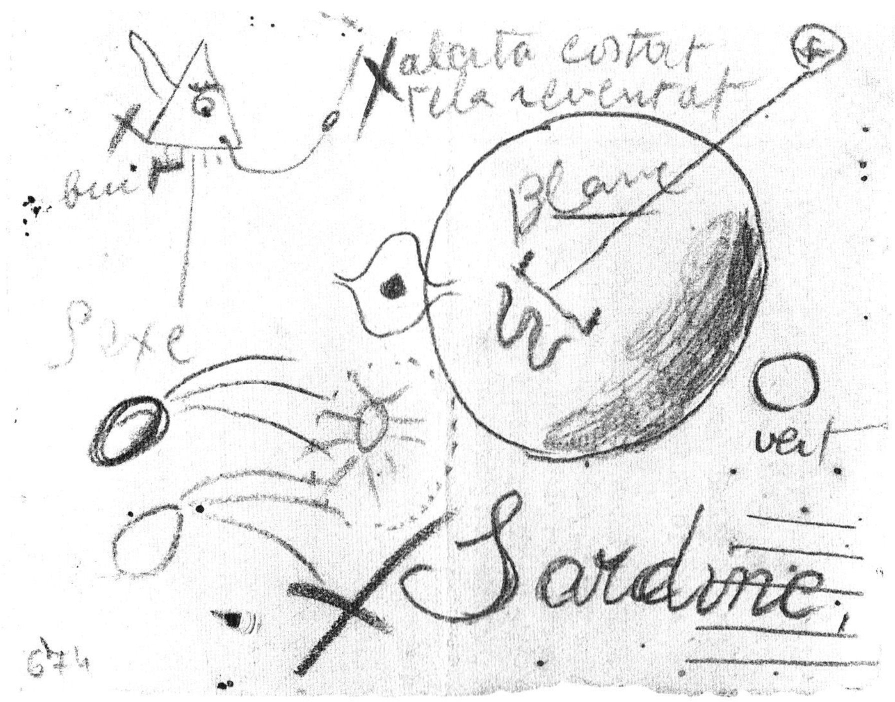

23. Study for *The Hunter (Catalan Landscape)*, ca. 1923

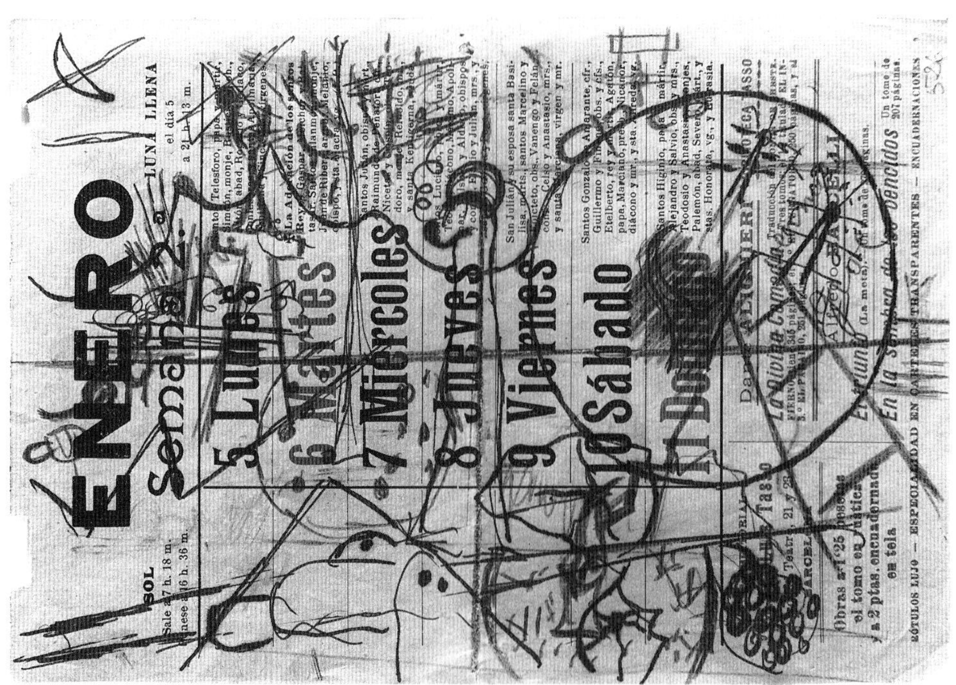

24. Study for *The Hunter (Catalan Landscape)*, ca. 1923

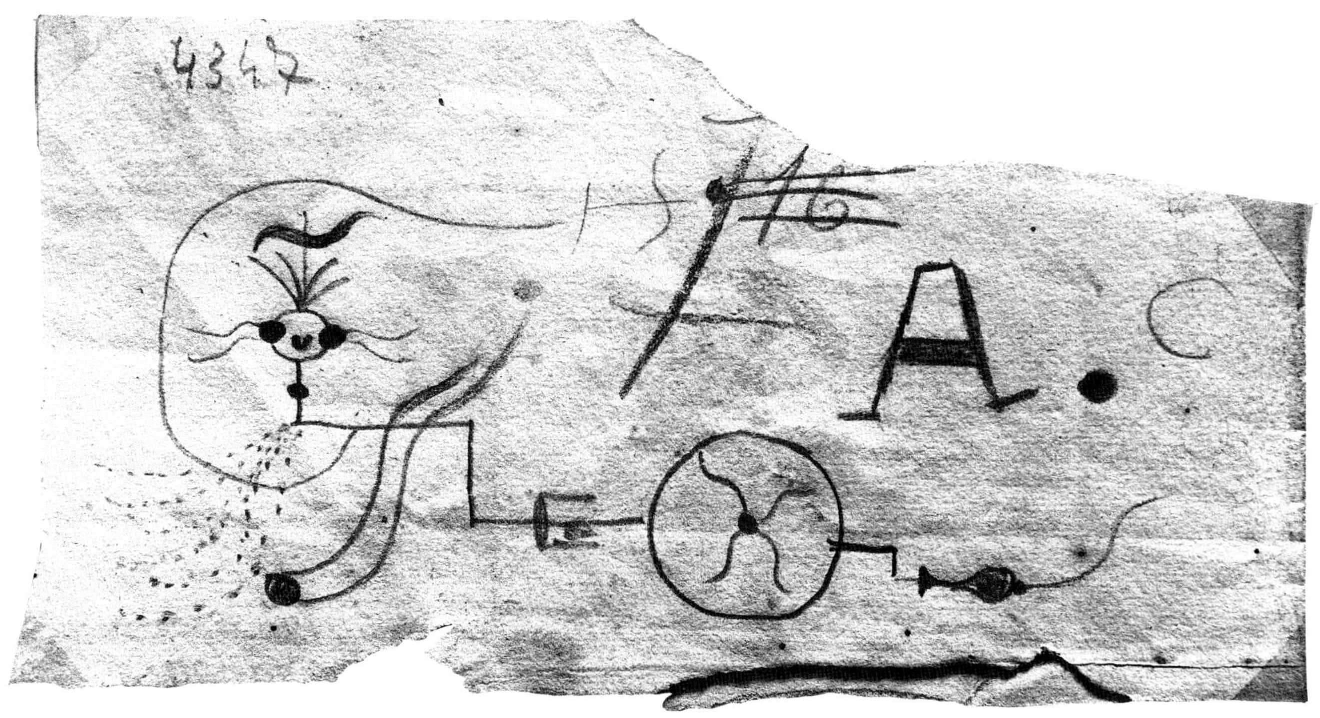

25. Study for *Automaton*, ca. 1924

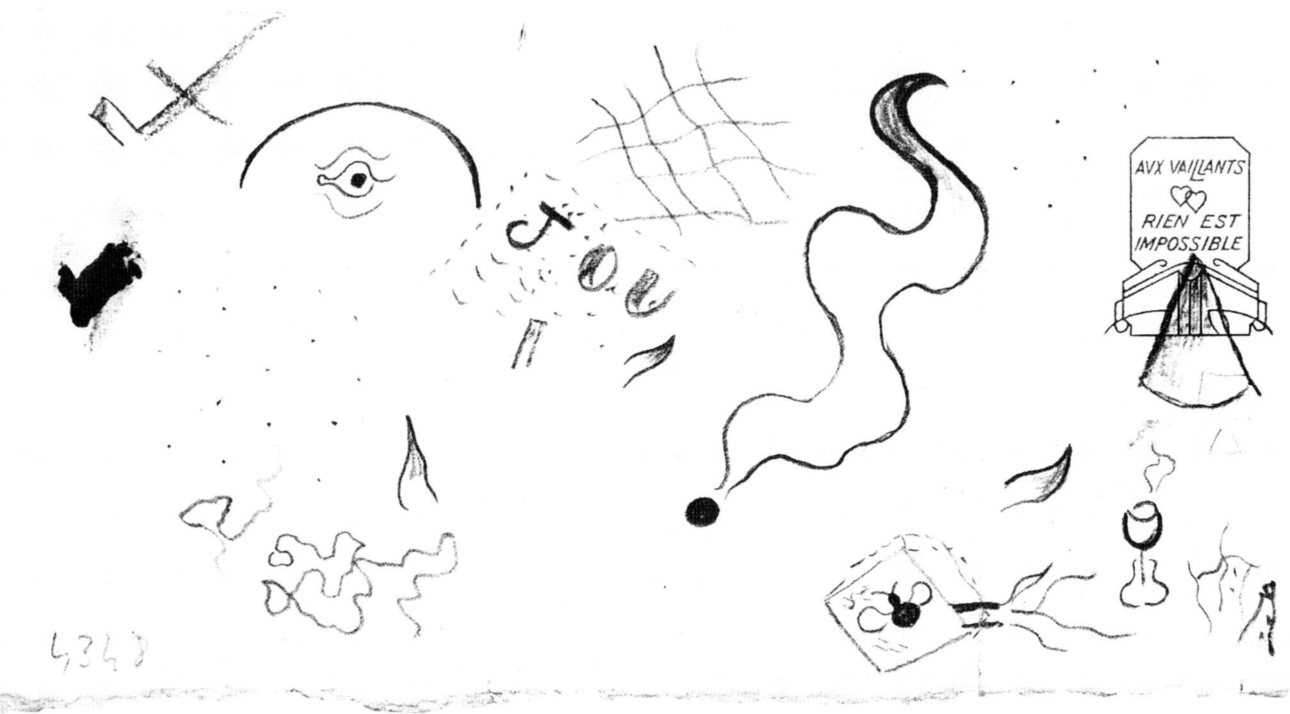

26. Study for *Head of a Smoker*, ca. 1924

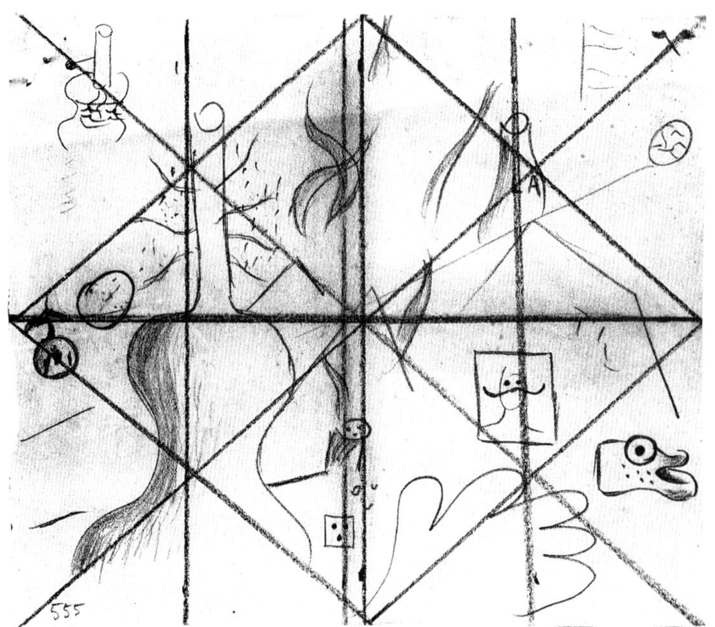

27. Study for *The Gas Lamp*, ca. 1924

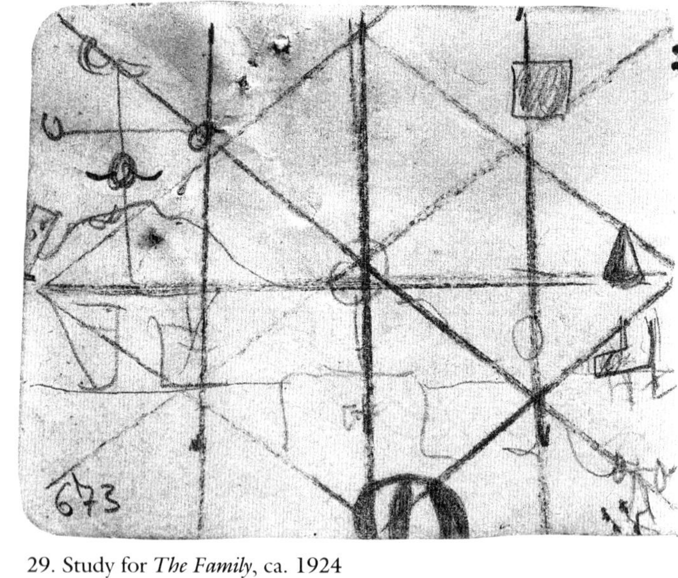

29. Study for *The Family*, ca. 1924

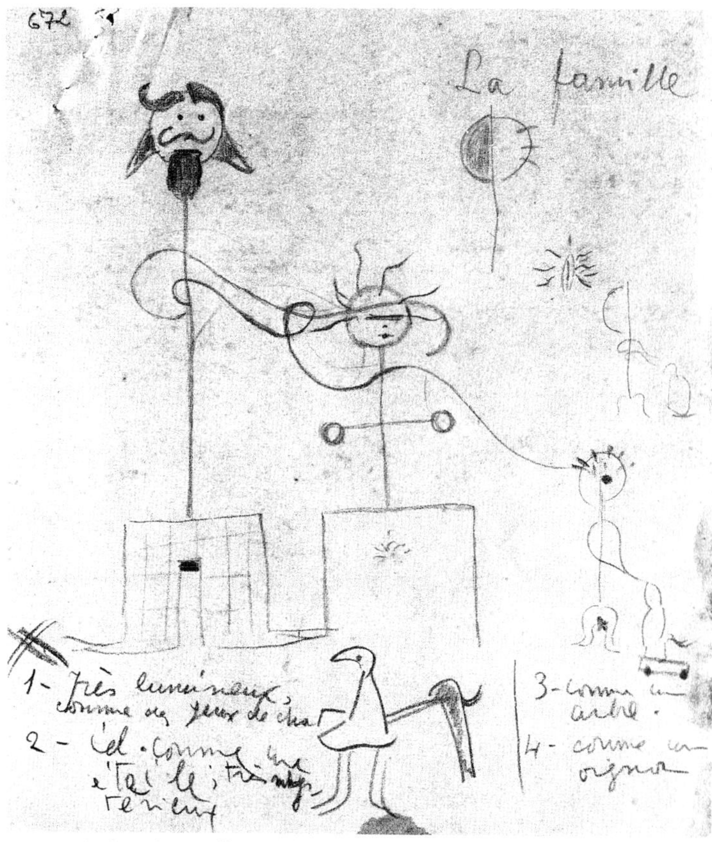

28. Study for *The Family*, ca. 1924

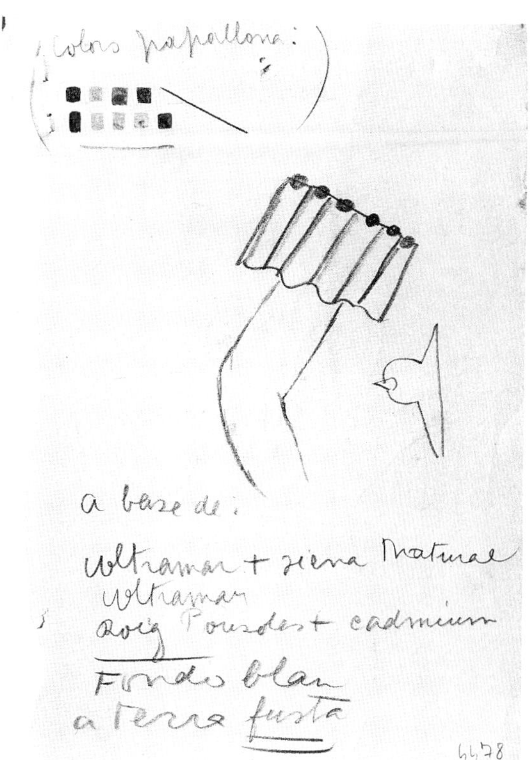

30. Study for *The Spanish Dancer*, ca. 1924

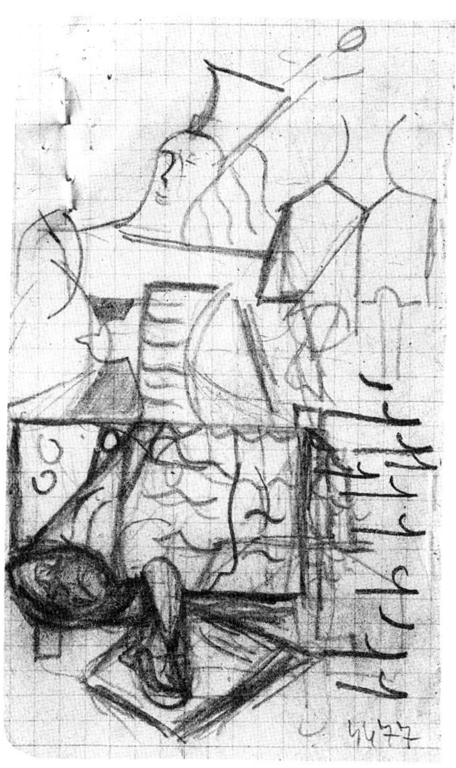

31. Study for *The Spanish Dancer*, ca. 1924

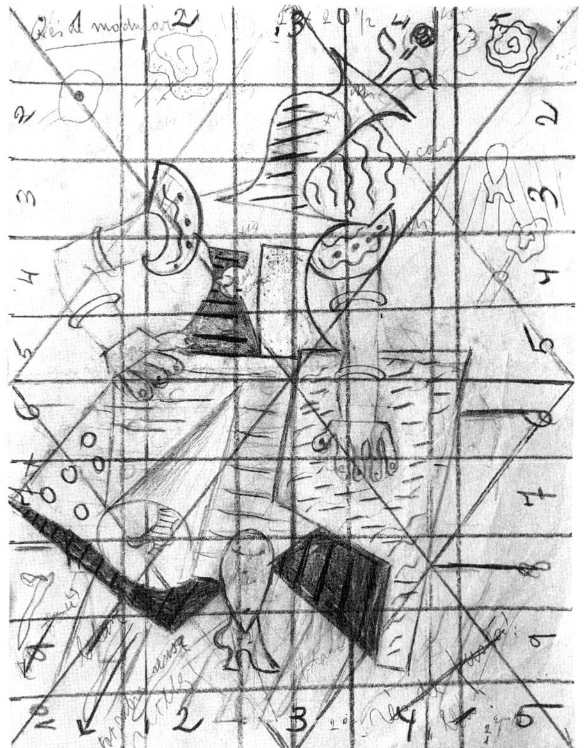

32. Study for *The Spanish Dancer*, ca. 1924

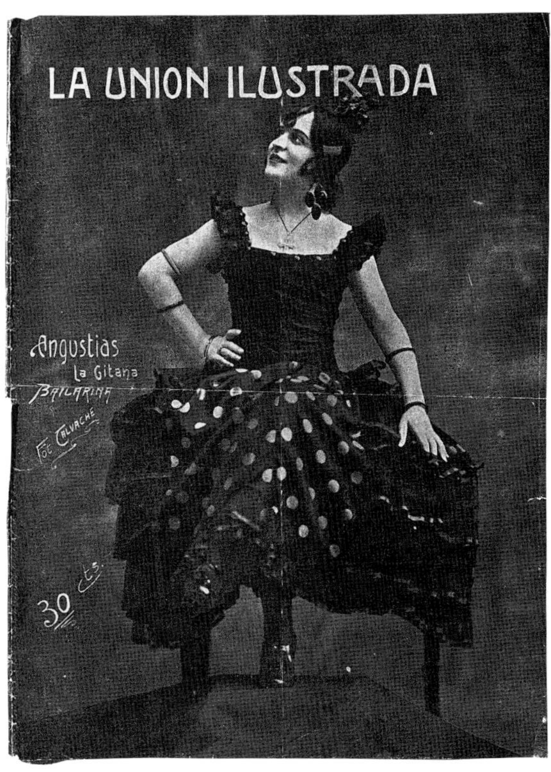

Figure B. Magazine cover used as a source for *The Spanish Dancer*

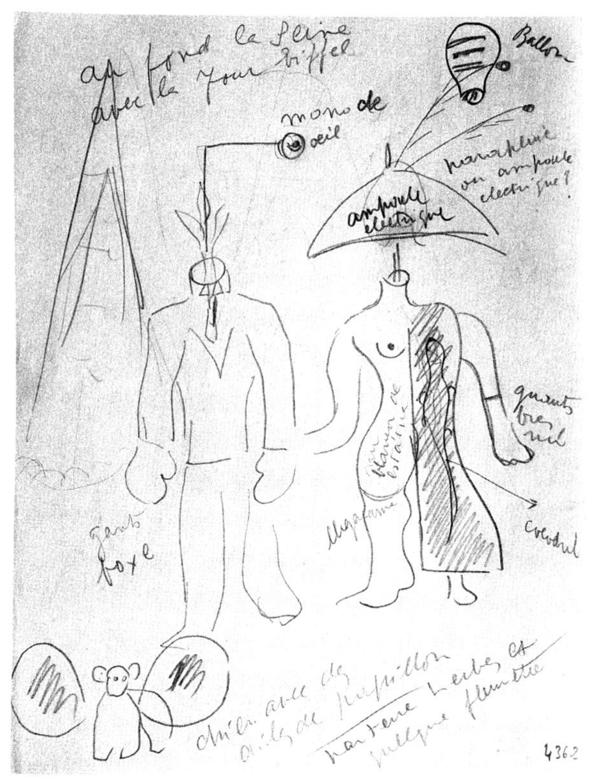

33. Study for *Carnival of Harlequin*, ca. 1924

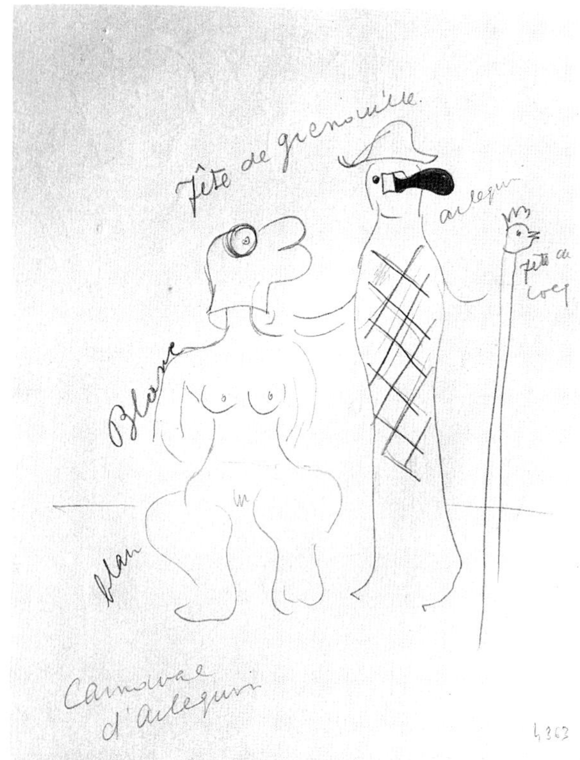

34. Study for *Carnival of Harlequin*, ca. 1924

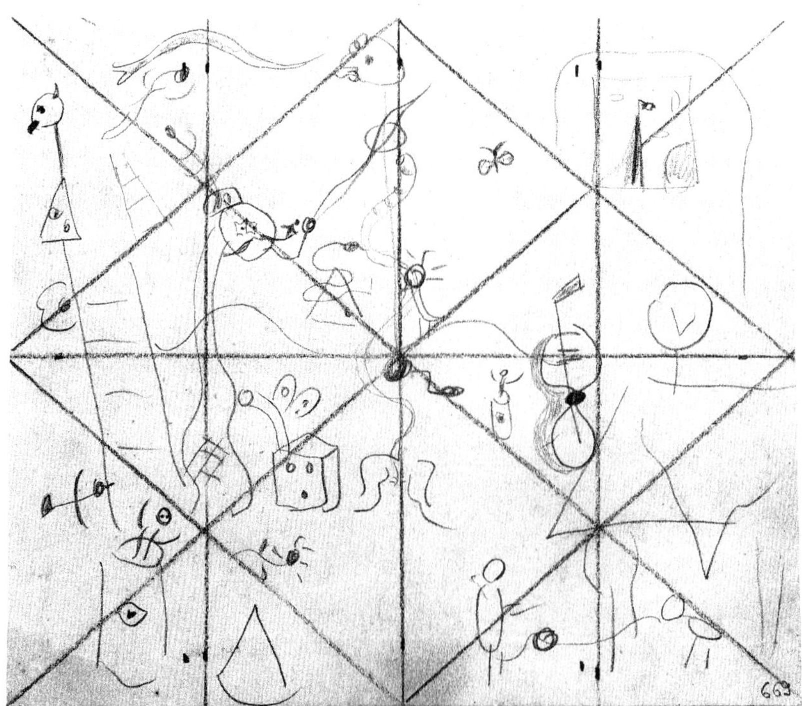

35. Study for *Carnival of Harlequin*, ca. 1924

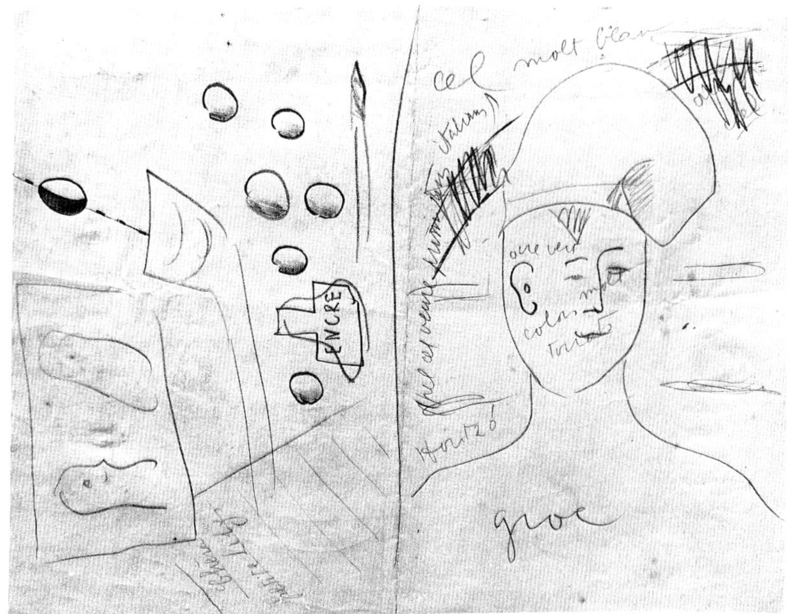

36. Study for *Head of a Catalan Peasant*, ca. 1925

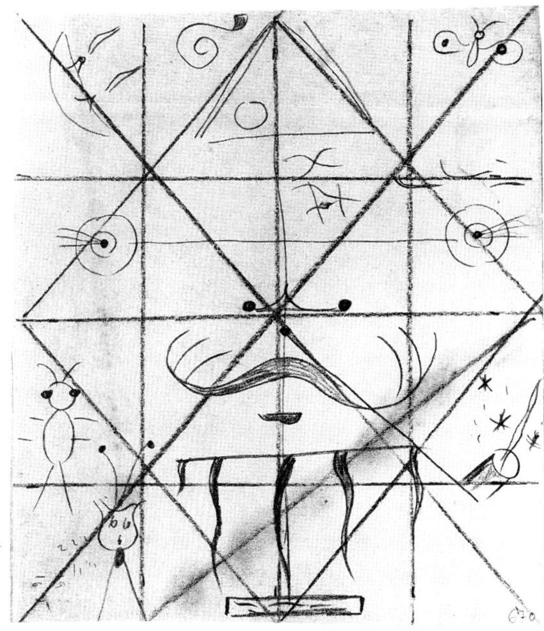

37. Study for *Head of a Catalan Peasant*, ca. 1925

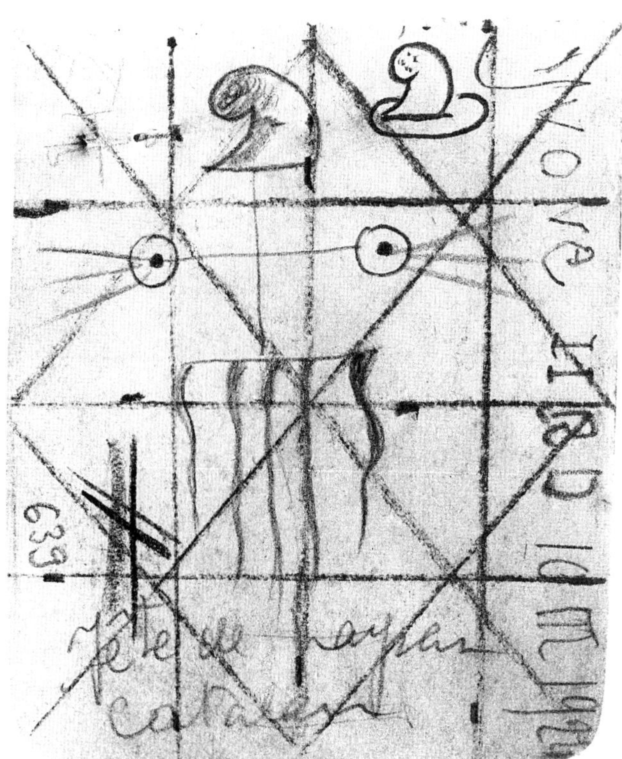

38. Study for *Head of a Catalan Peasant*, ca. 1925

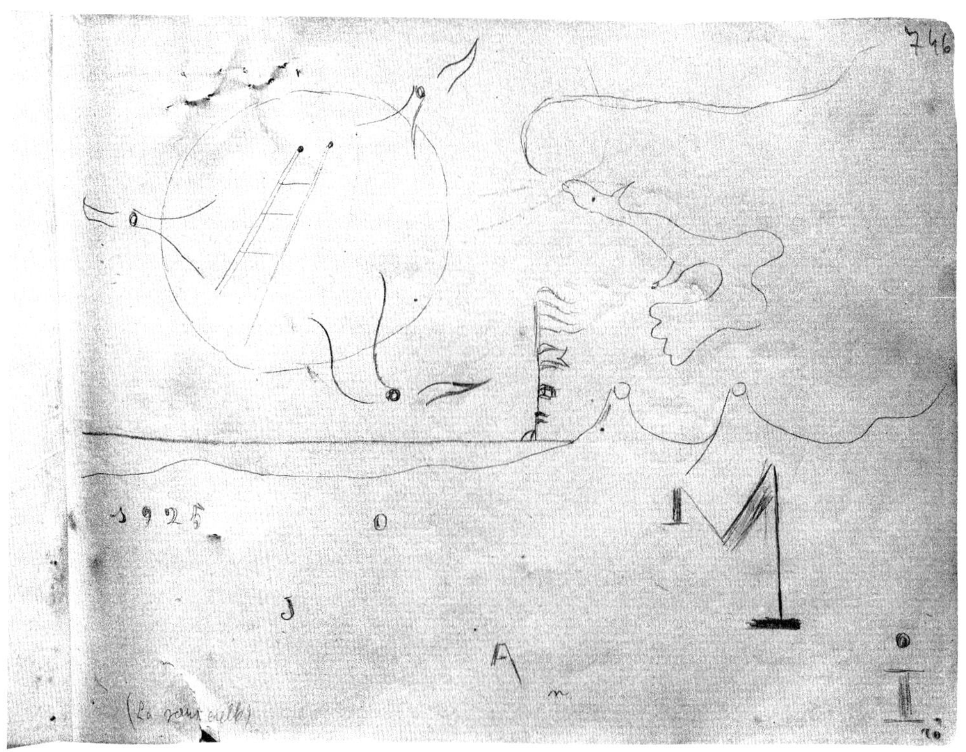

39. Page from a notebook, ca. 1925-26

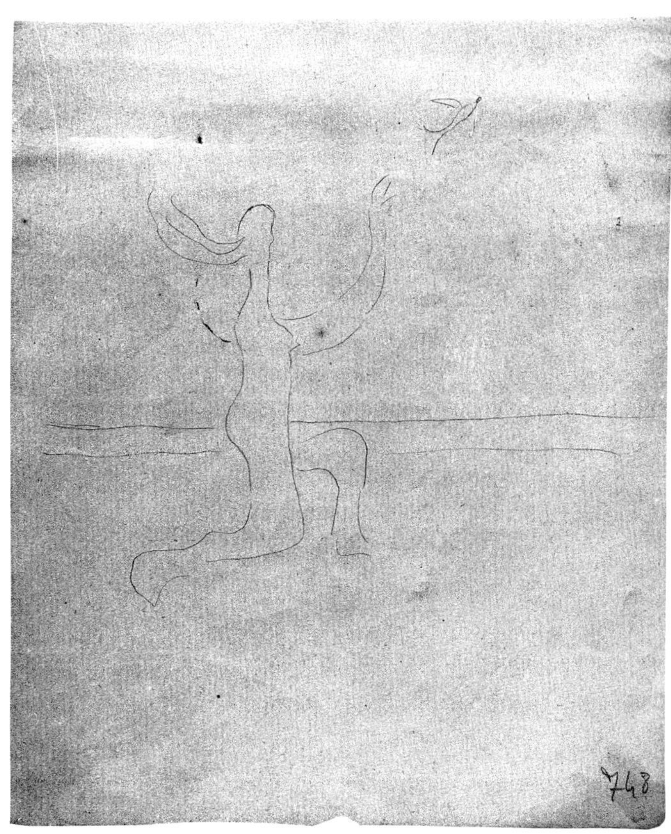

40. Page from a notebook, ca. 1925-26

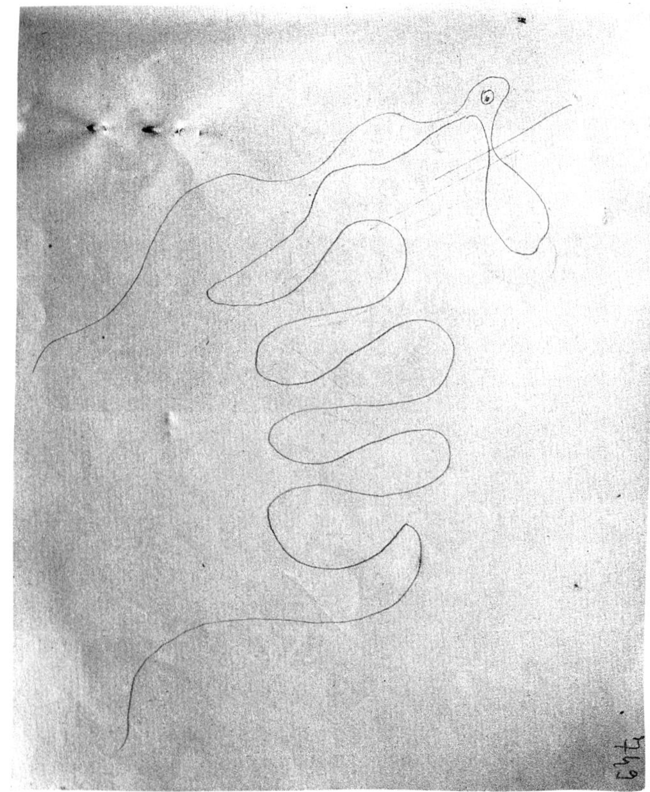

41. Page from a notebook, ca. 1925-26

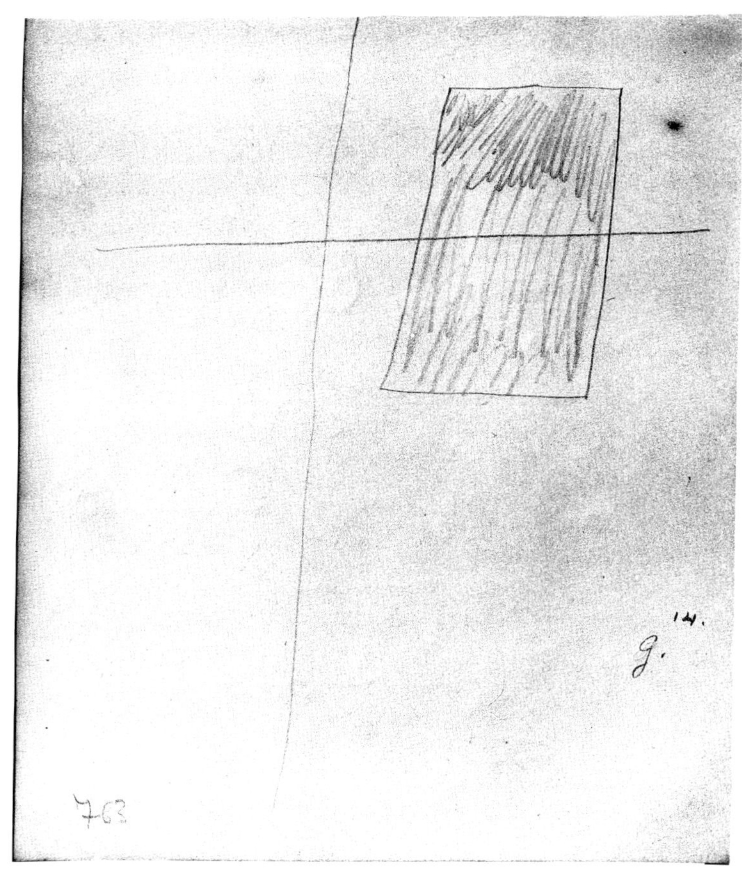

42. Page from a notebook, ca. 1925-26

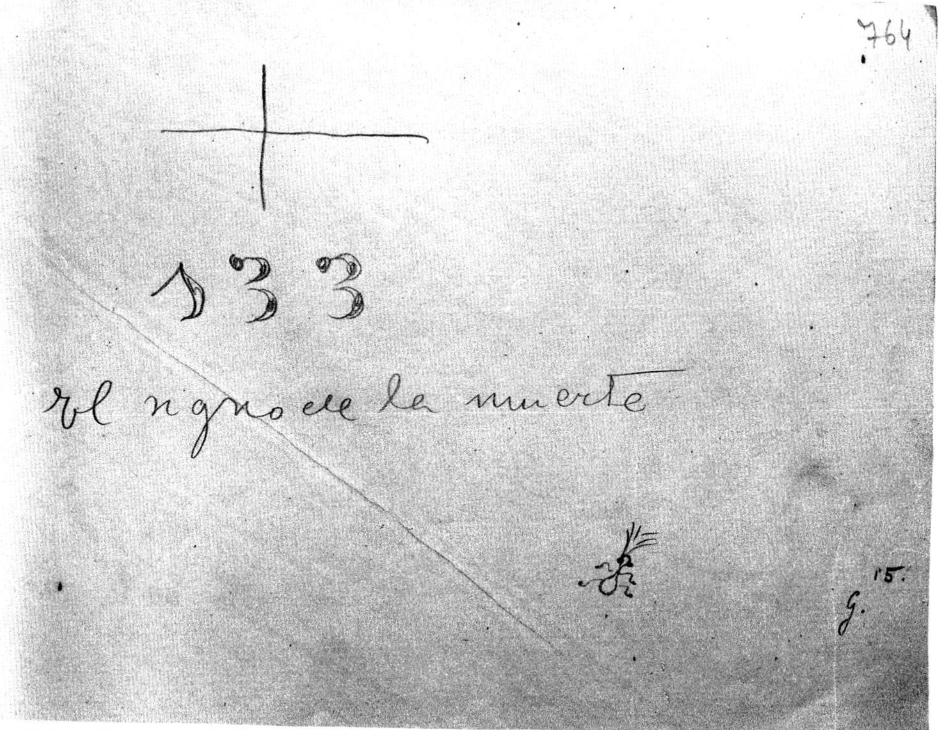

43. Page from a notebook, ca. 1925-26

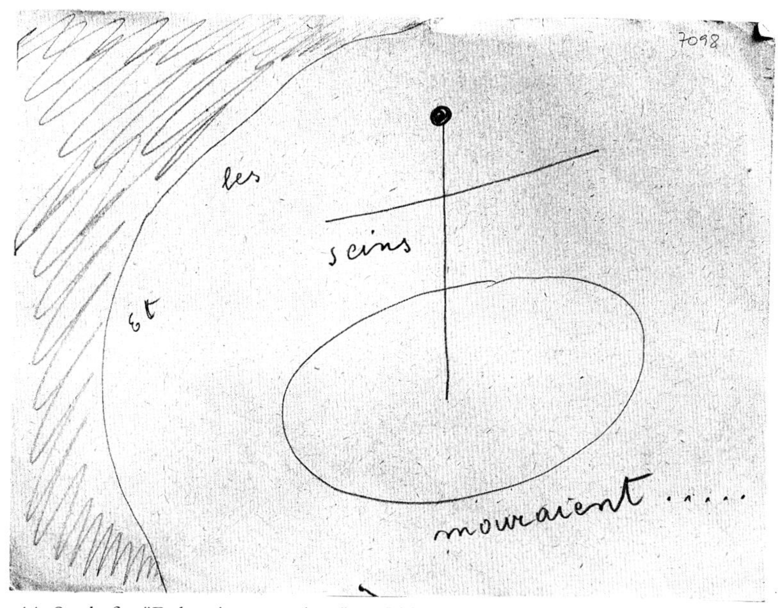

44. Study for *"Et les seins mouraient,"* ca. 1927

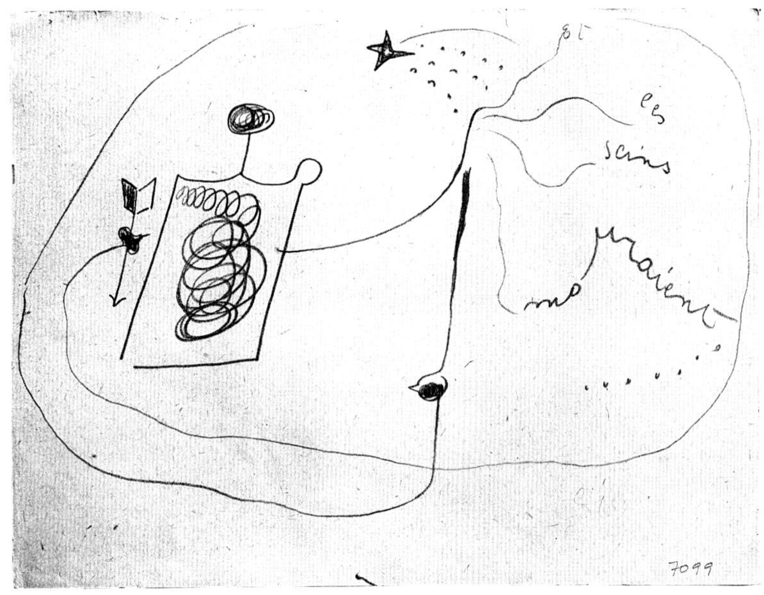

45. Study for *"Et les seins mouraient,"* ca. 1927

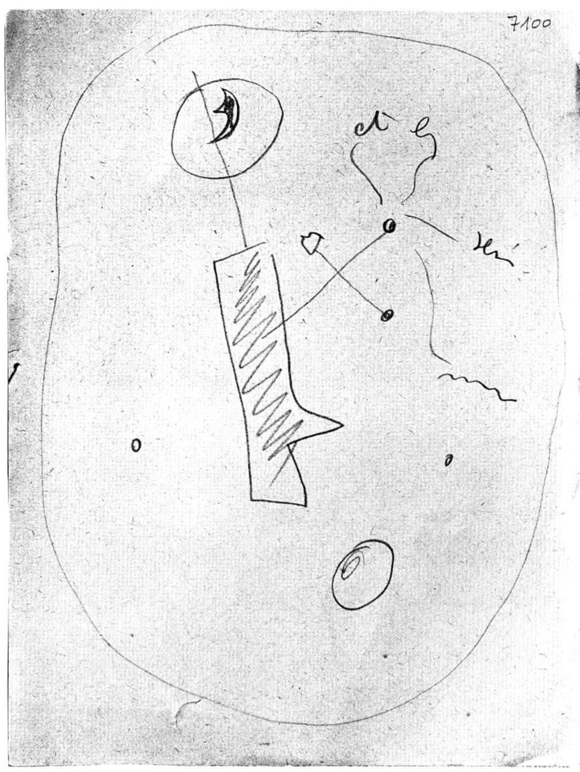

46. Study for *"Et les seins mouraient,"* ca. 1927

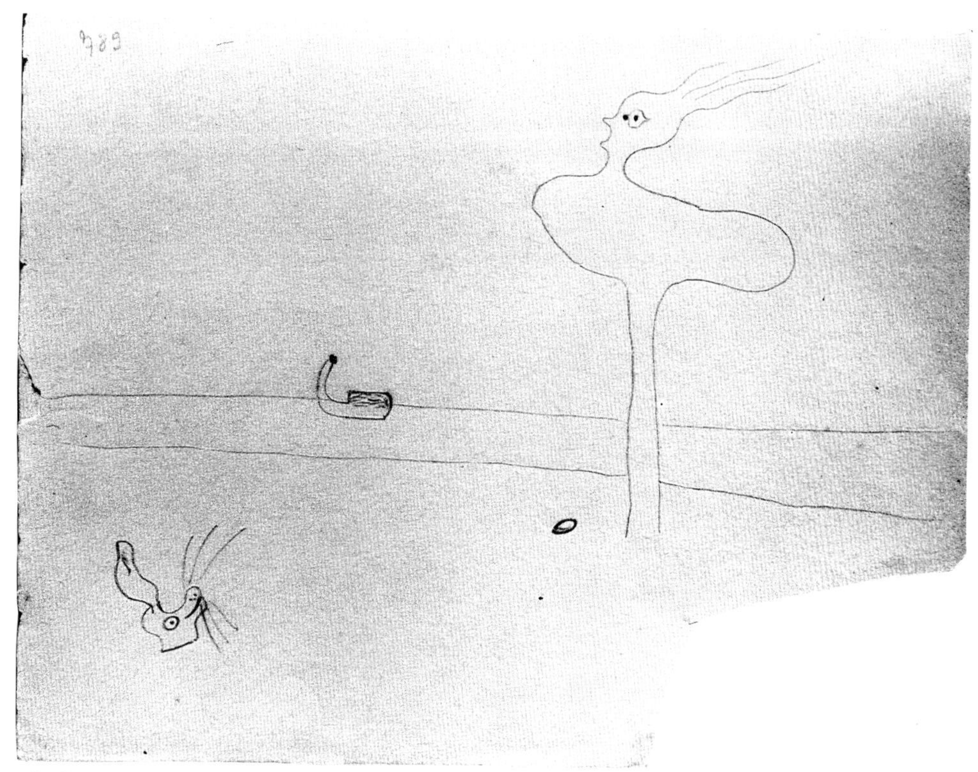

47. Study for *Landscape*, ca. 1927

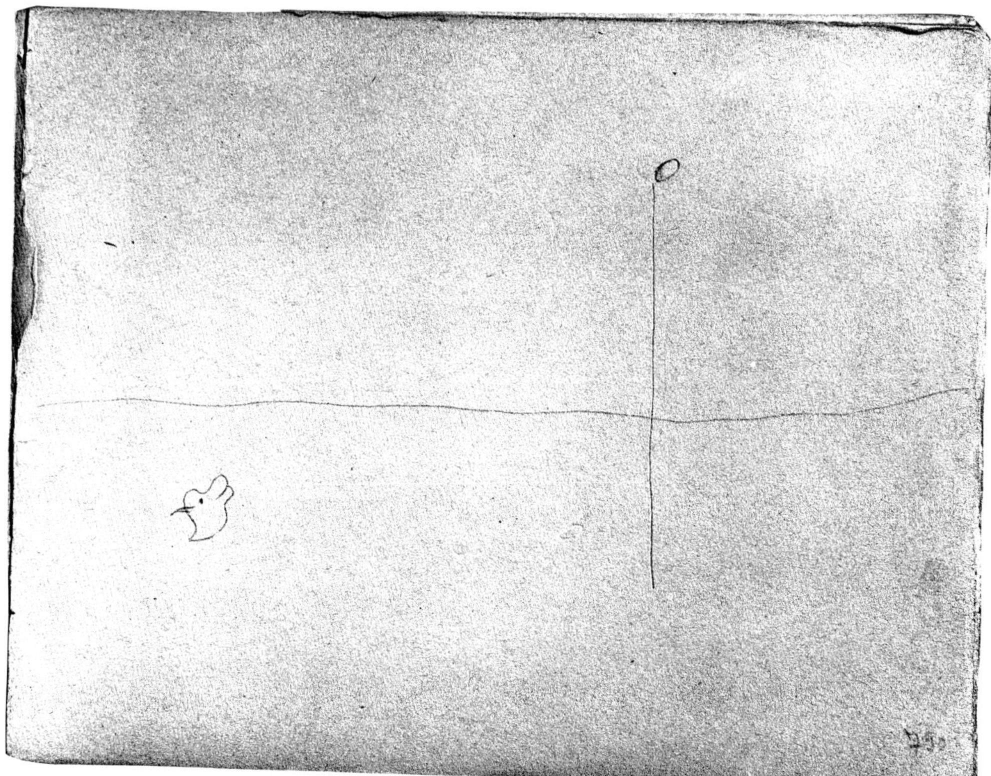

48. Study for *Landscape*, ca. 1927

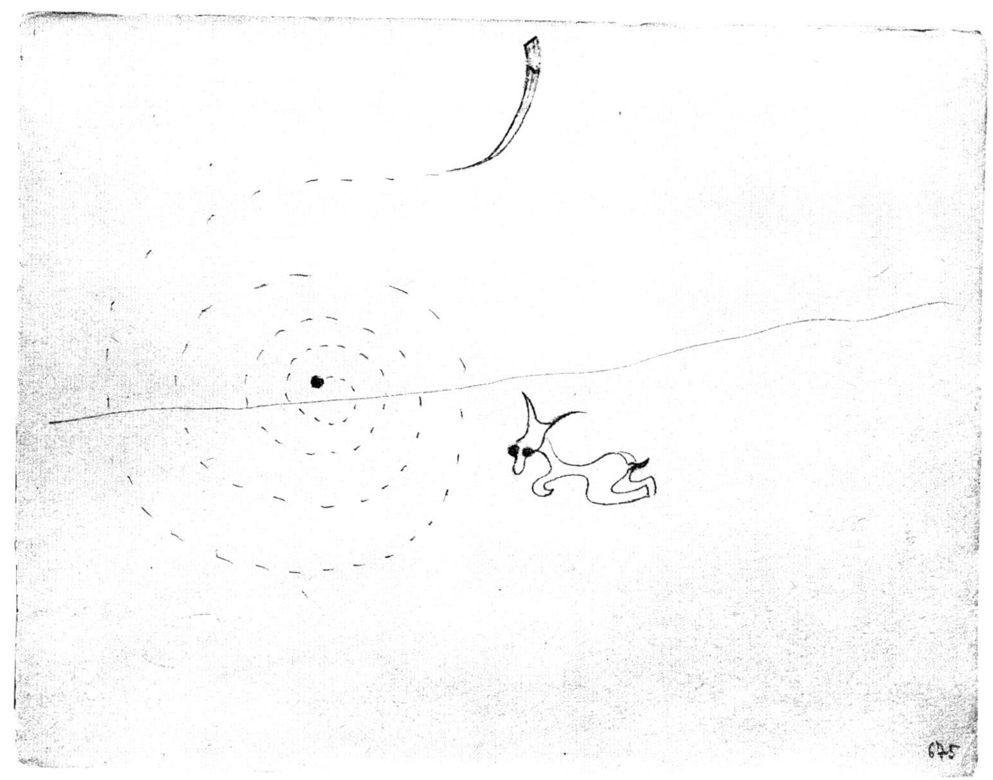

49. Study for *Landscape, The Hare*, 1927

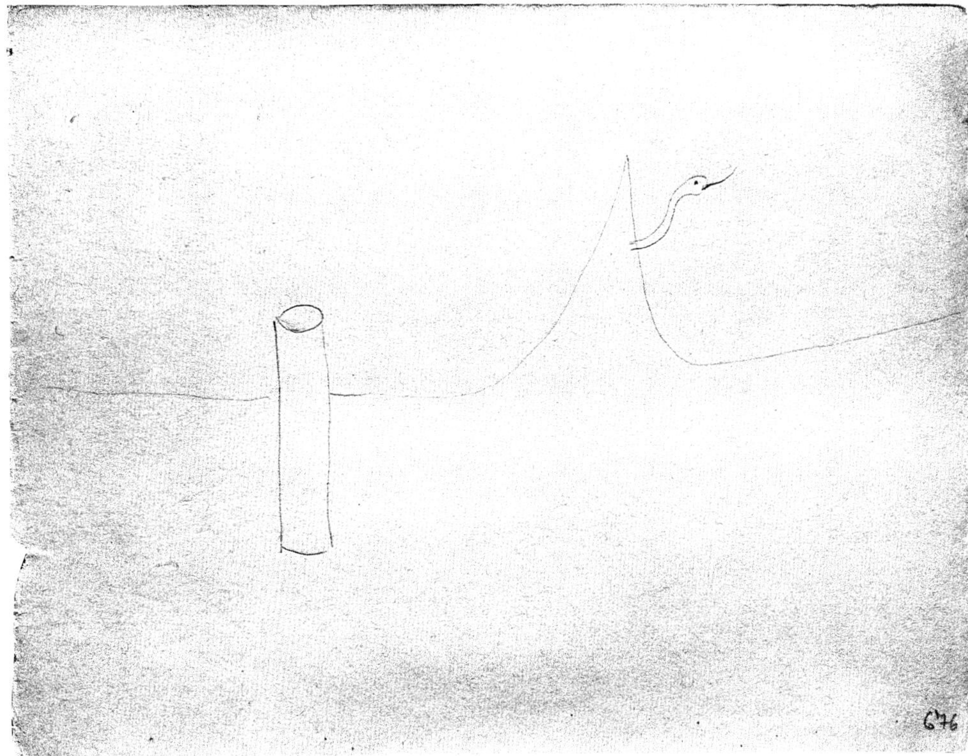

50. Study for *Landscape, The Snake*, 1927

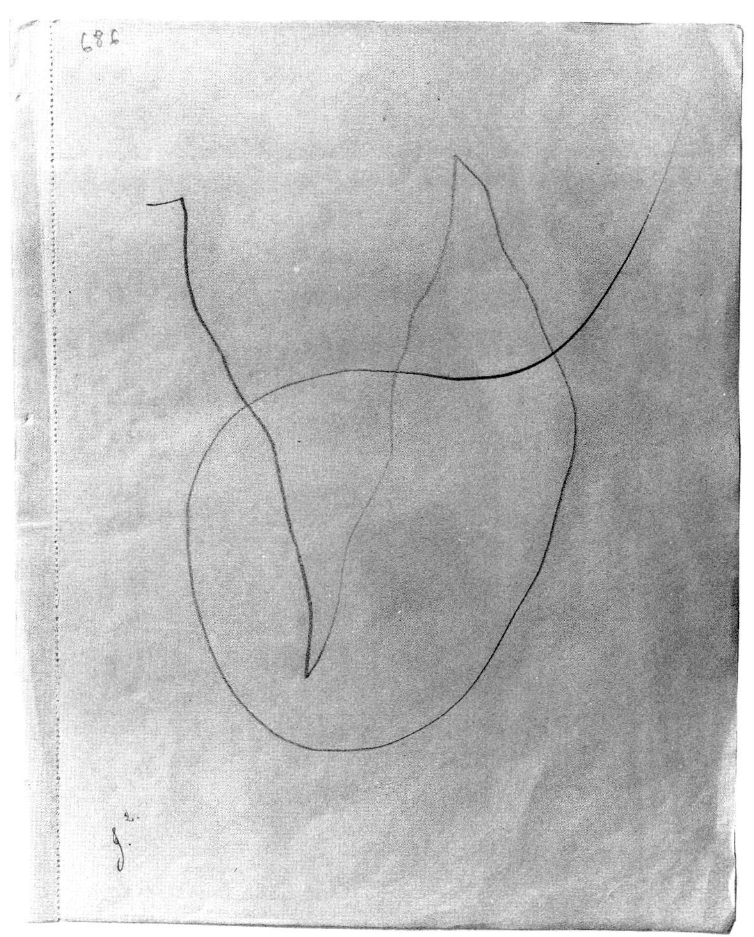

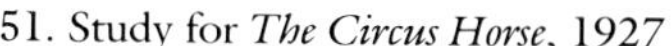

51. Study for *The Circus Horse*, 1927

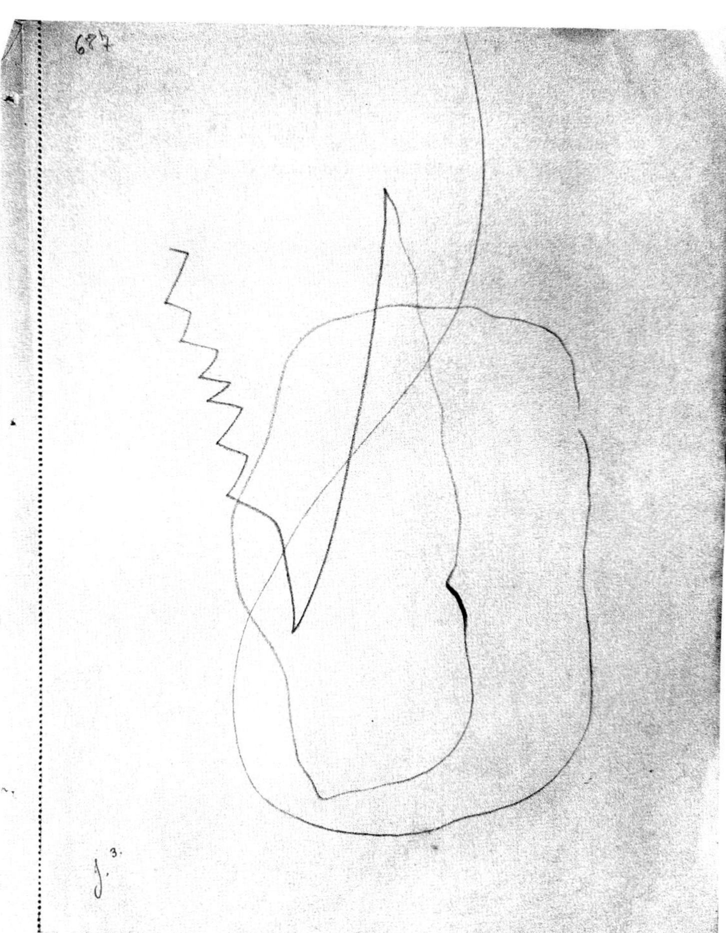

52. Study for *The Circus Horse*, 1927

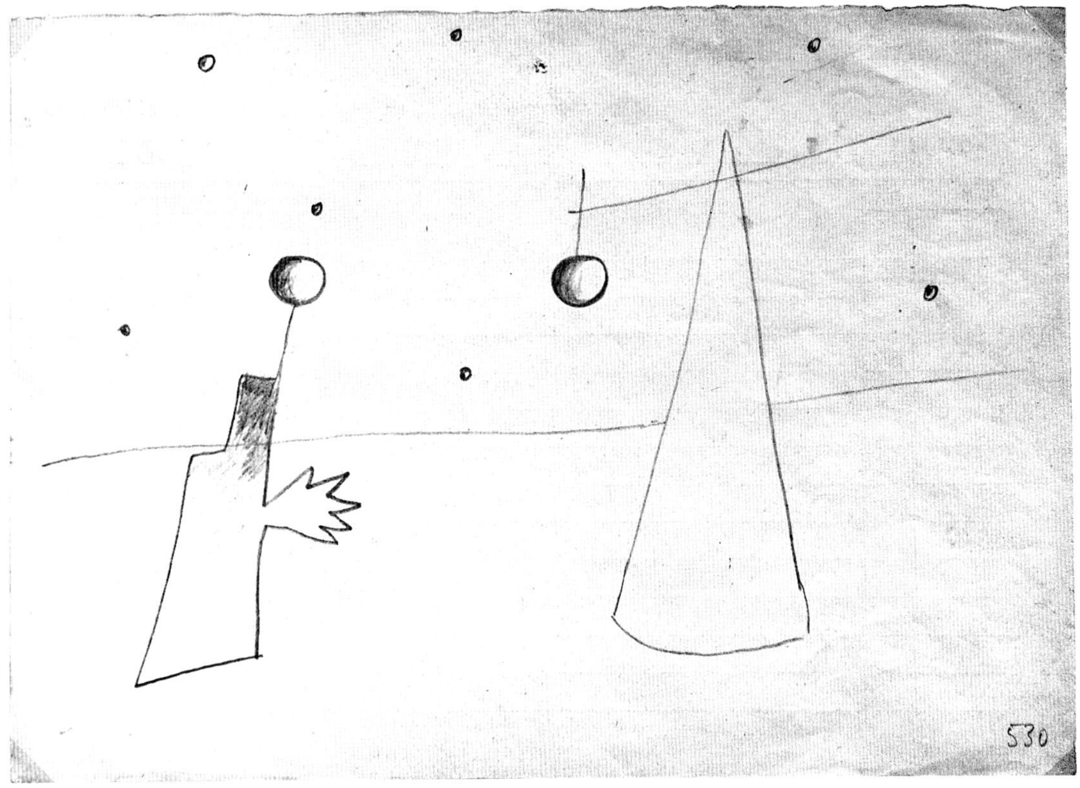

53. Drawing, ca. 1927

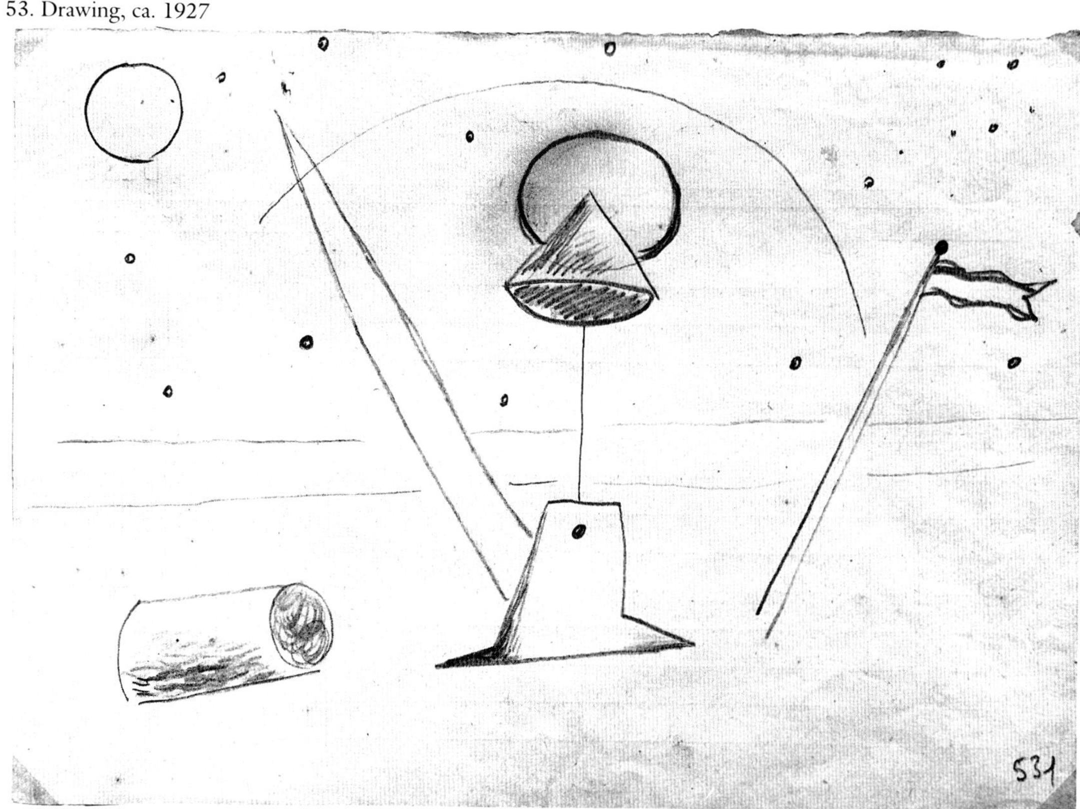

54. Drawing, ca. 1927

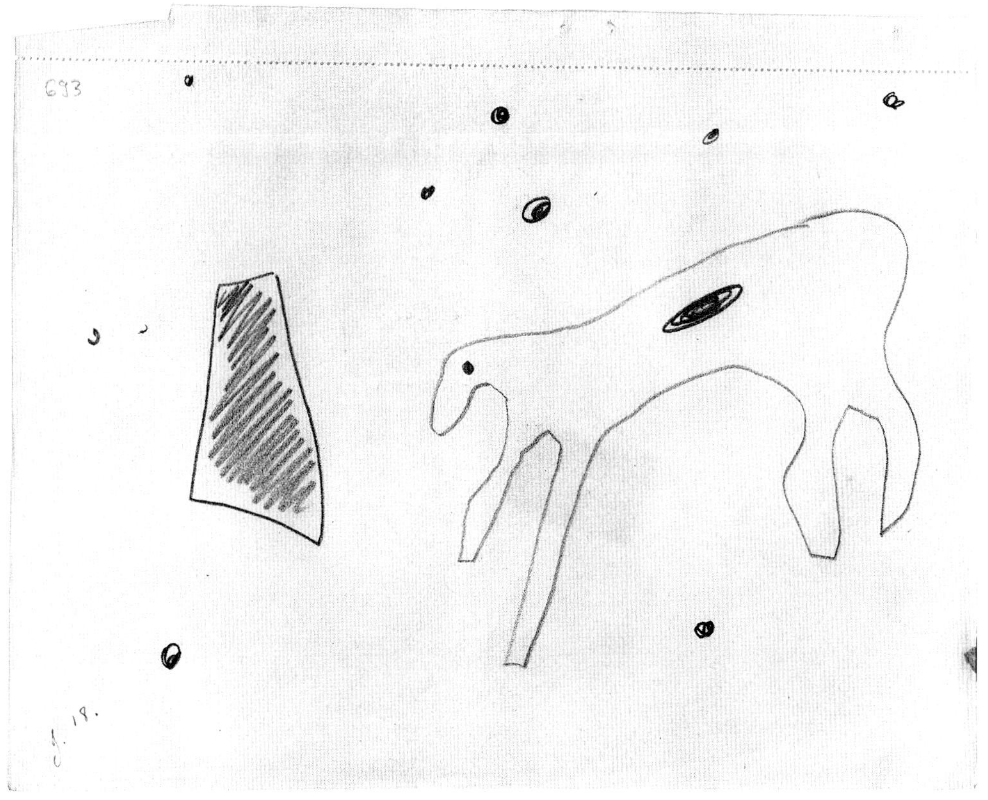

55. Study for *Painting on White Ground, The Dog*, 1927

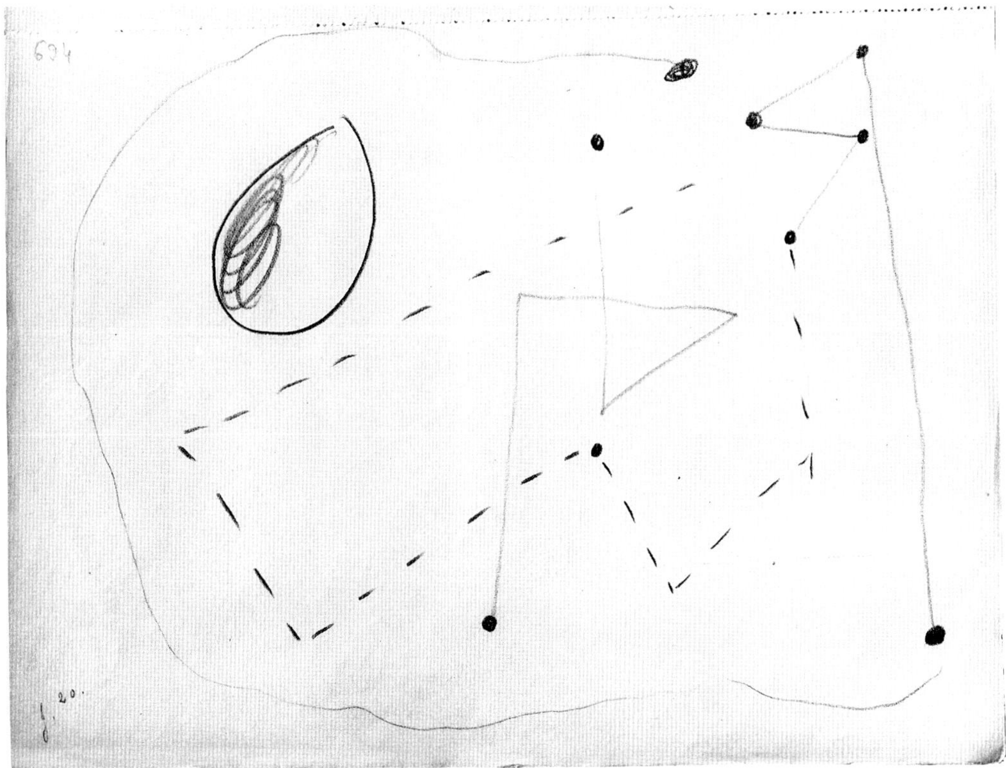

56. Study for *Painting on White Ground*, 1927

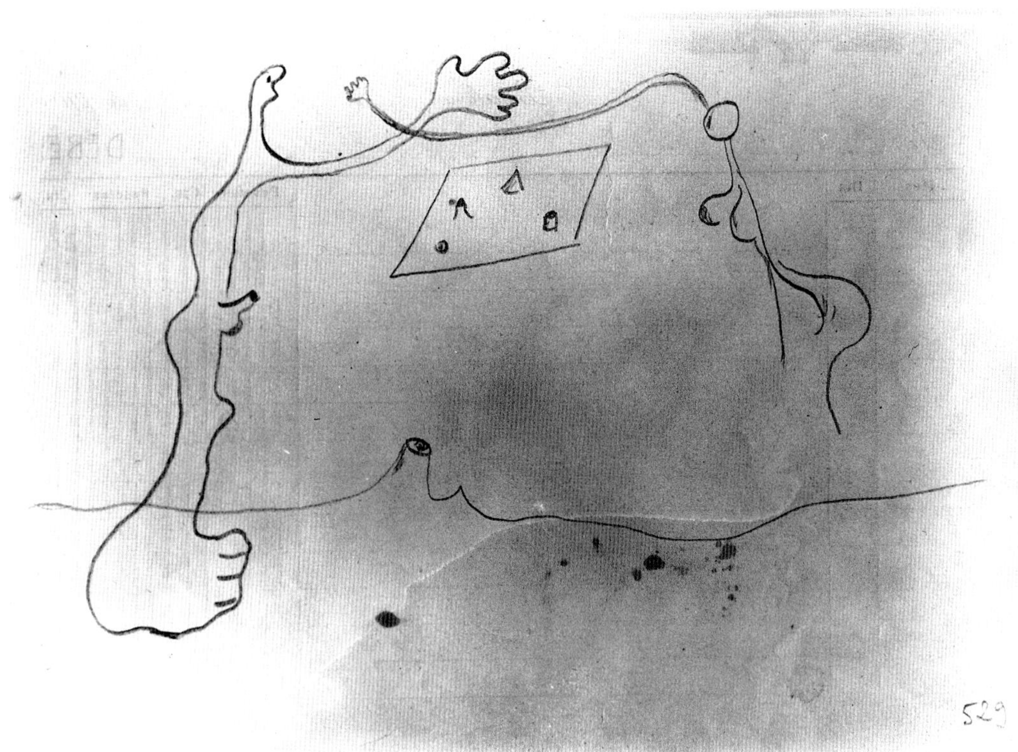

57. Drawing, ca. 1928

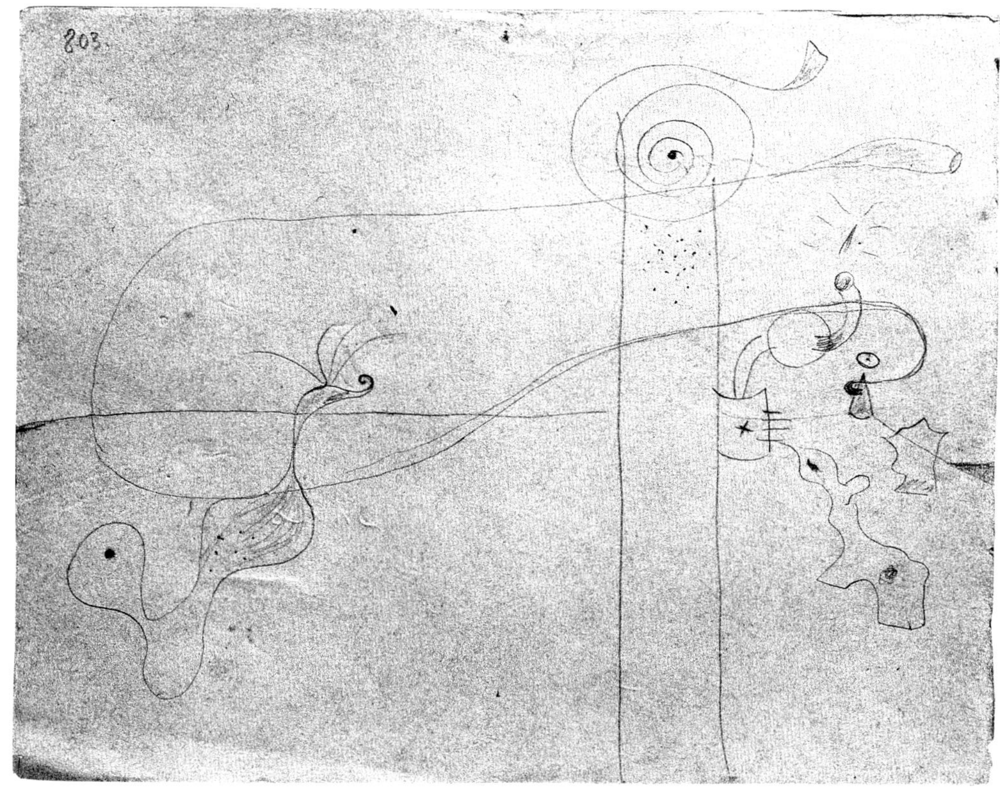

58. Study for *Still Life with Gas Lamp*, 1928

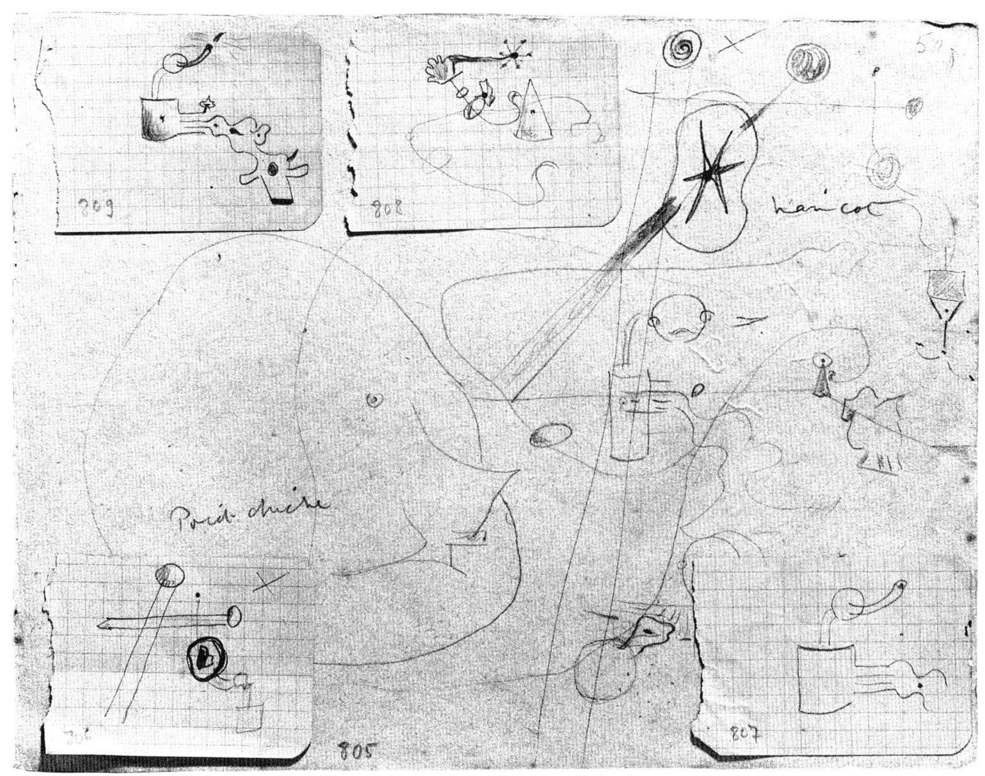

59. Study for *Still Life with Gas Lamp*, 1928

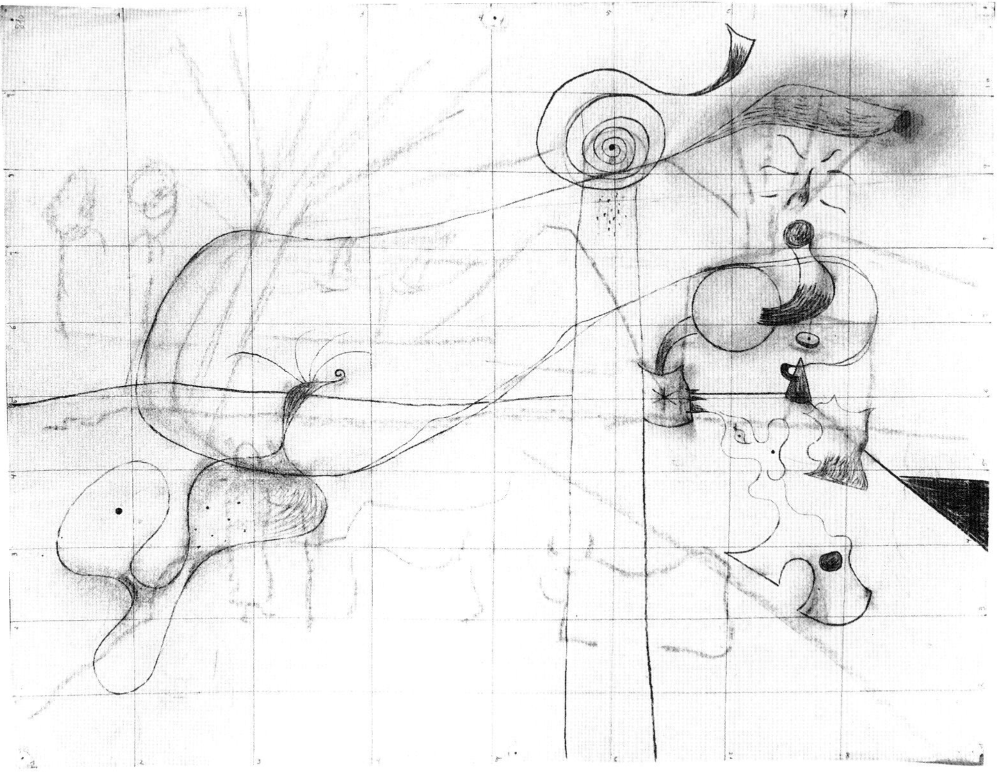

60. Study for *Still Life with Gas Lamp*, 1928

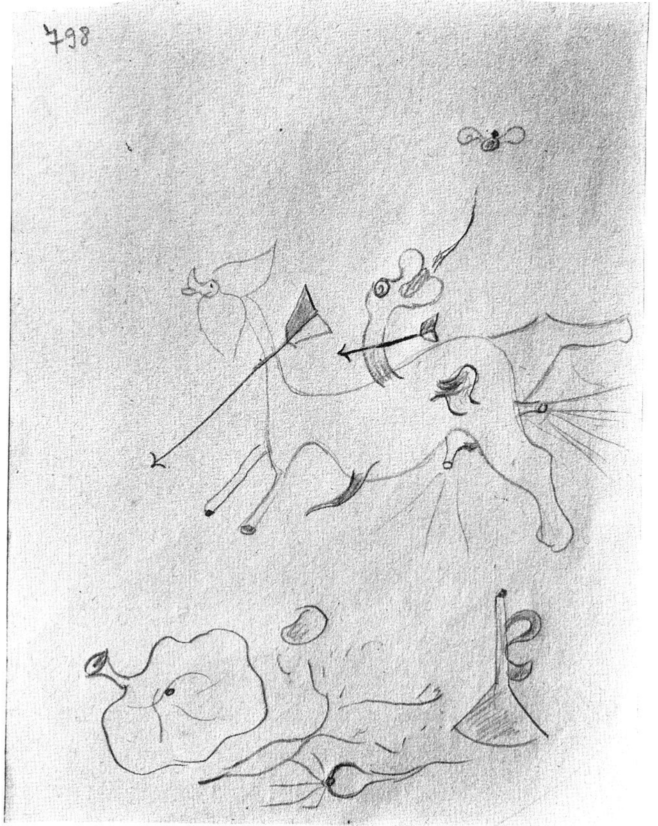

61. Study for *Dutch Interior II*, 1928

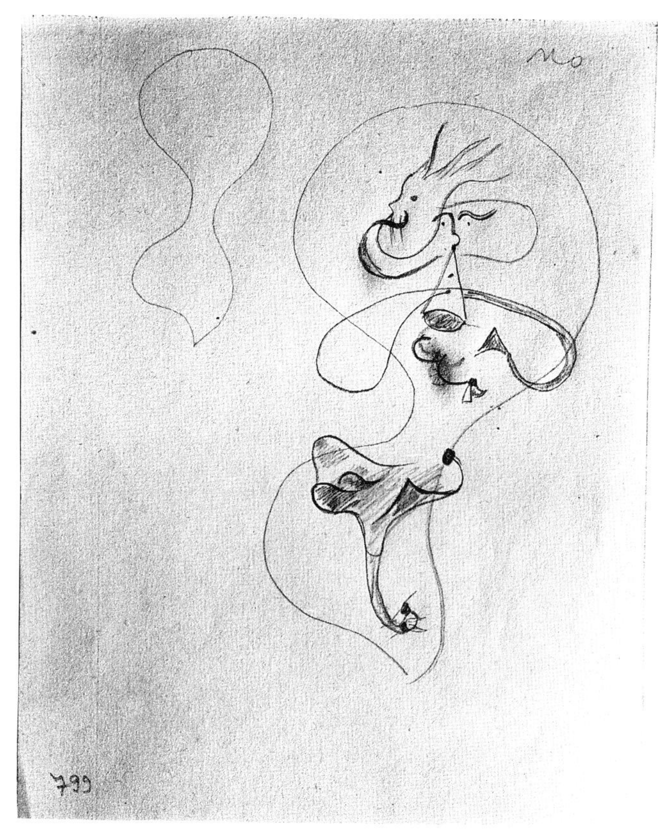

62. Study for *Dutch Interior II*, 1928

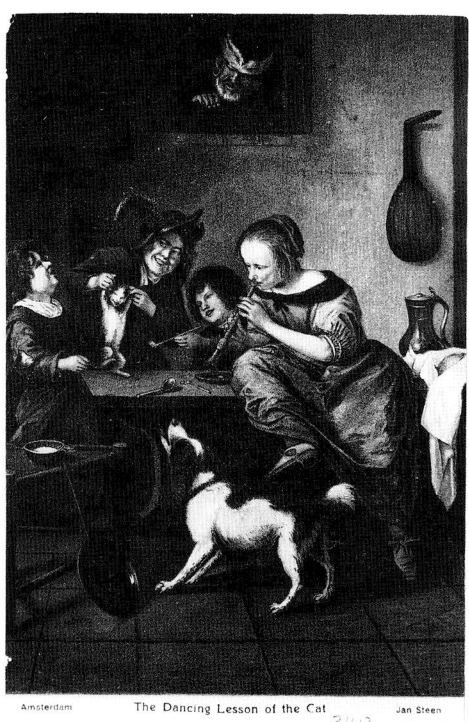

Figure D. Postcard of *The Dancing Lesson of the Cat* by Jan Steen.

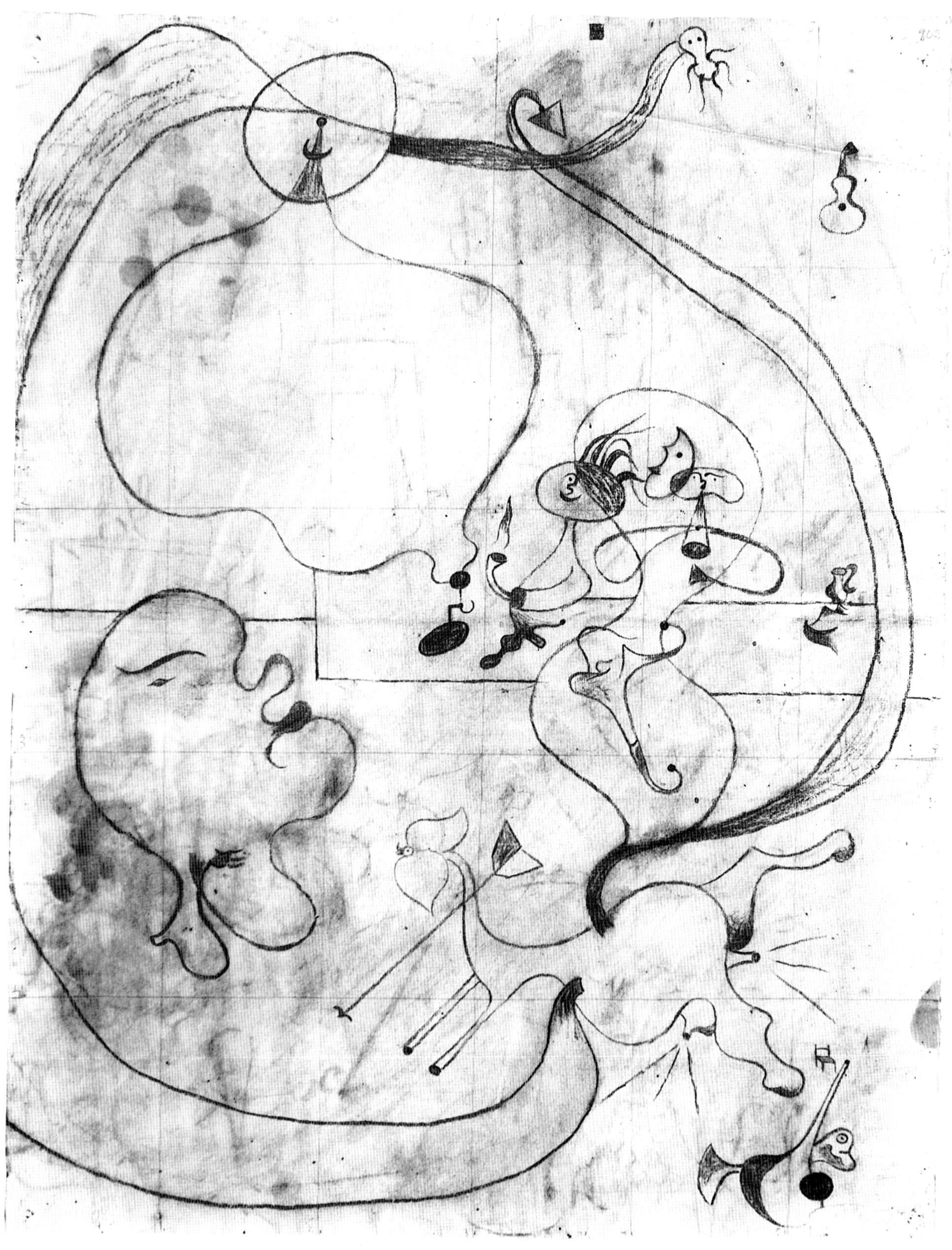

63. Study for *Dutch Interior II*, 1928

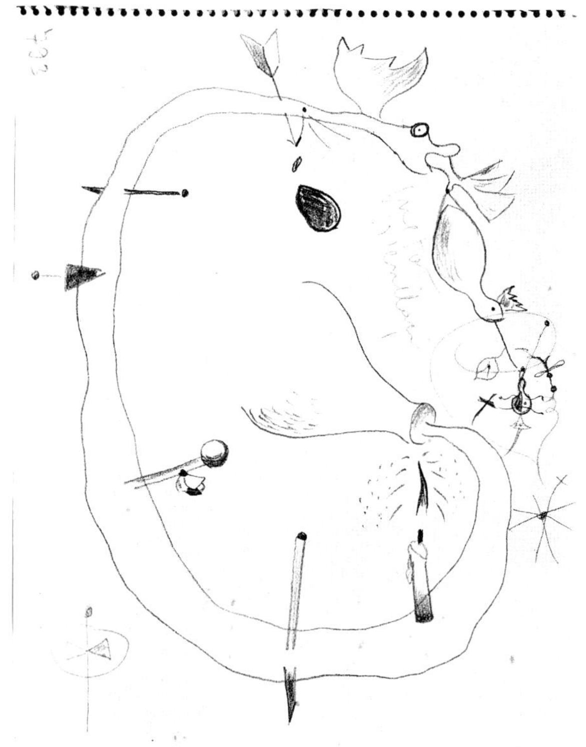

64. Study for *The Potato,* 1928

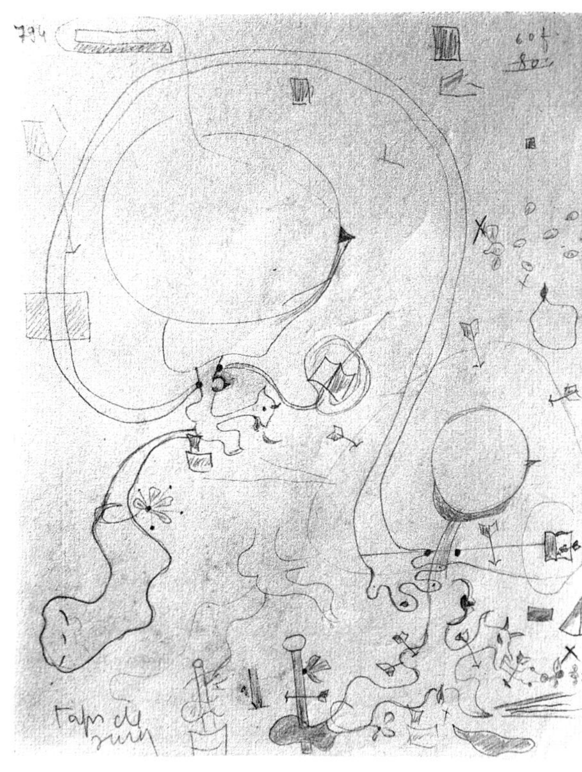

65. Study for *Dutch Interior III*, 1928

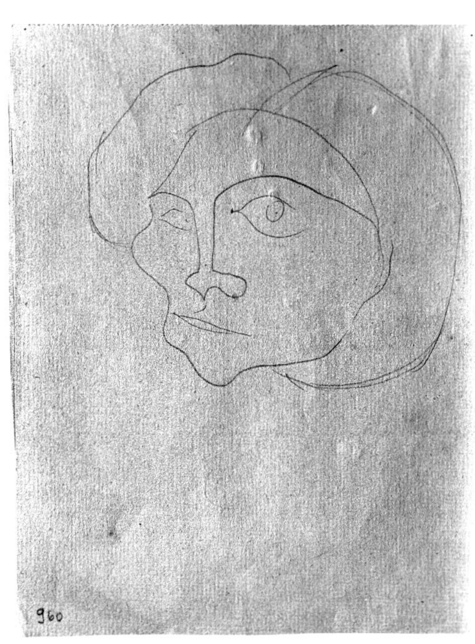

67. Study for *Portrait of a Lady in 1820*, 1929

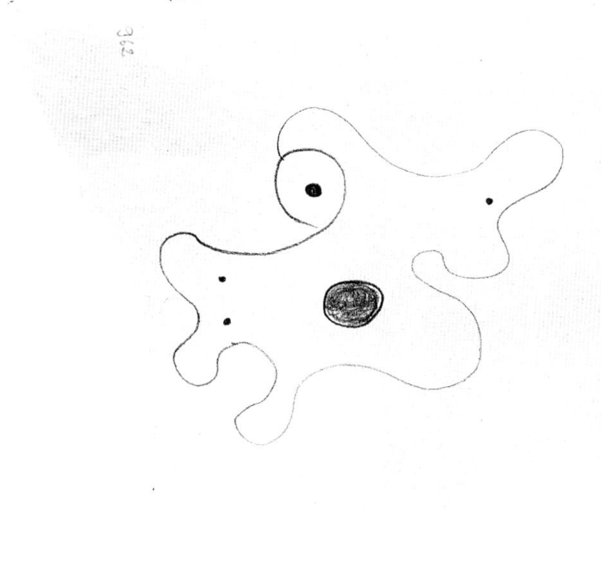

68. Study for *Portrait of a Lady in 1820*, 1929

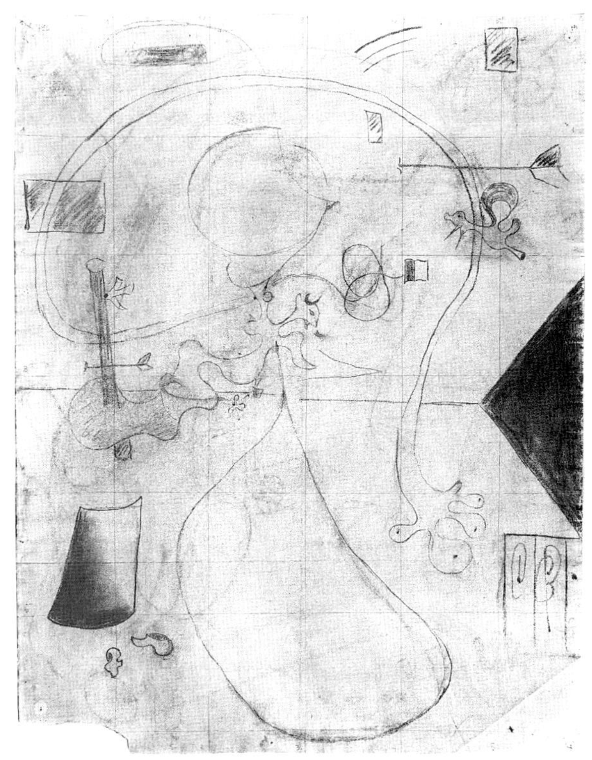

66. Study for *Dutch Interior III*, 1928

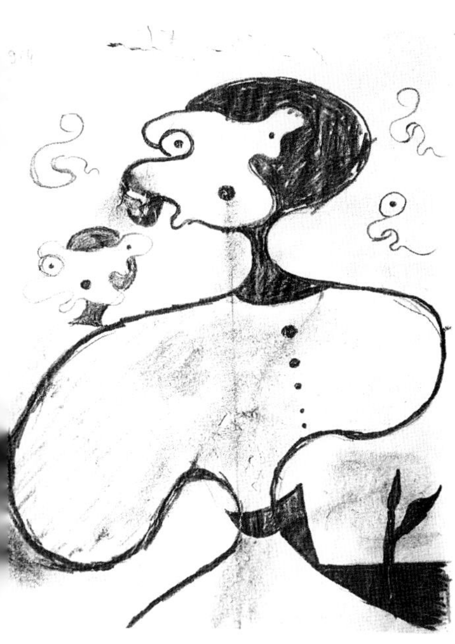

9. Study for *Portrait of a Lady in 1820*, 1929

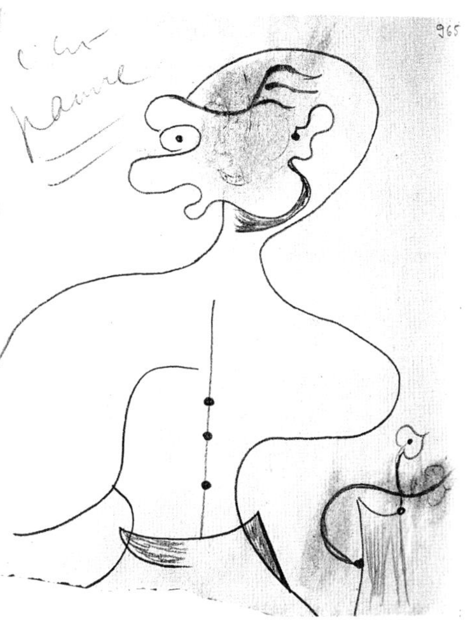

70. Study for *Portrait of a Lady in 1820*, 1929

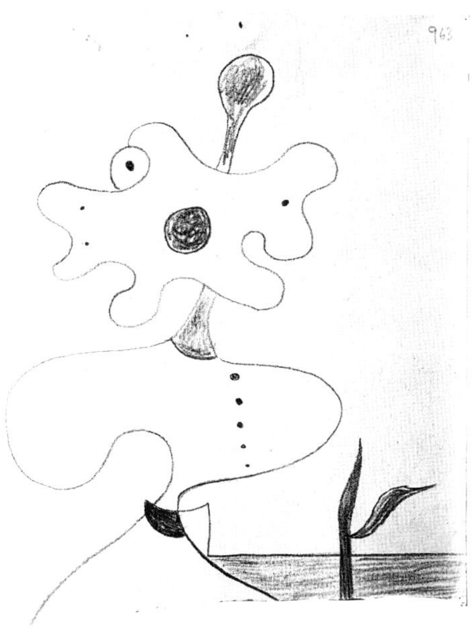

71. Study for *Portrait of a Lady in 1820*, 1929

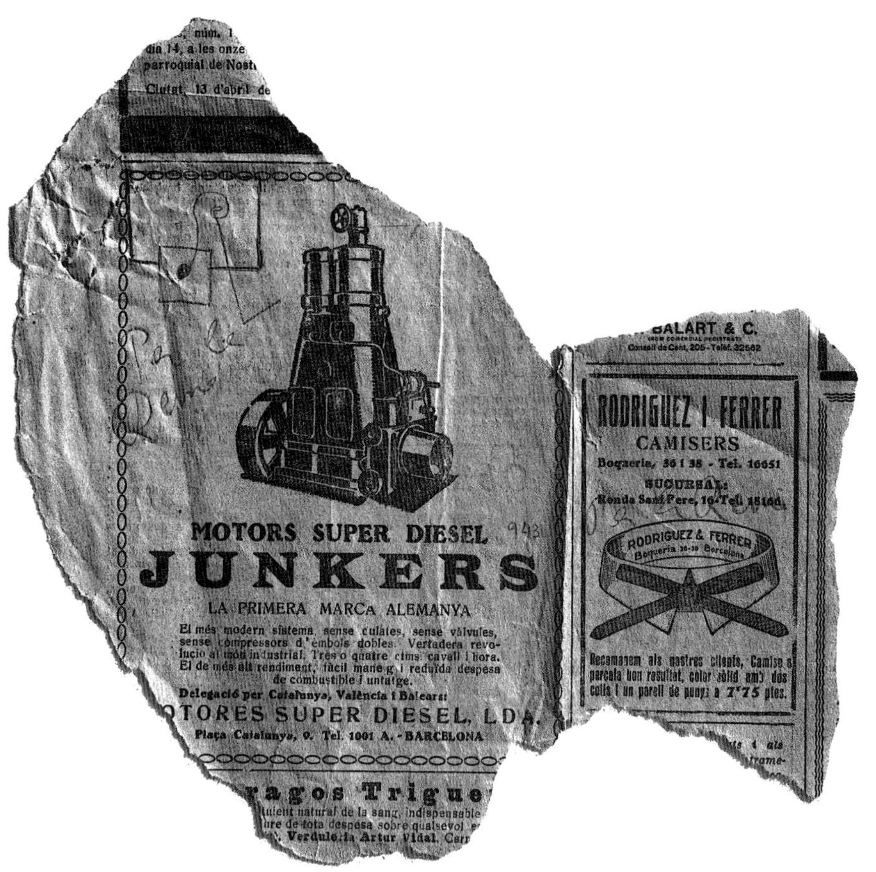

72. Study for *Queen Louise of Prussia*, 1929

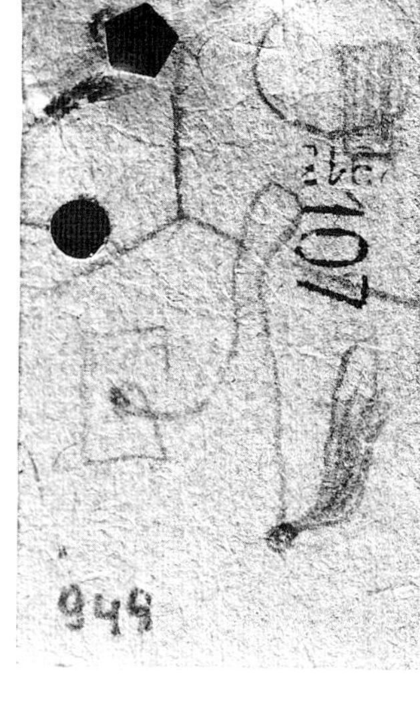

73. Study for *Queen Louise of Prussia*, 1929

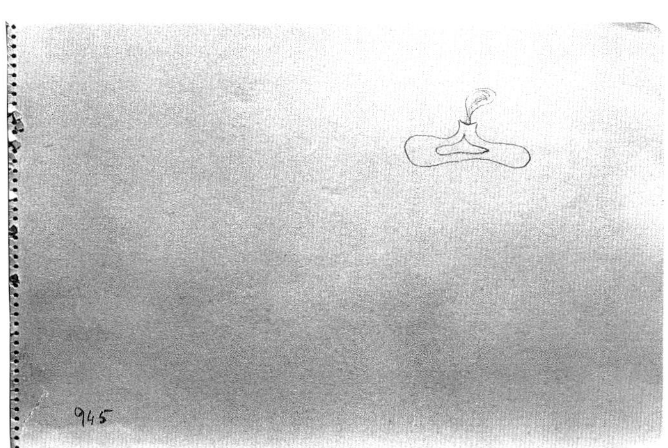

74. Study for *Queen Louise of Prussia*, 1929

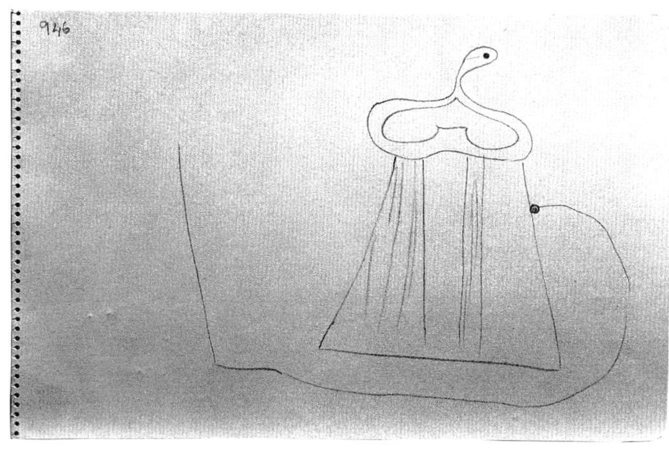

75. Study for *Queen Louise of Prussia*, 1929

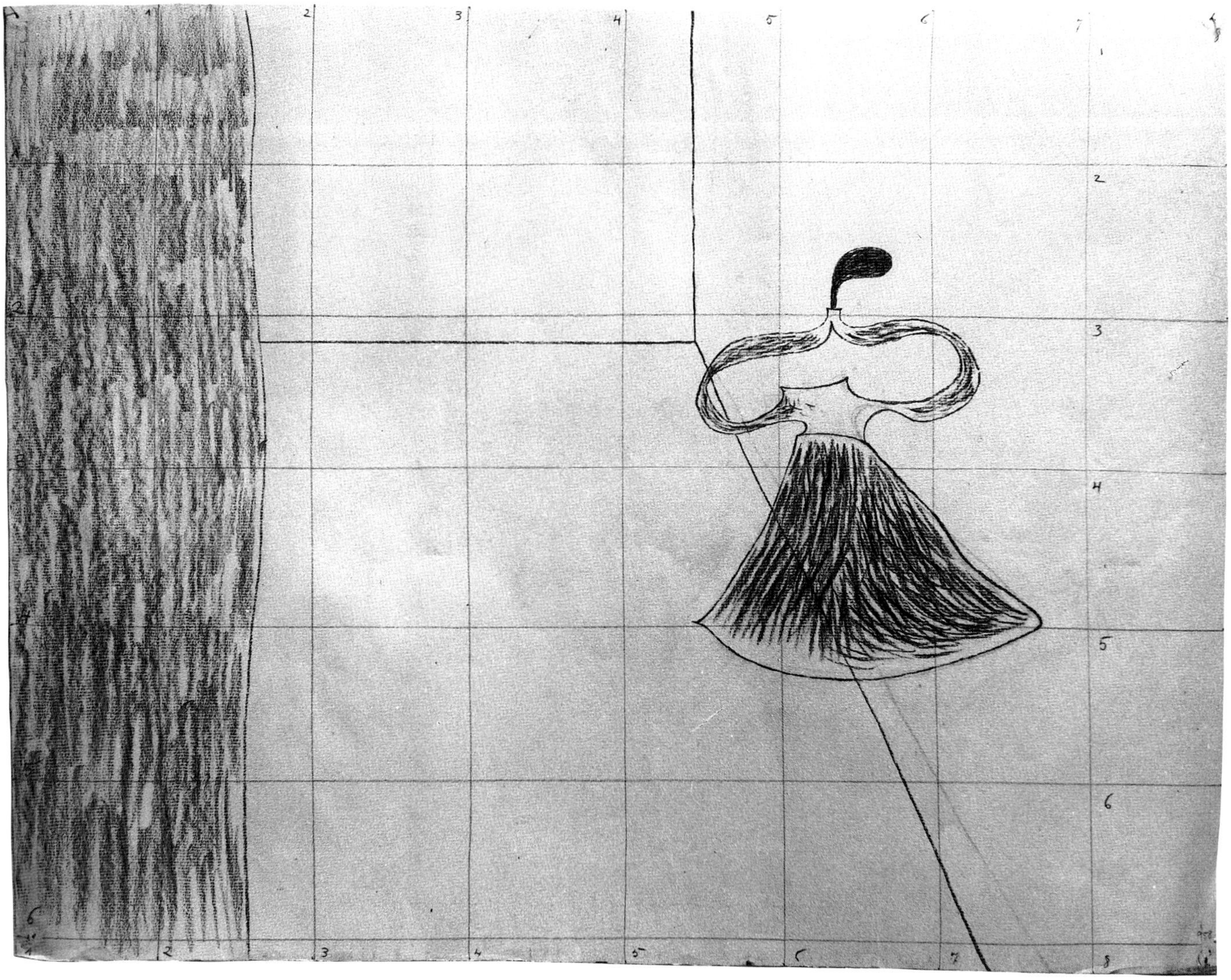

78. Study for *Queen Louise of Prussia*, 1929

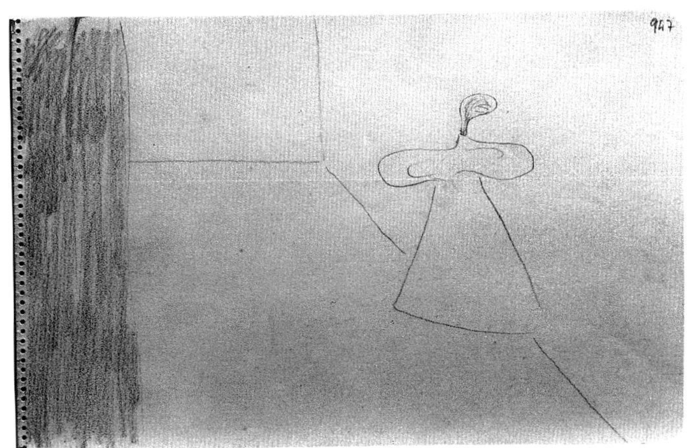

76. Study for *Queen Louise of Prussia*, 1929

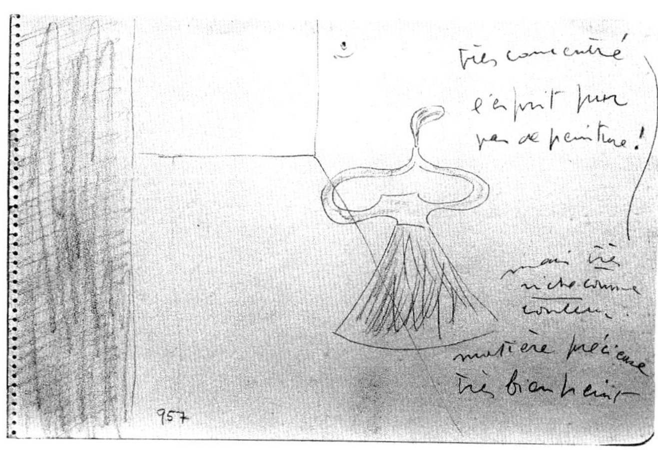

77. Study for *Queen Louise of Prussia*, 1929

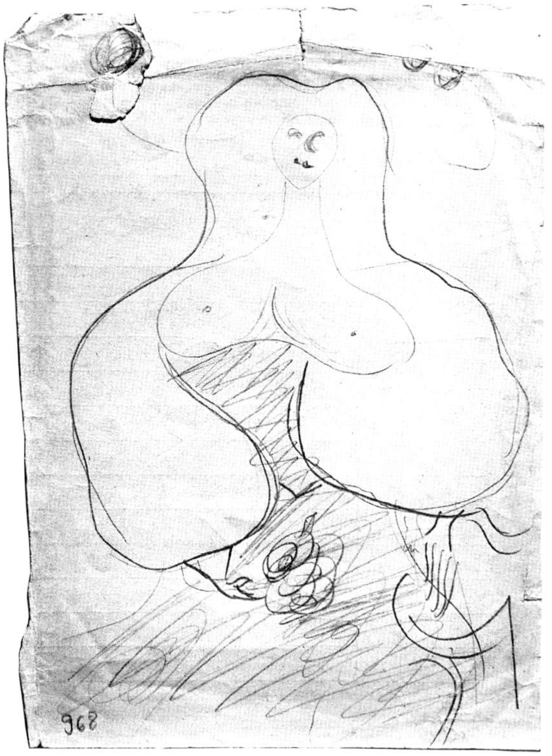

79. Study for *La Fornarina*, 1929

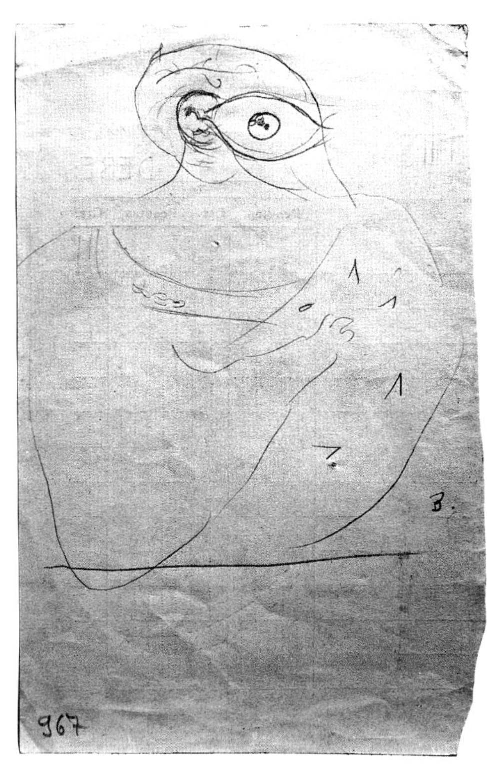

80. Study for *La Fornarina*, 1929

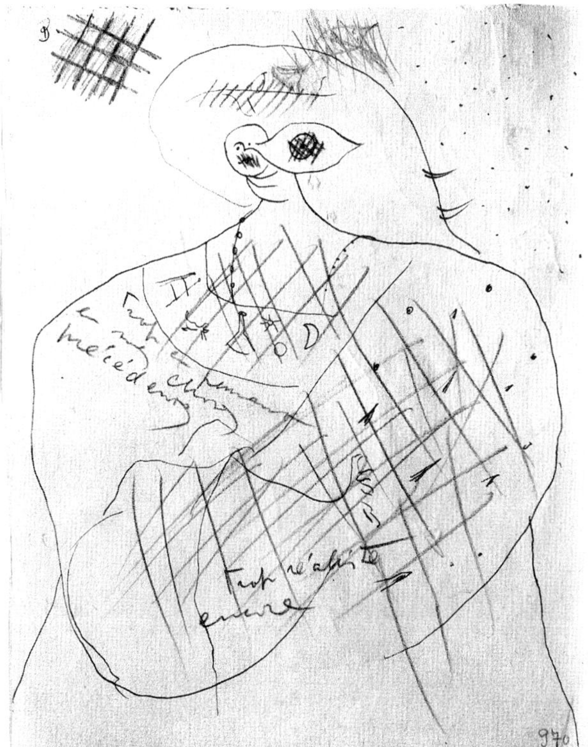

81. Study for *La Fornarina*, 1929

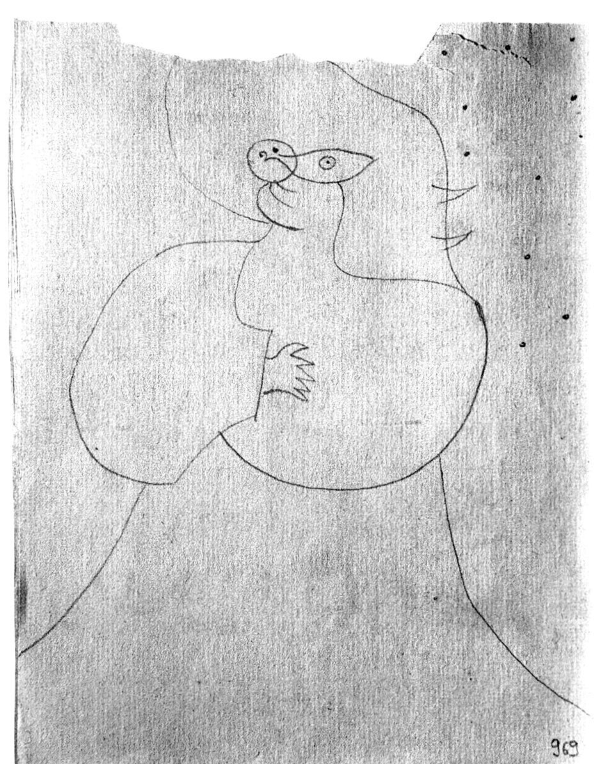

82. Study for *La Fornarina*, 1929

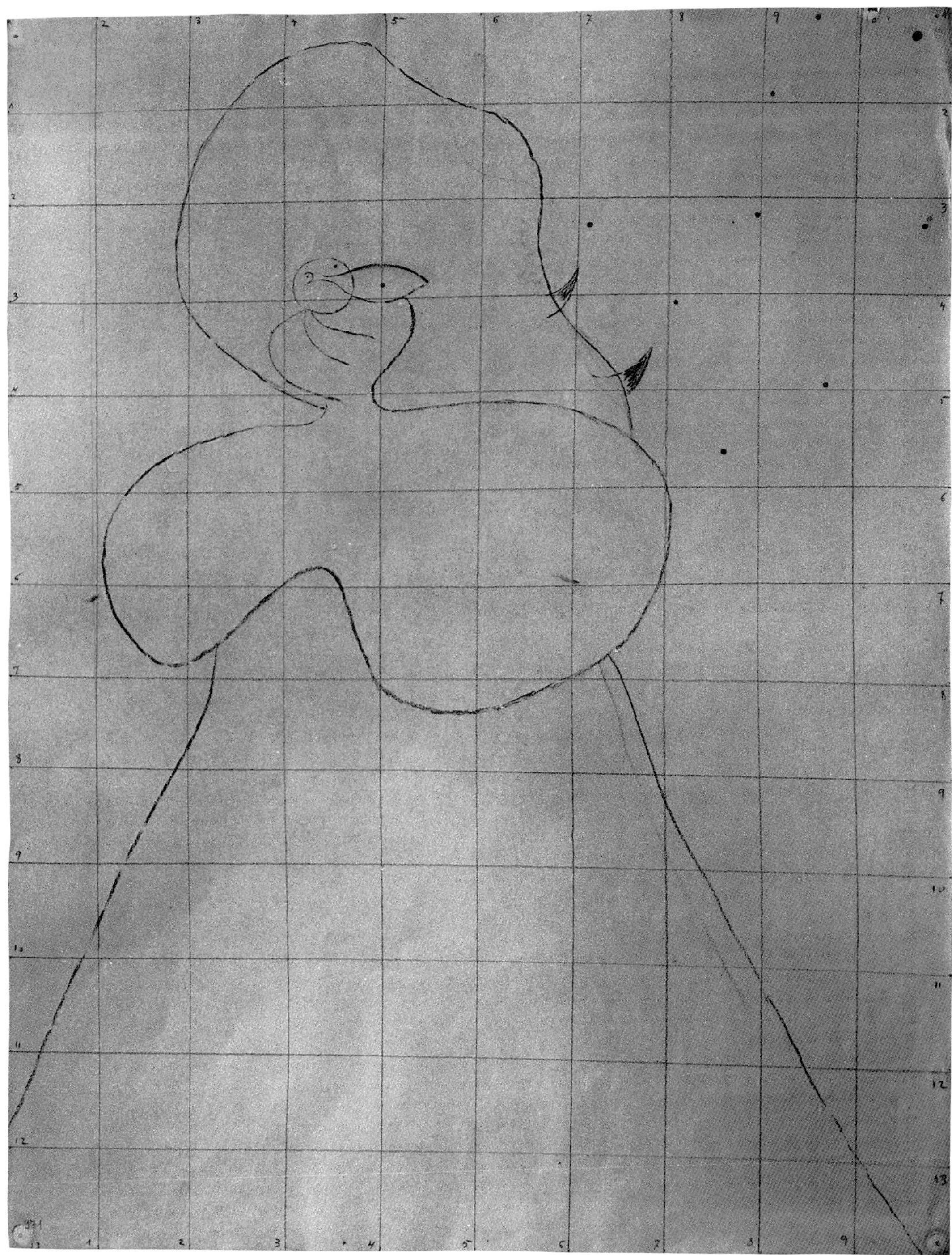

83. Study for *La Fornarina*, 1929

Series of Preparatory Collages for Paintings, 1933

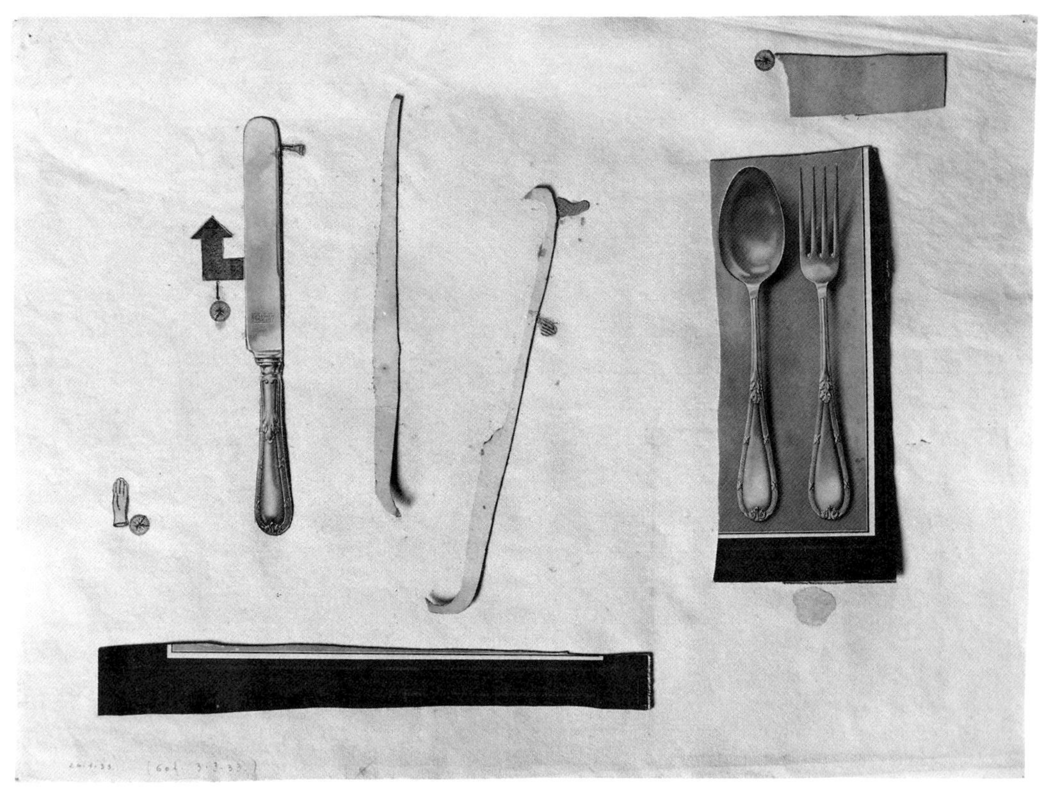

84. Collage, 26 January 1933

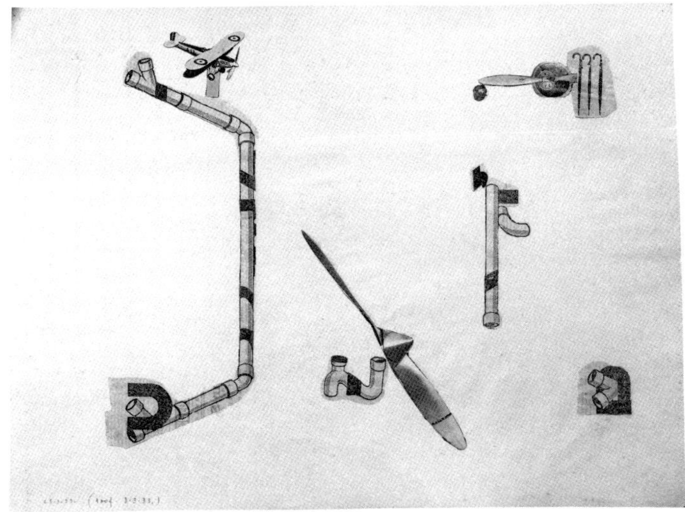

85. Collage, 28 January 1933

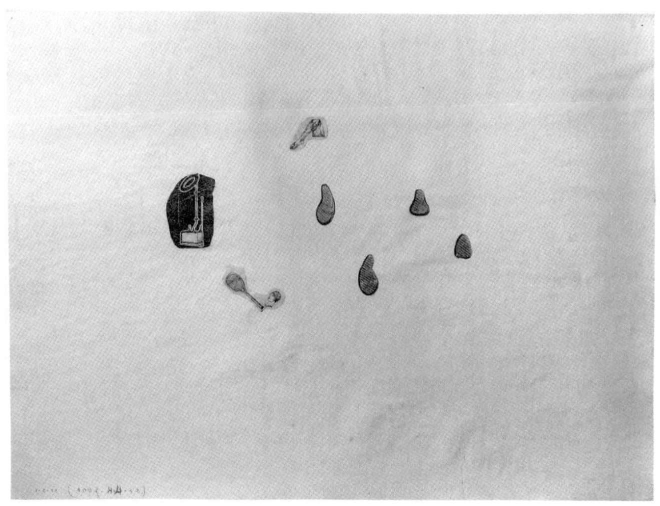

86. Collage, 1 February 1933

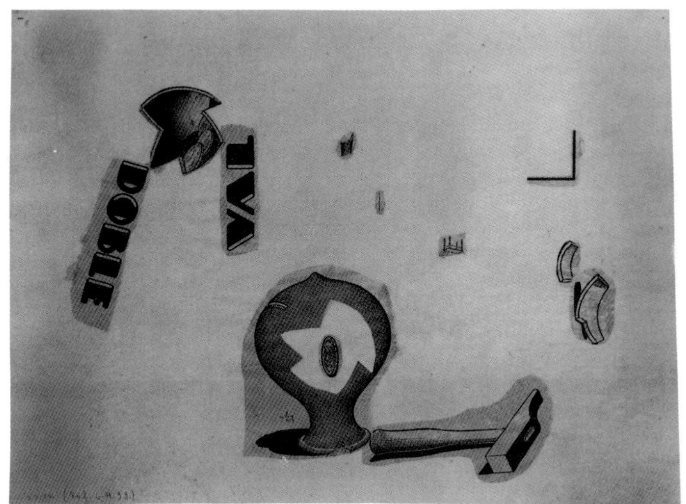

87. Collage, 2 February 1933

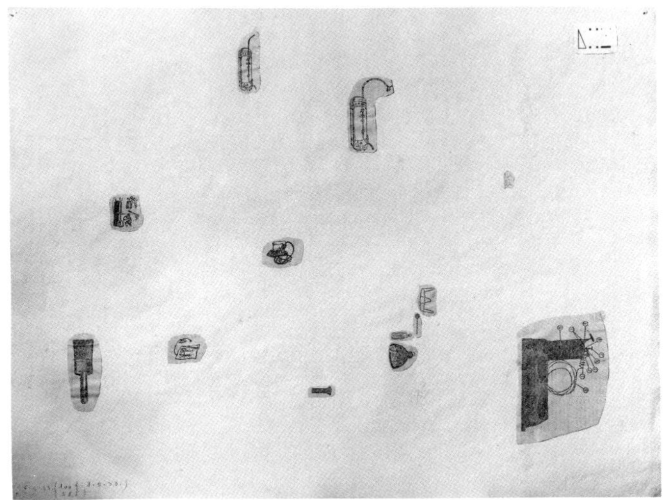

88. Collage, 6 February 1933

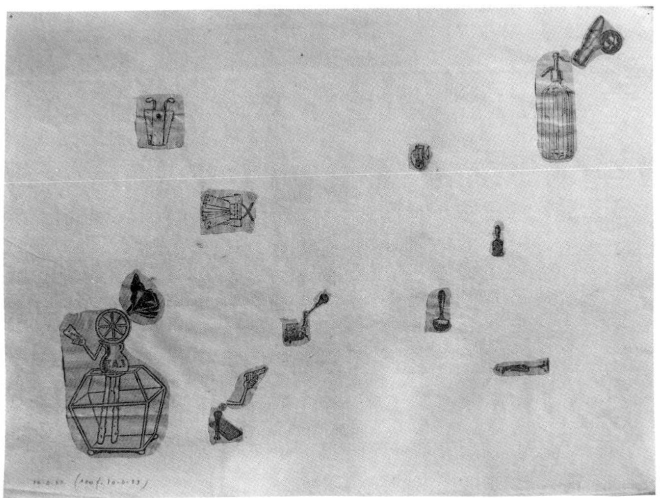

89. Collage, 10 February 1933

Legend of the Minotaur, 1933

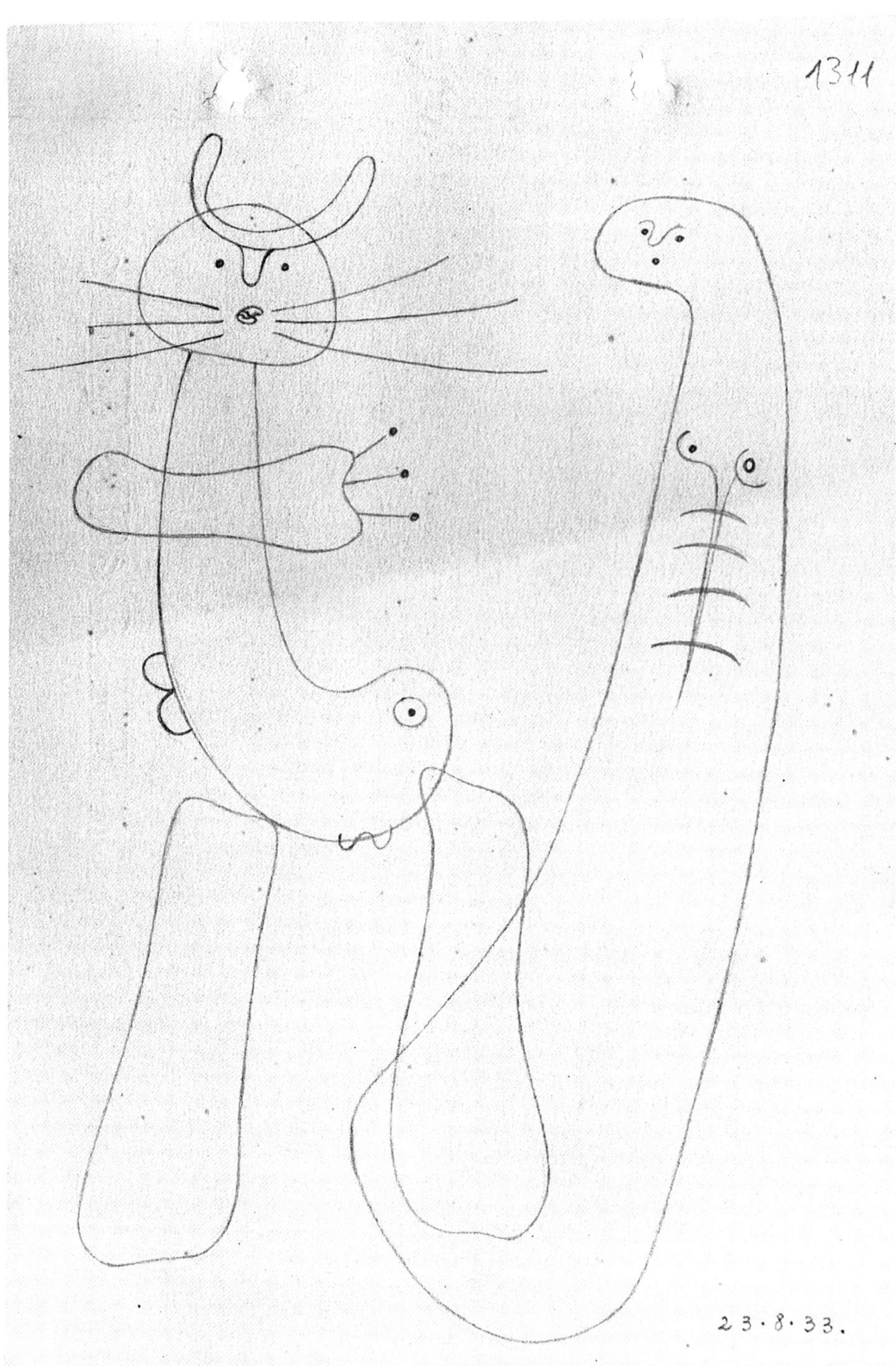

90. Study, 23 August 1933

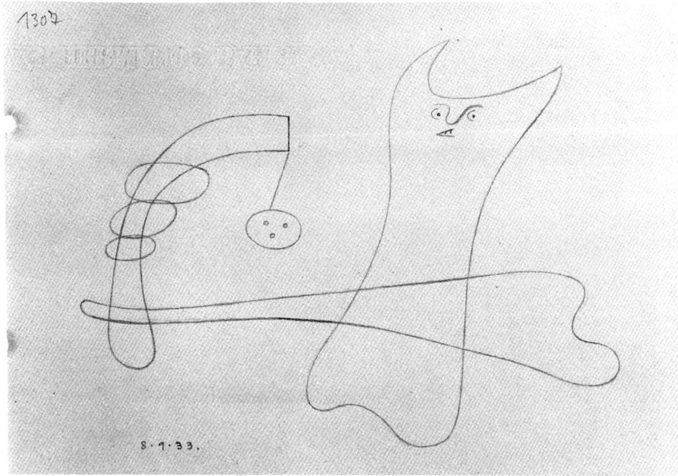

91. Study, 8 September 1933

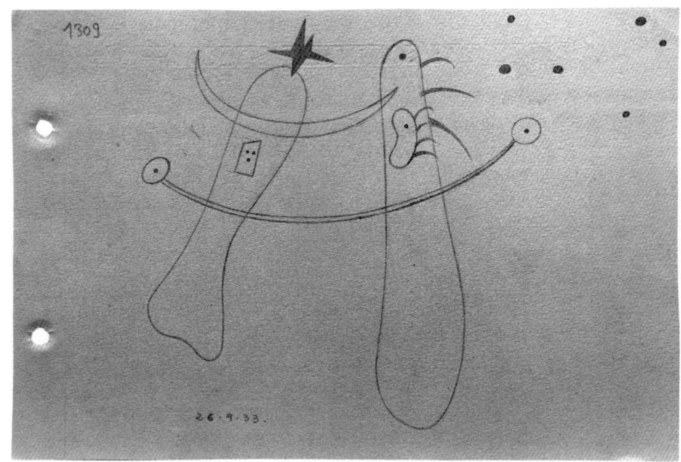

92. Study, 26 September 1933

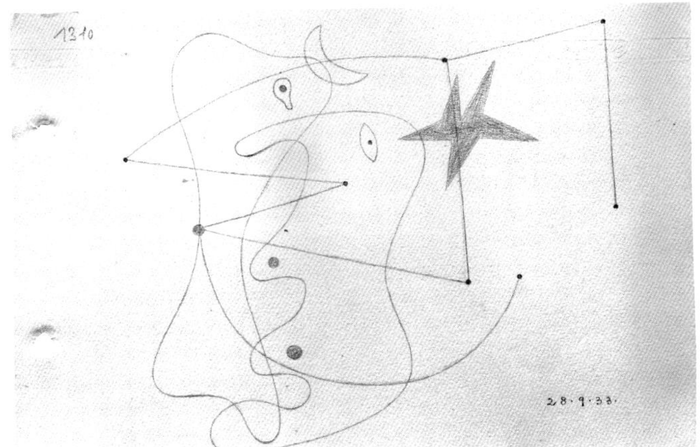

93. Study, 28 September 1933

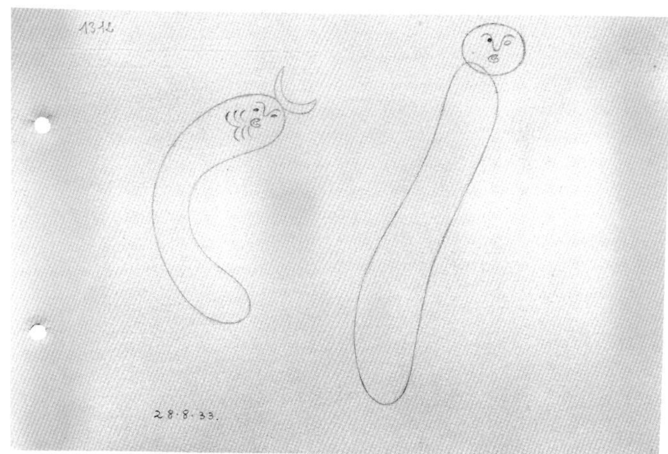

94. Study, 28 August 1933

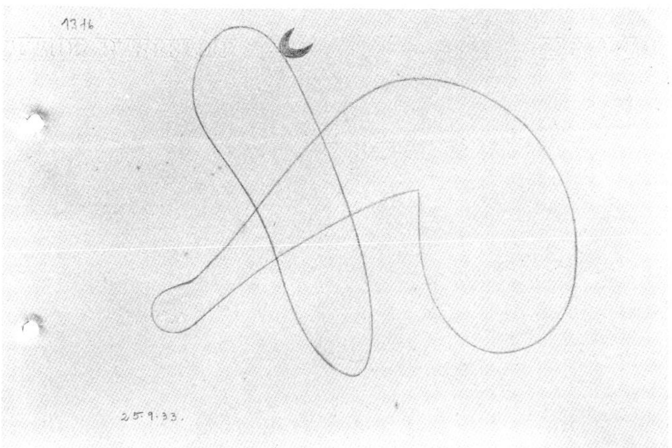

95. Study, 25 September 1933

Wartime Studies, 1937-42

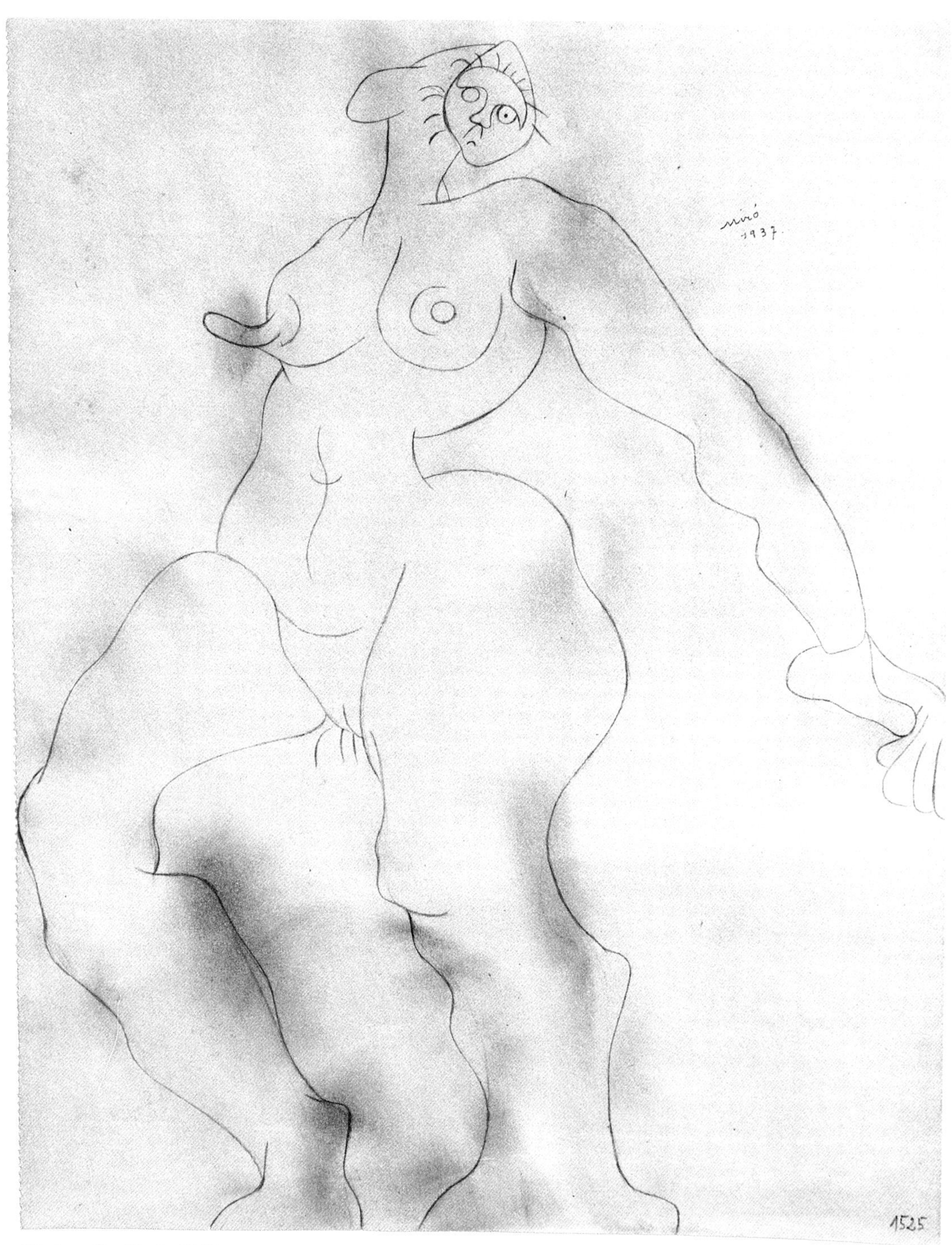

96. *Standing Nude*, 1937

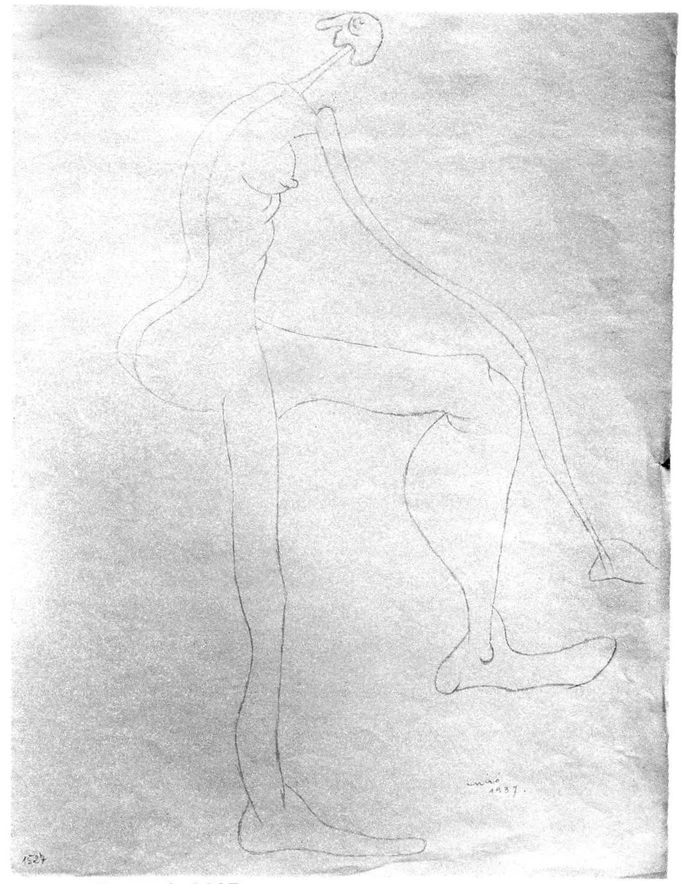

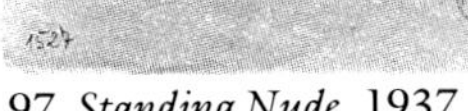

97. *Standing Nude*, 1937

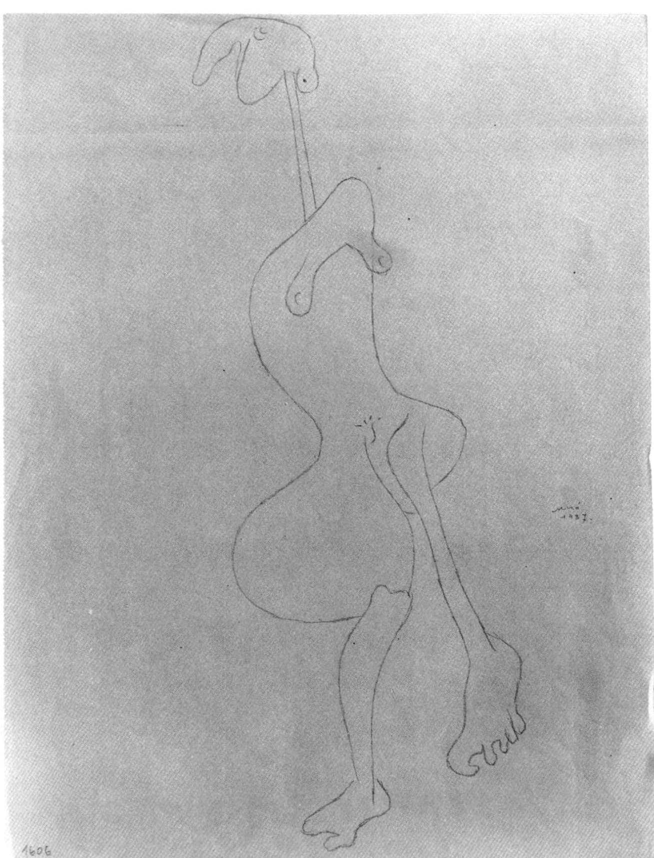

98. *Standing Nude*, 1937

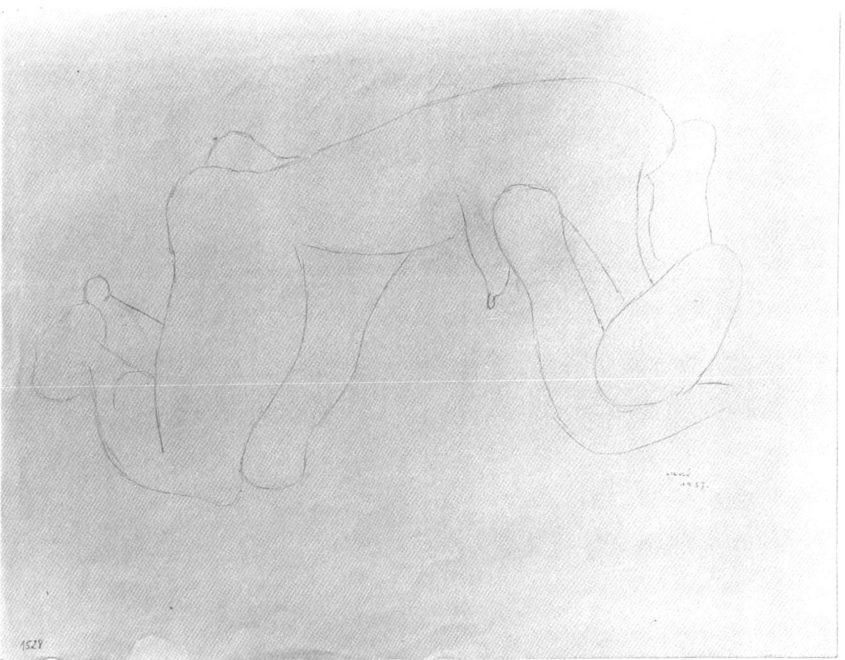

99. *Kneeling Female Nude*, 1937

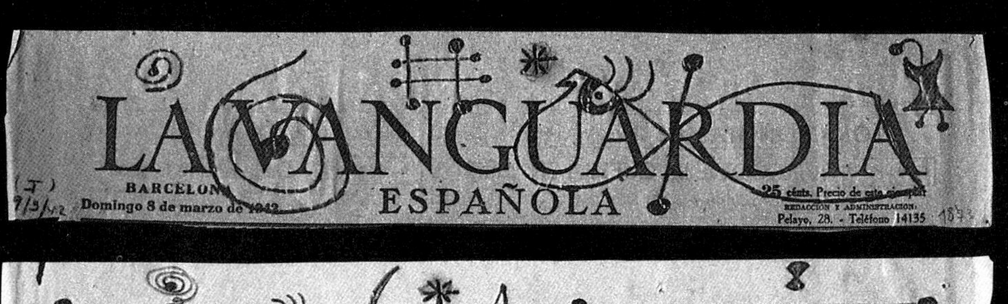
LA VANGUARDIA
ESPAÑOLA
BARCELONA
Domingo 8 de marzo de 1942
25 cénts. Precio de este ejemplar
REDACCIÓN Y ADMINISTRACIÓN:
Pelayo, 28. - Teléfono 14135

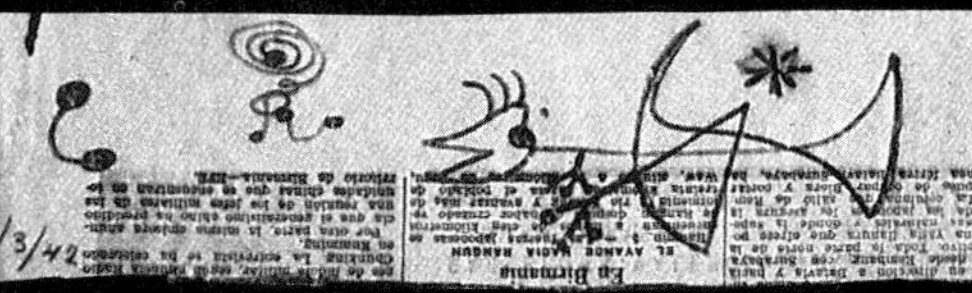

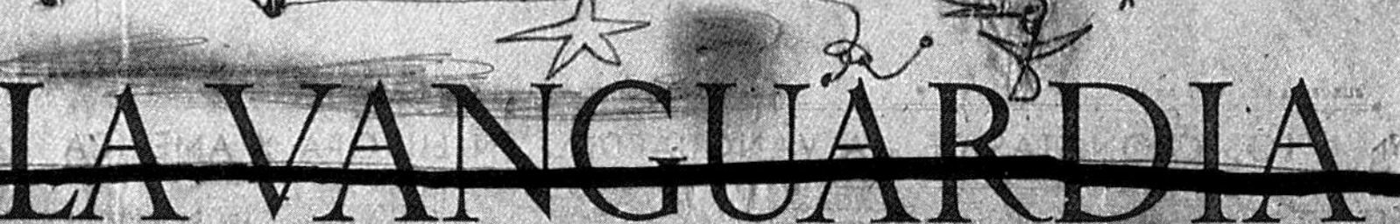
LA VANGUARDIA
ESPAÑOLA
BARCELONA
Jueves 5 de marzo de 1942
25 cénts. Precio de este ejemplar
Pelayo, 28. - Teléfono 14135
FUNDADORES: DON CARLOS Y DON BARTOLOMÉ GODÓ
Año LVIII. - Número 23.560
DIRECTOR: LUIS DE GALINSOGA
LA AVIACIÓN INGLESA BOMBARDEA INTENSAMENTE VARIOS BARRIOS DE PARIS
600 muertos, más de 1.000 heridos y 200 casas destruídas
Los ingleses afirman que el bombardeo tenía por objetivo las fábricas «Renault» y otras que construyen material de guerra para los alemanes»
La lucha prosigue encarnizadamente en Java, donde los nipones progresan lentamente venciendo la tenaz resistencia anglo-yanqui-neerlandesa
PARTES OFICIALES DE GUERRA NEERLANDESES

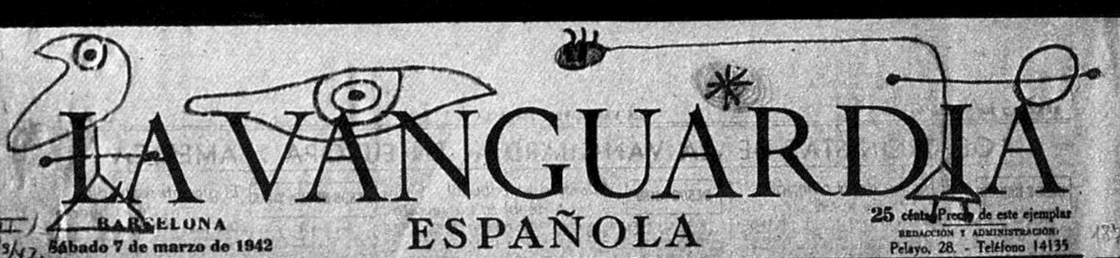
LA VANGUARDIA
ESPAÑOLA
BARCELONA
Sábado 7 de marzo de 1942
25 cénts. Precio de este ejemplar
REDACCIÓN Y ADMINISTRACIÓN:
Pelayo, 28. - Teléfono 14135

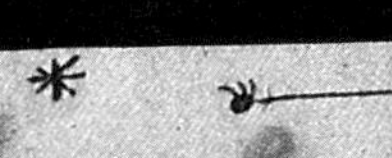

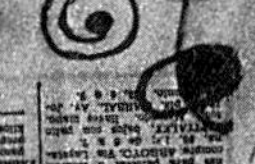
LA VANGUARDIA
ESPAÑOLA
BARCELONA
Martes 10 de marzo de 1942
25 cénts. Precio de este ejemplar
Pelayo, 28. - Teléfono 14135
FUNDADORES: DON CARLOS Y DON BARTOLOMÉ GODÓ
DIRECTOR: LUIS DE GALINSOGA

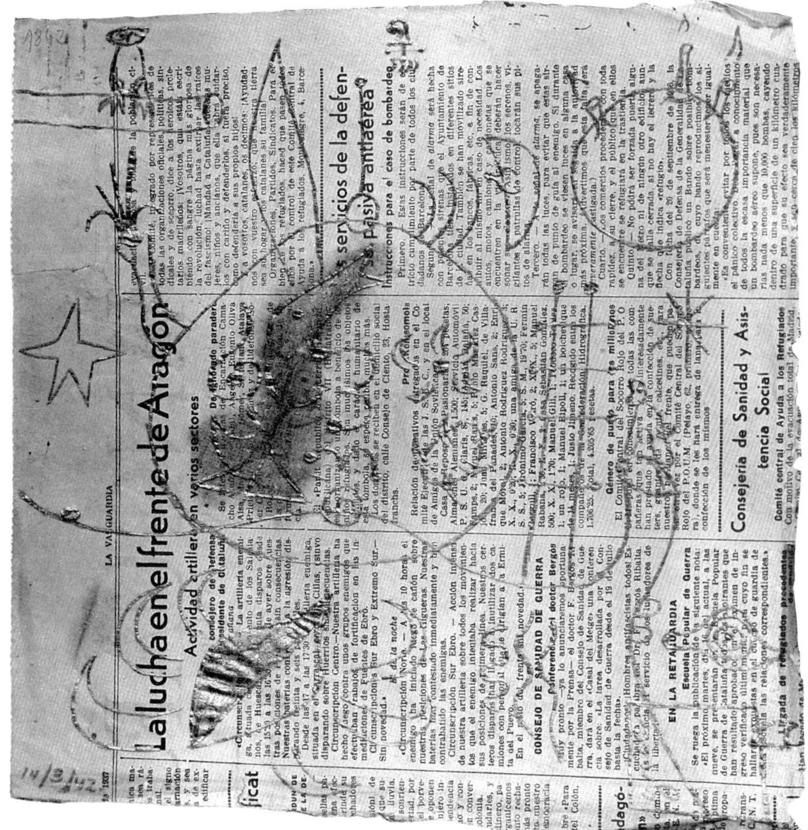

101. *Self-Portrait*, 14 March 1942

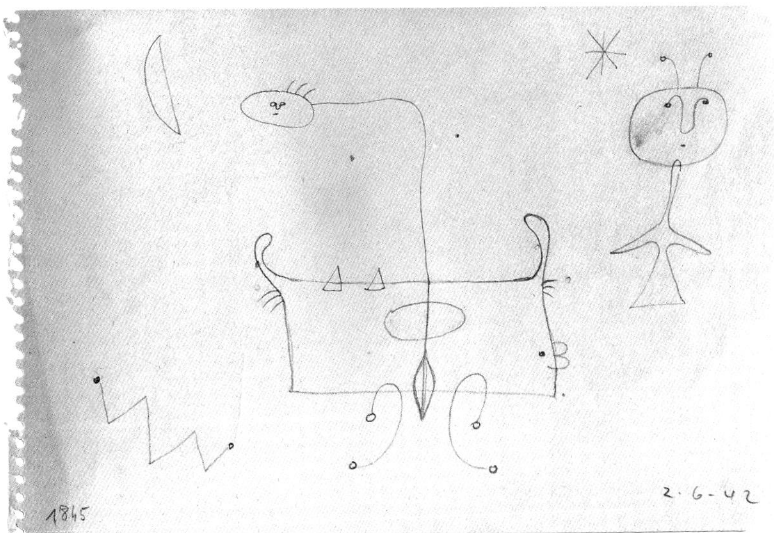

102. Study, 2 June 1942

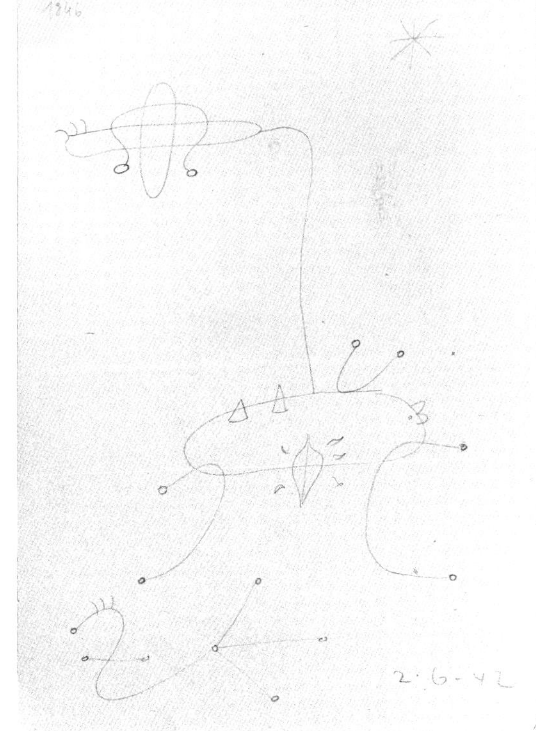

100. Eight studies, March 1942

103. Study, 2 June 1942

Studies for Sculptures, 1945-56

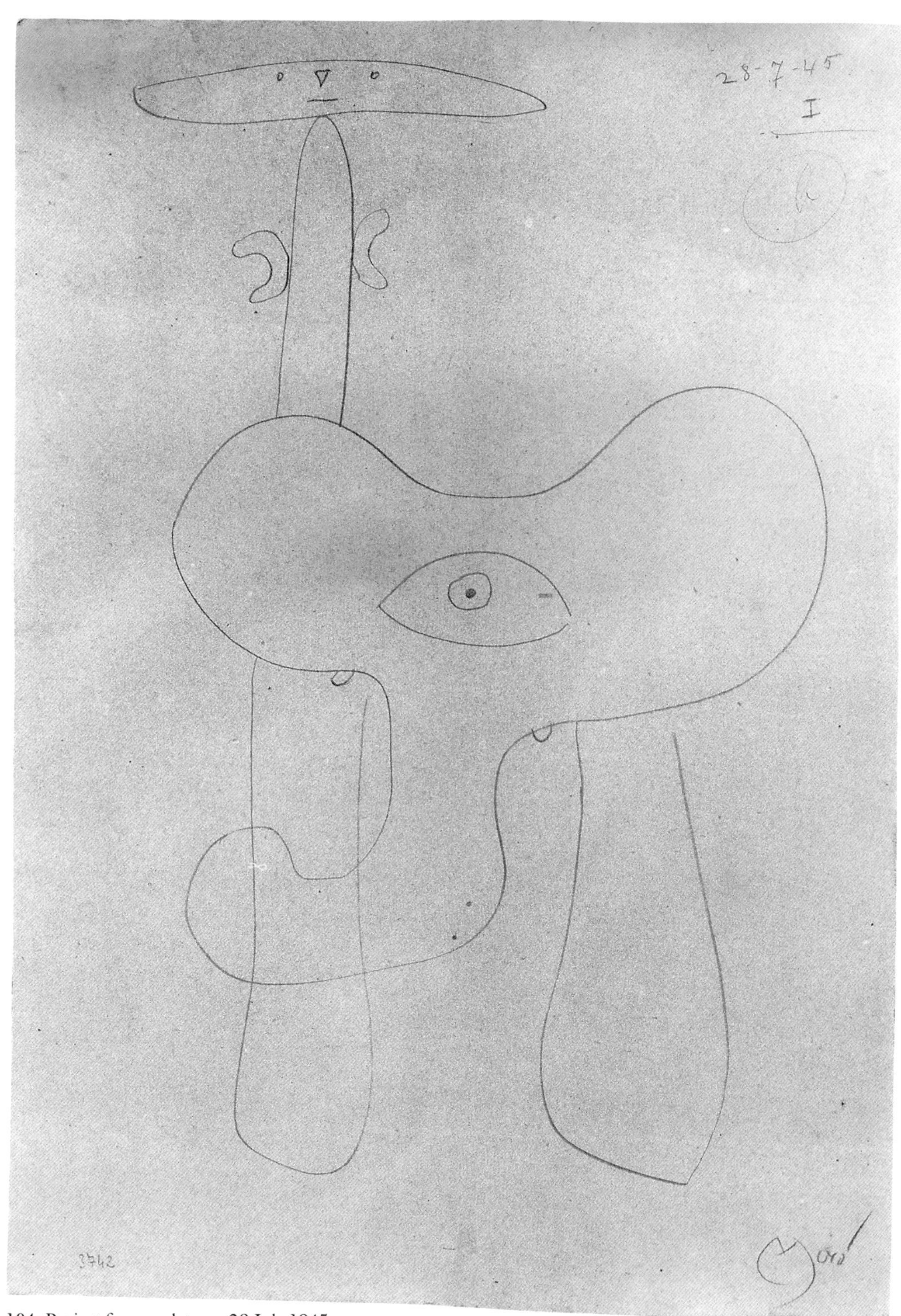

104. Project for a sculpture, 28 July 1945

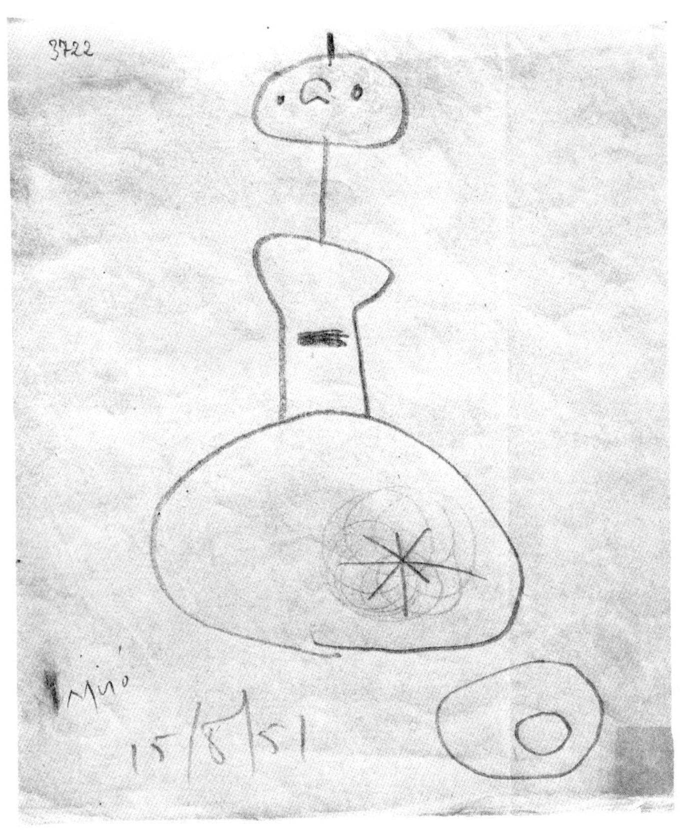

105. Study for *Project for a Monument*, 15 August 1951

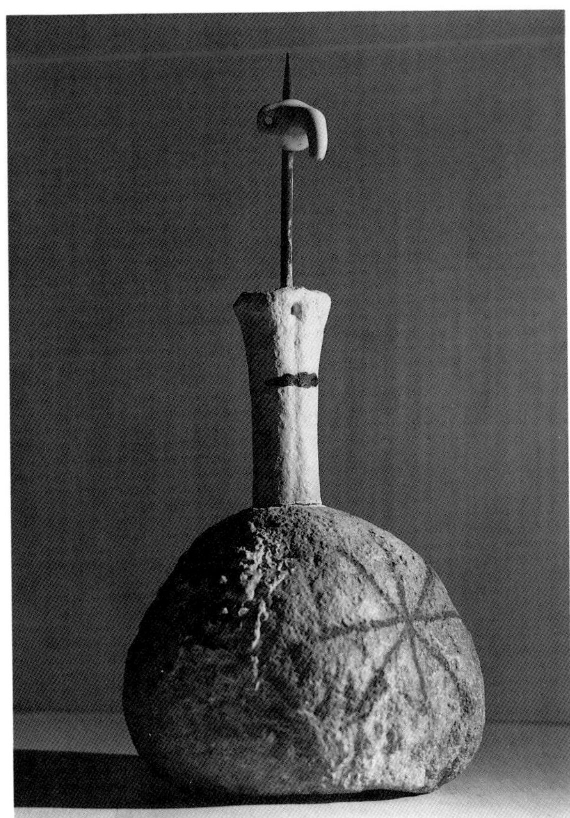

Figure G. Joan Miró. *Project for a Monument*, 1954

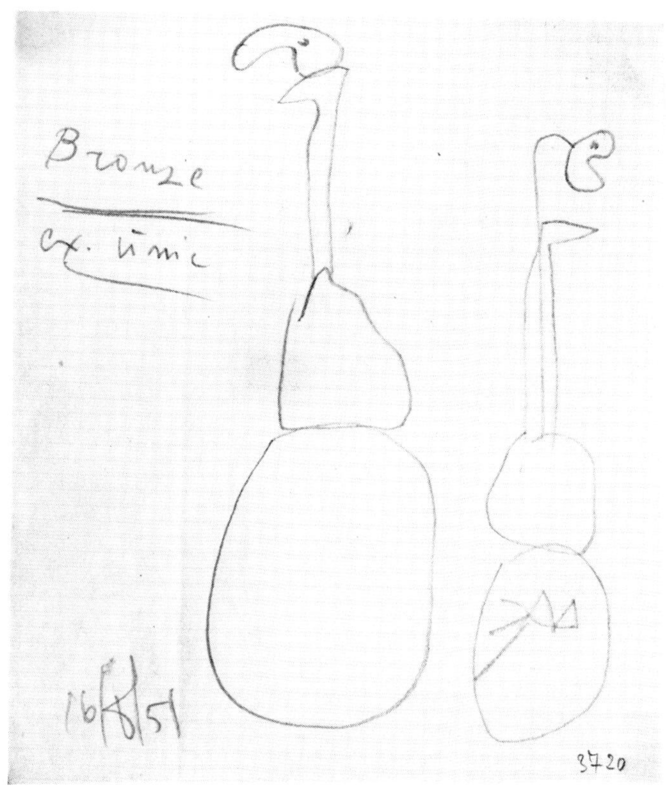

106. Study for *Project for a Monument*, 16 August 1951

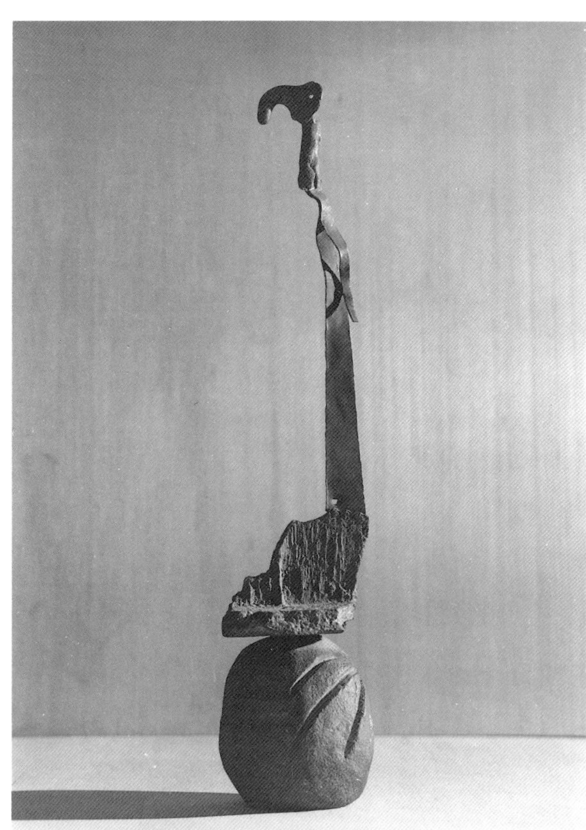

Figure H. Joan Miró. *Project for a Monument*, 1954

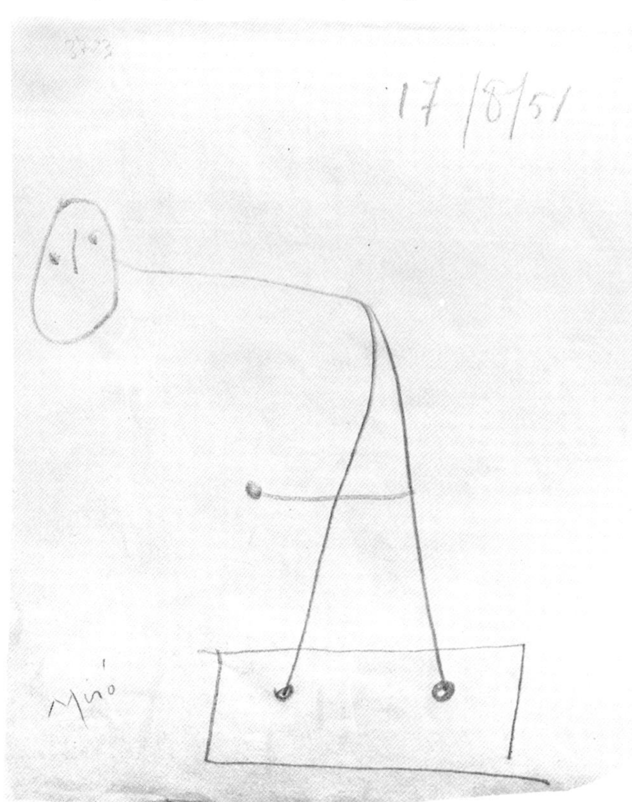

107. Study for *Project for a Monument*, 17 August 1951

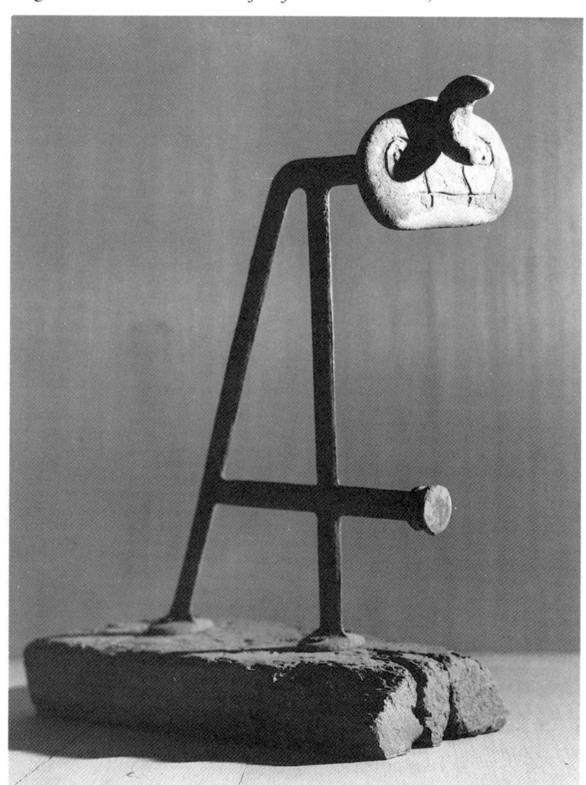

Figure I. Joan Miró. *Project for a Monument*: *Personnage*, 1954

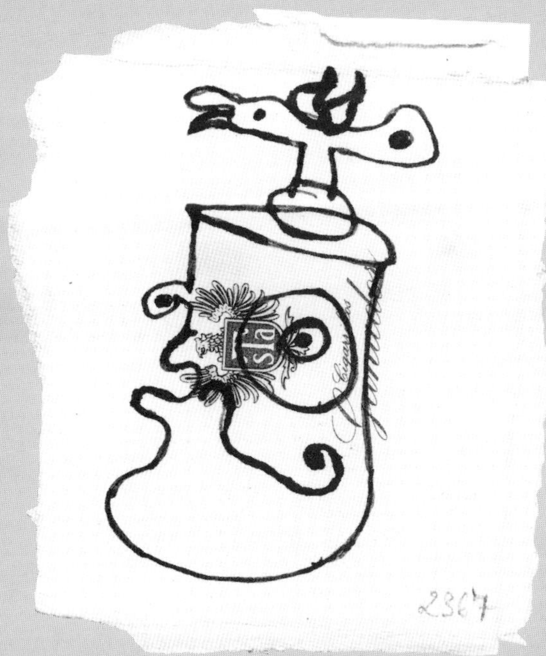

108. Study for ceramic sculpture, ca. 1956

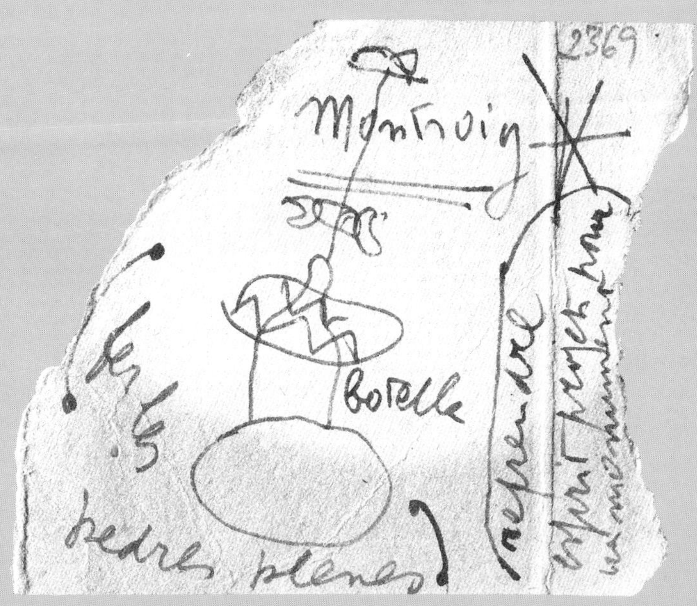

109. Study for ceramic sculpture, ca. 1956

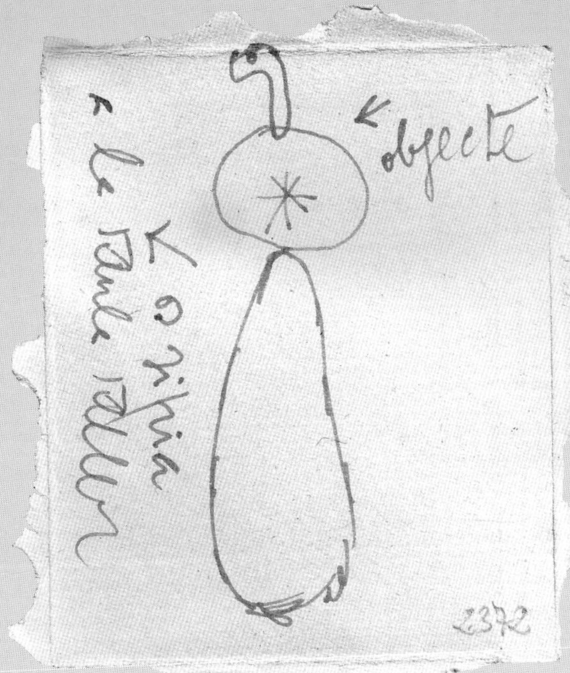

110. Study for ceramic sculpture, ca. 1956

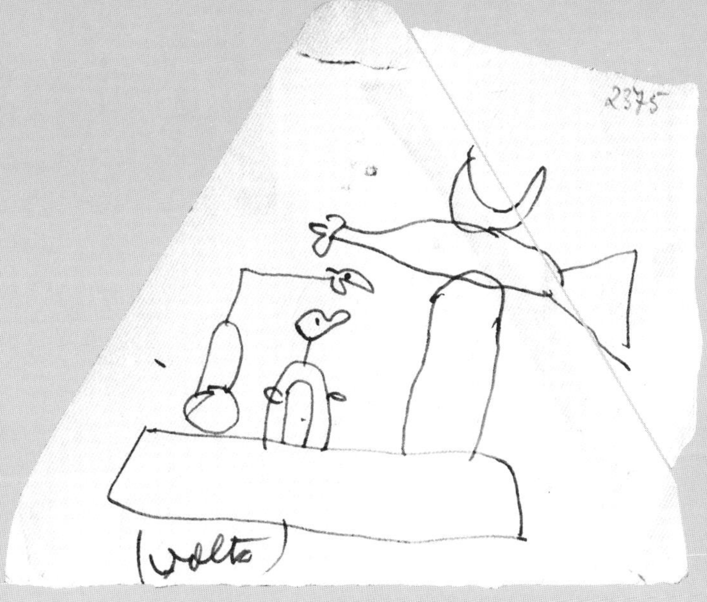

111. Study for ceramic sculpture, ca. 1956

1960s

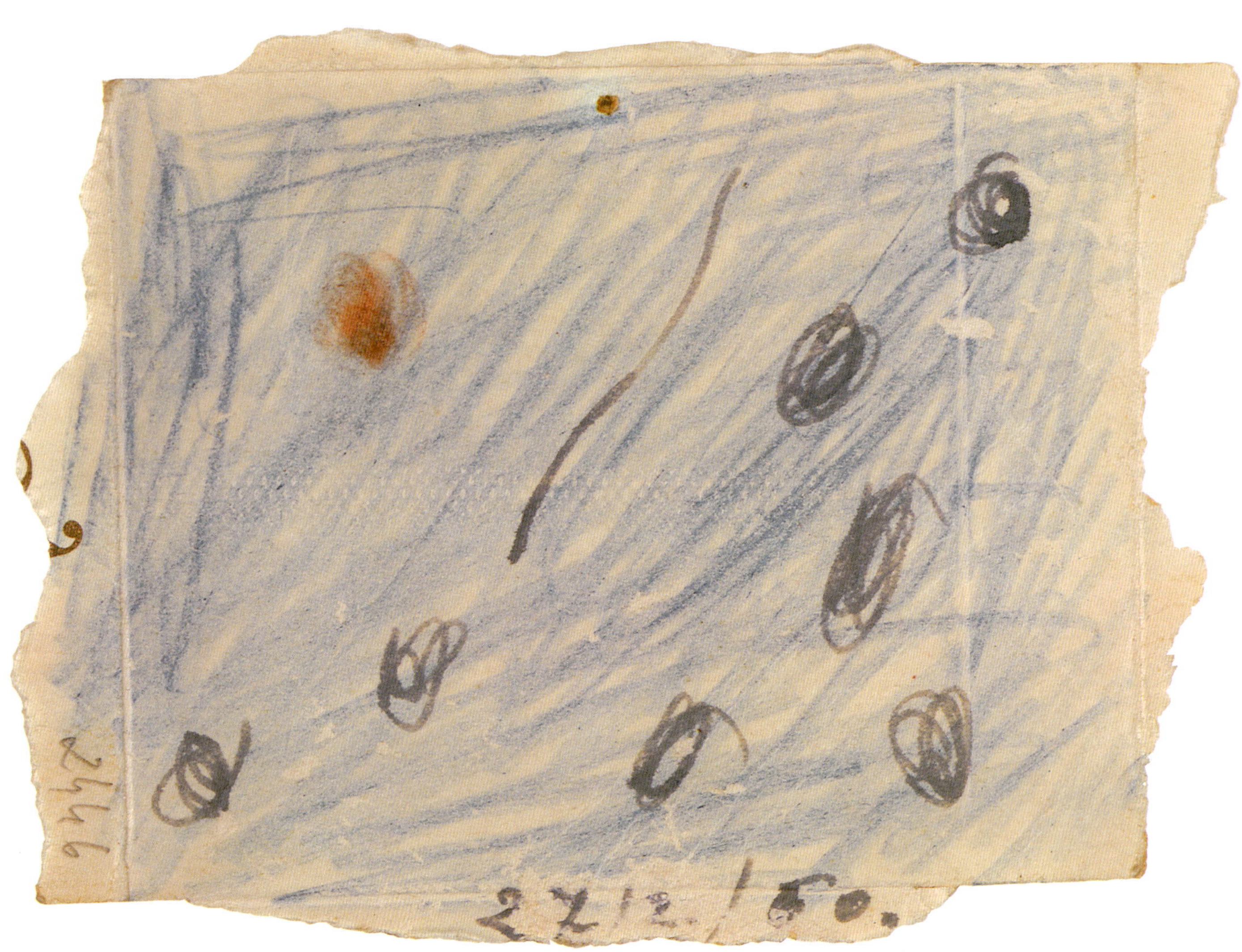

112. Study for *Blue I*, 27 February 1960

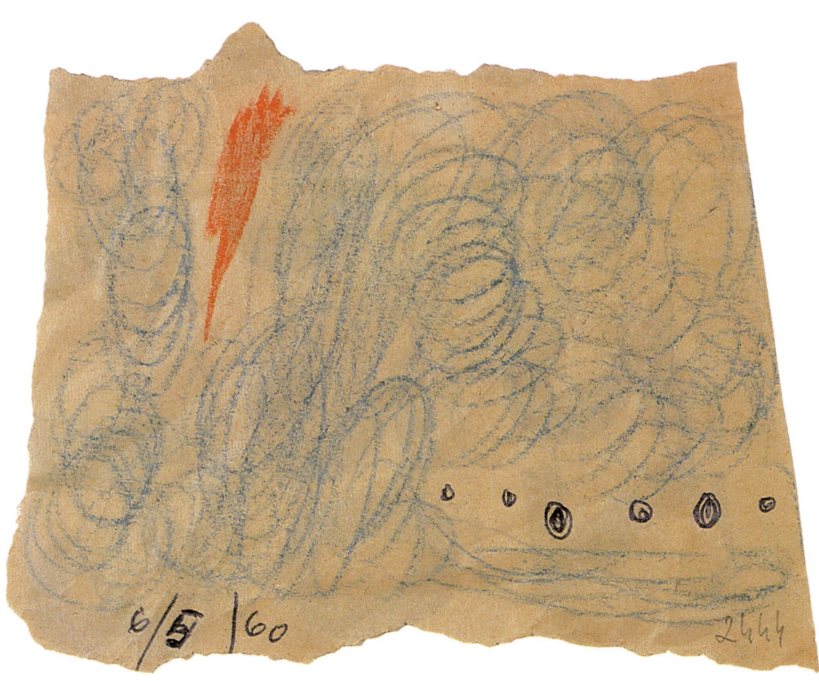

113. Study for *Blue II*, 6 May 1960

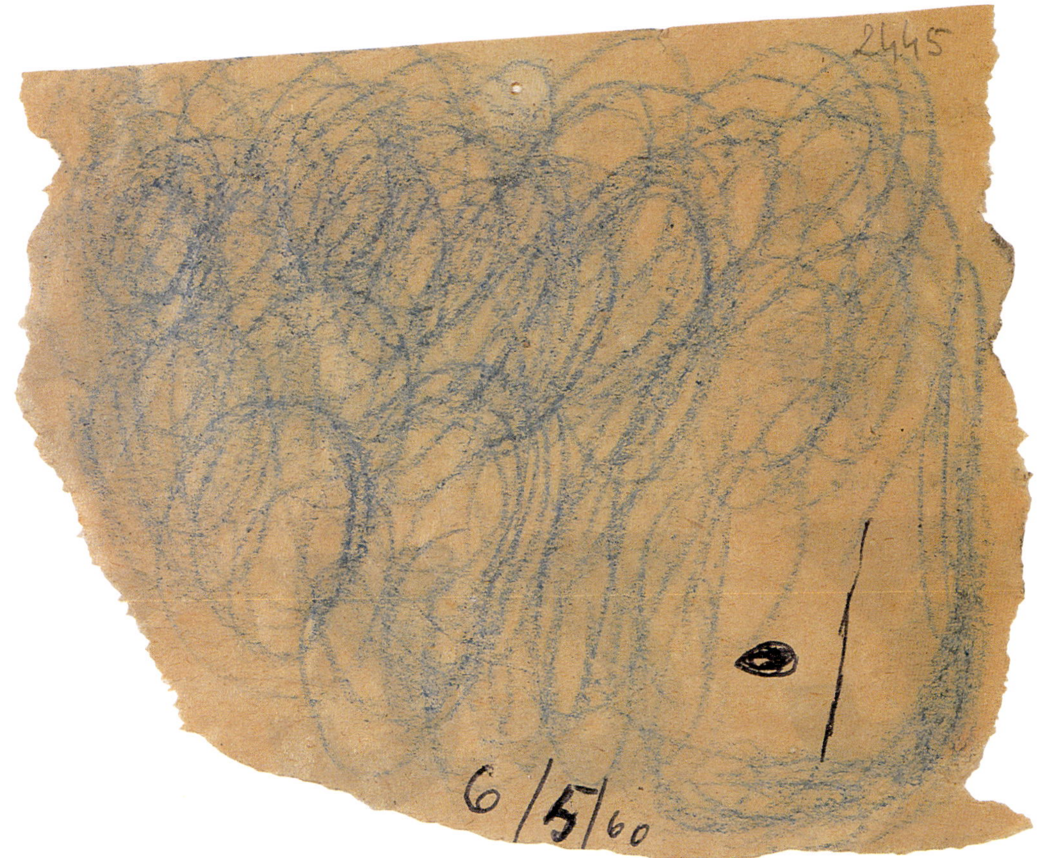

114. Study for *Blue III*, 6 May 1960

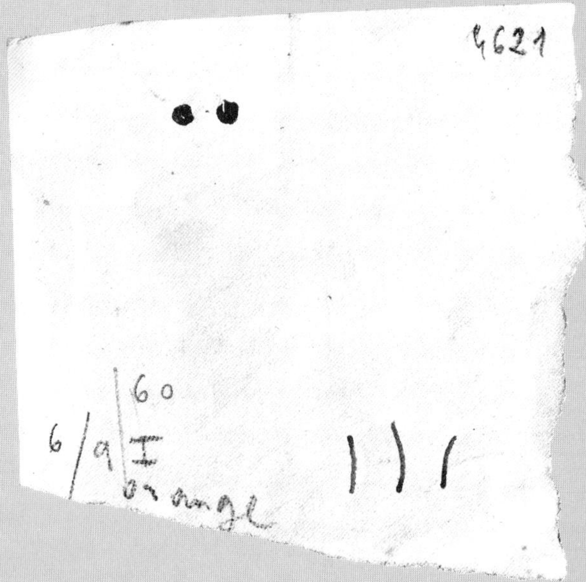

115. Study for *Mural Painting for a Temple I*, 6 September 1960

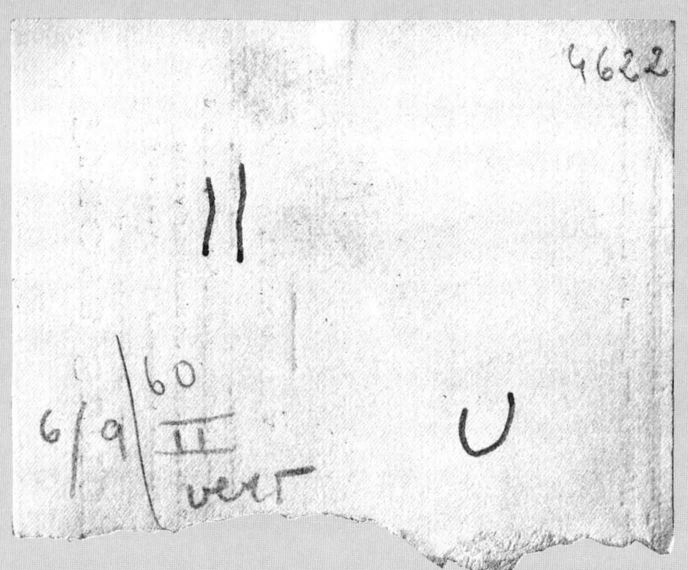

116. Study for *Mural Painting for a Temple II*, 6 September 1960

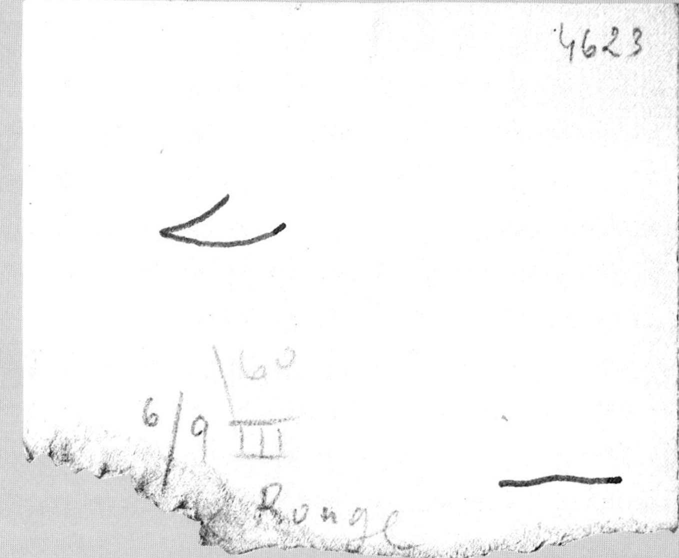

117. Study for *Mural Painting for a Temple III*, 6 September 1960

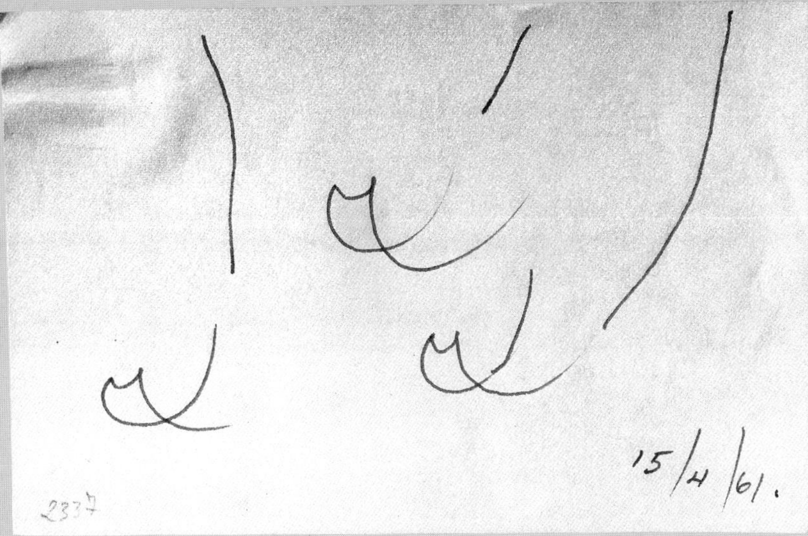

118. Drawing, 15 April 1961

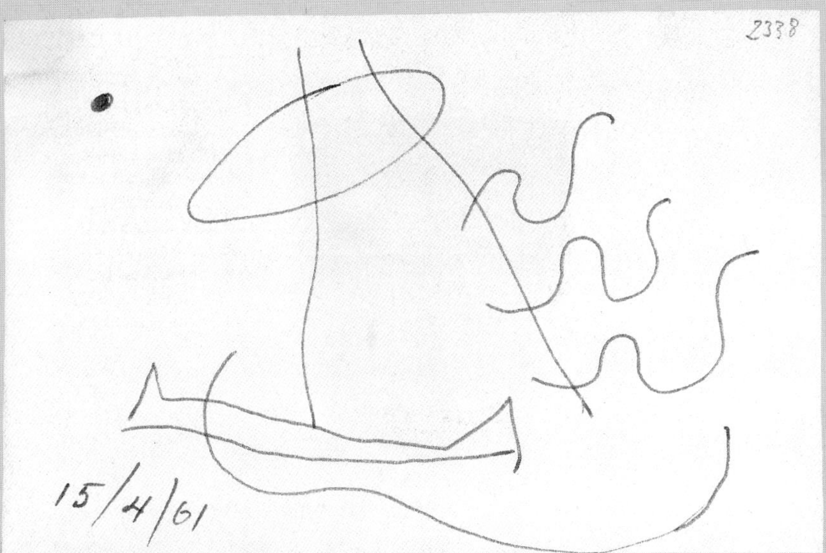

119. Drawing, 15 April 1961

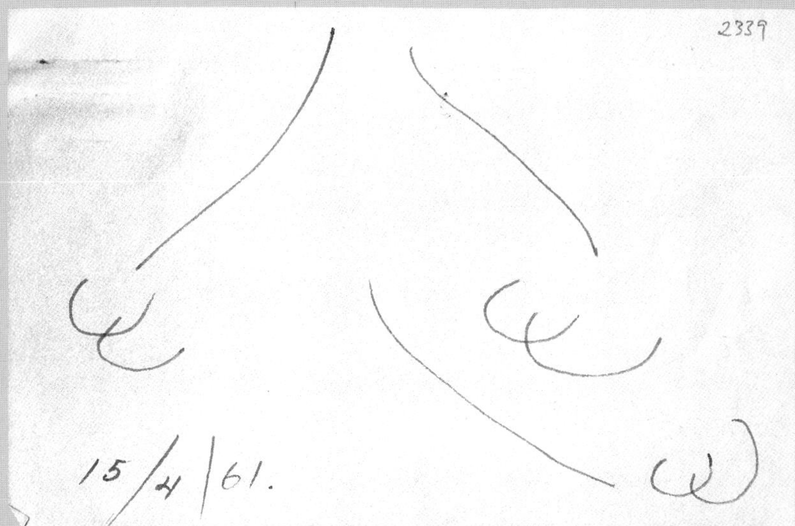

120. Drawing, 15 April 1961

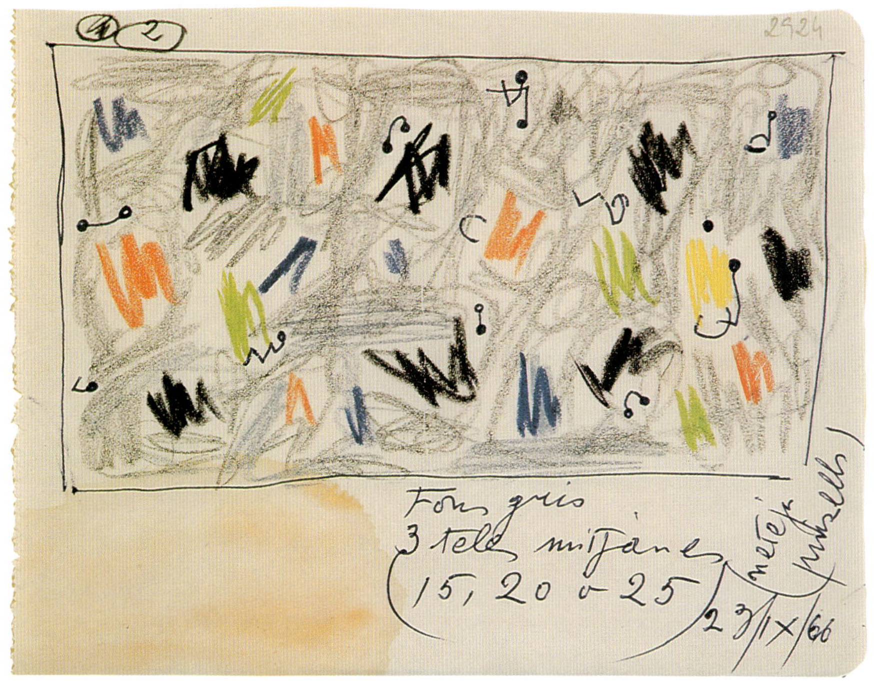

121. Drawing, 23 September 1966

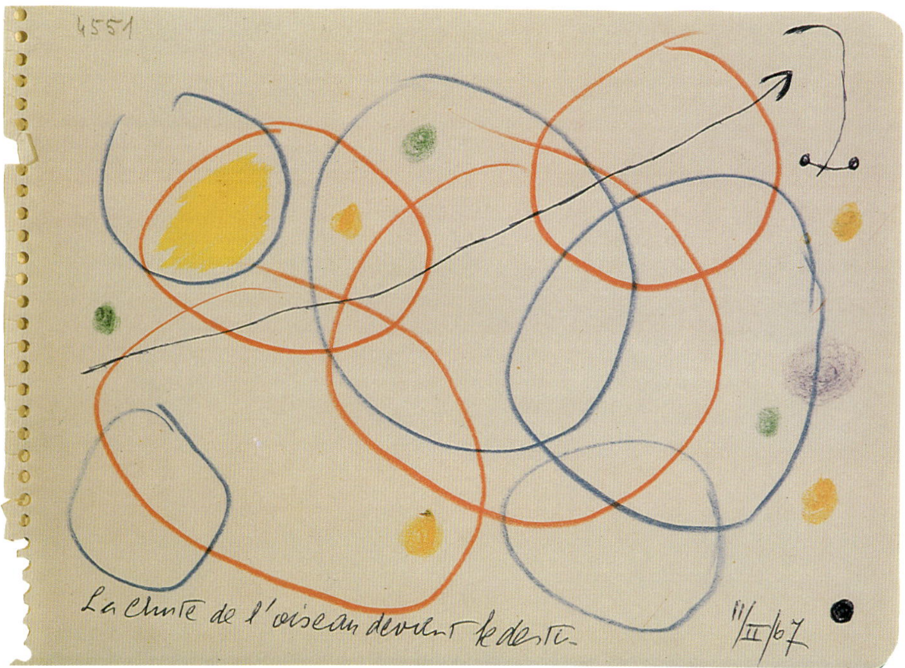

122. *The Fall of the Bird before Fate*, 11 February, 1967

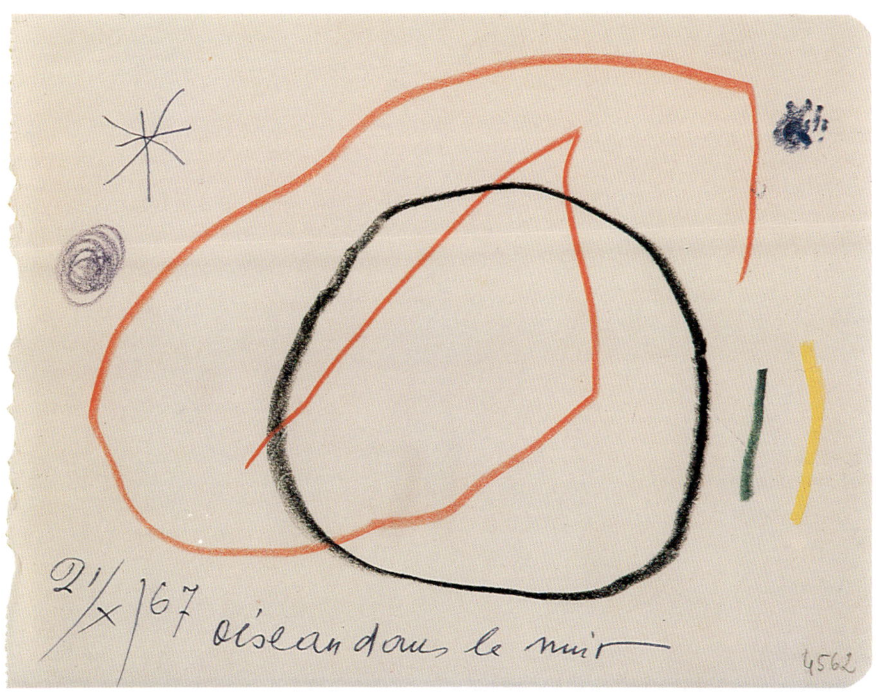

123. *Bird in the Night*, 21 October 1967

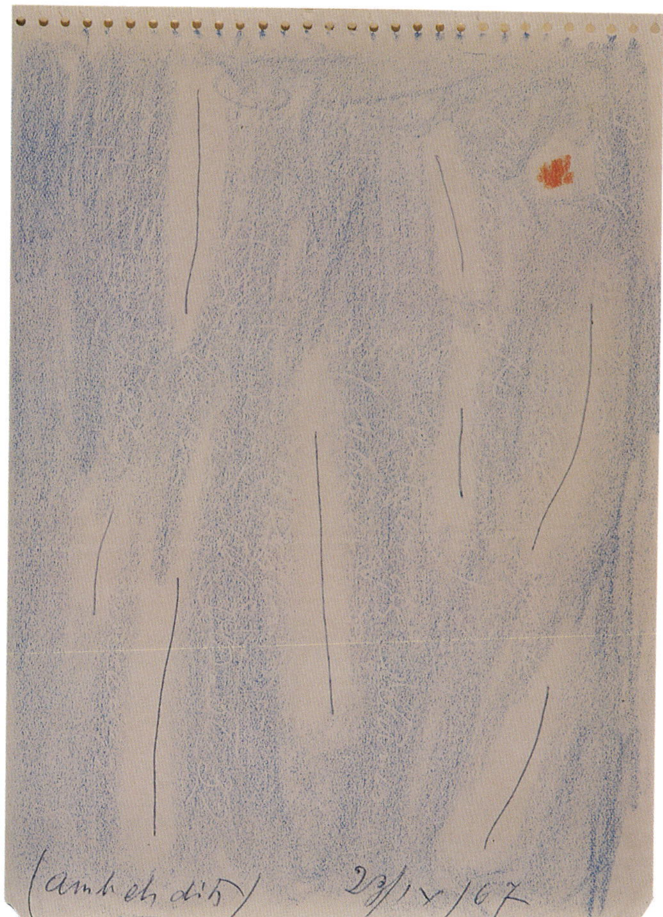

124. Study, 23 September 1967

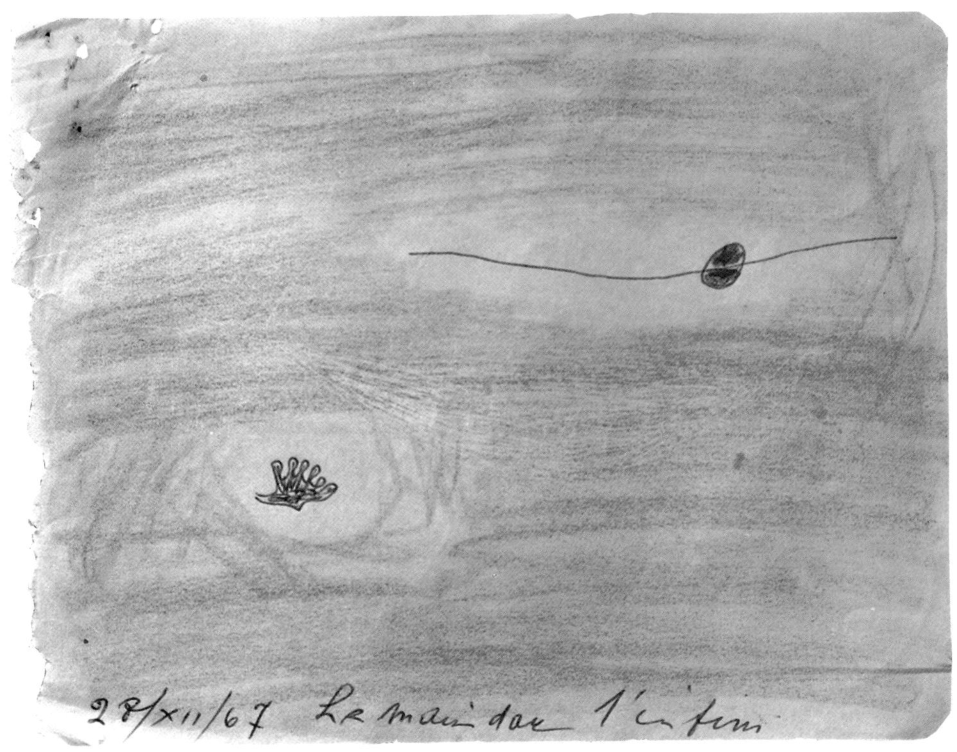

125. *The Hand in Infinity*, 28 December 1967

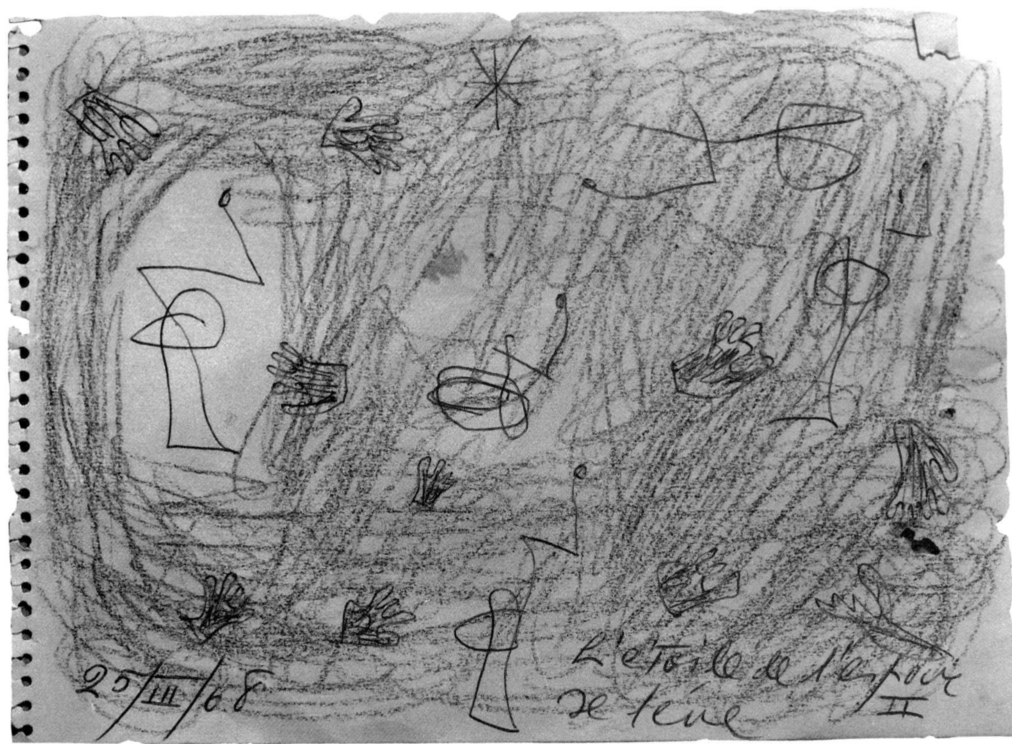

126. *The Star of Hope Rises II*, 25 March 1968

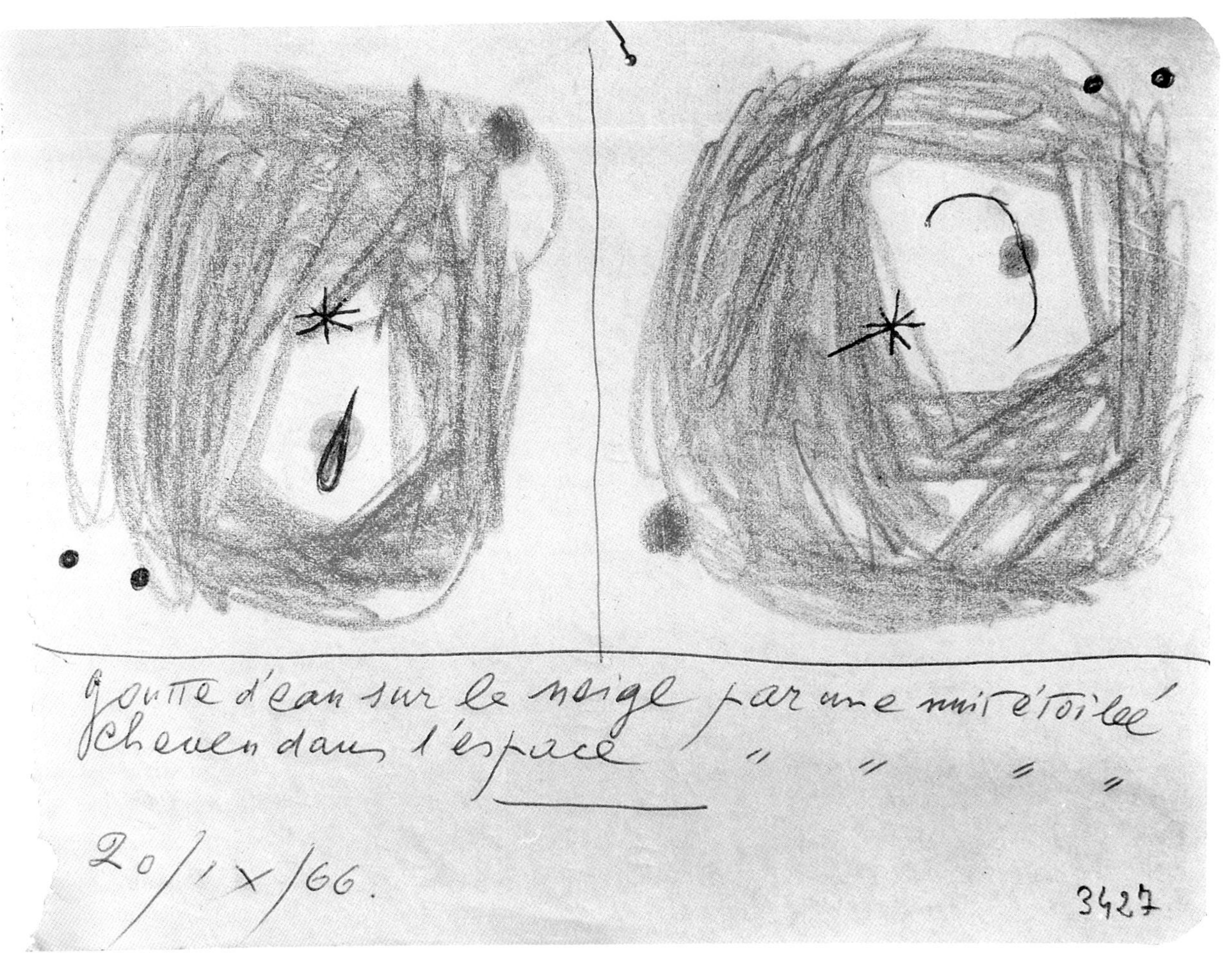

127. Studies for *Drop of Water on the Rose-colored Snow*, 20 September 1966

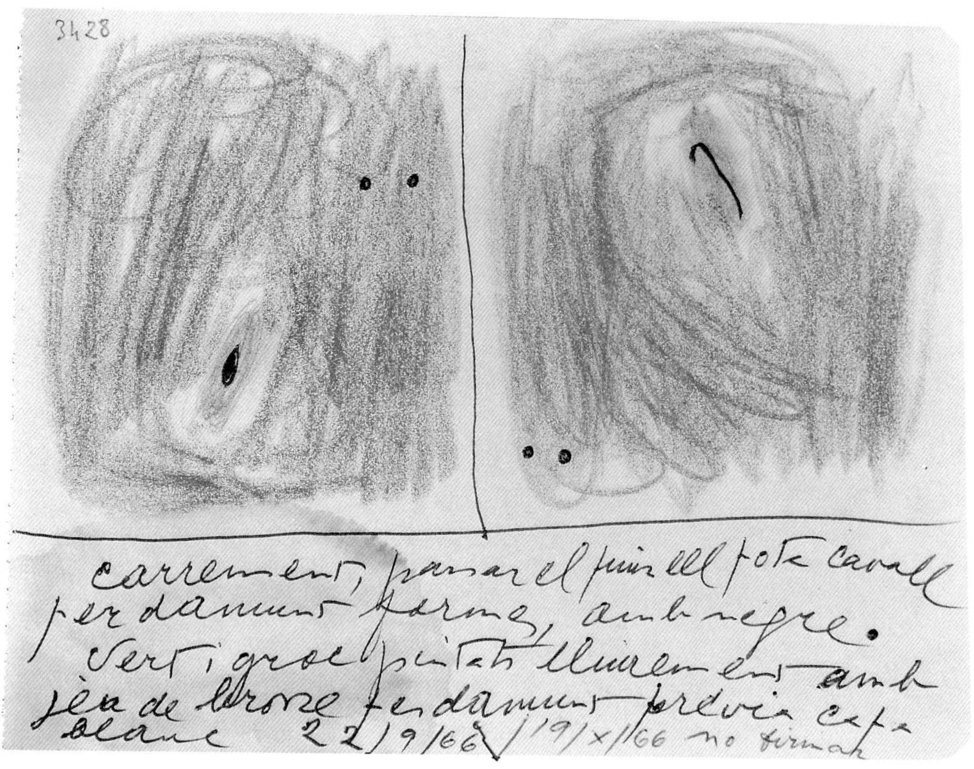

128. Studies for *Hair Pursued by Two Planets*, 22 September/19 October 1966

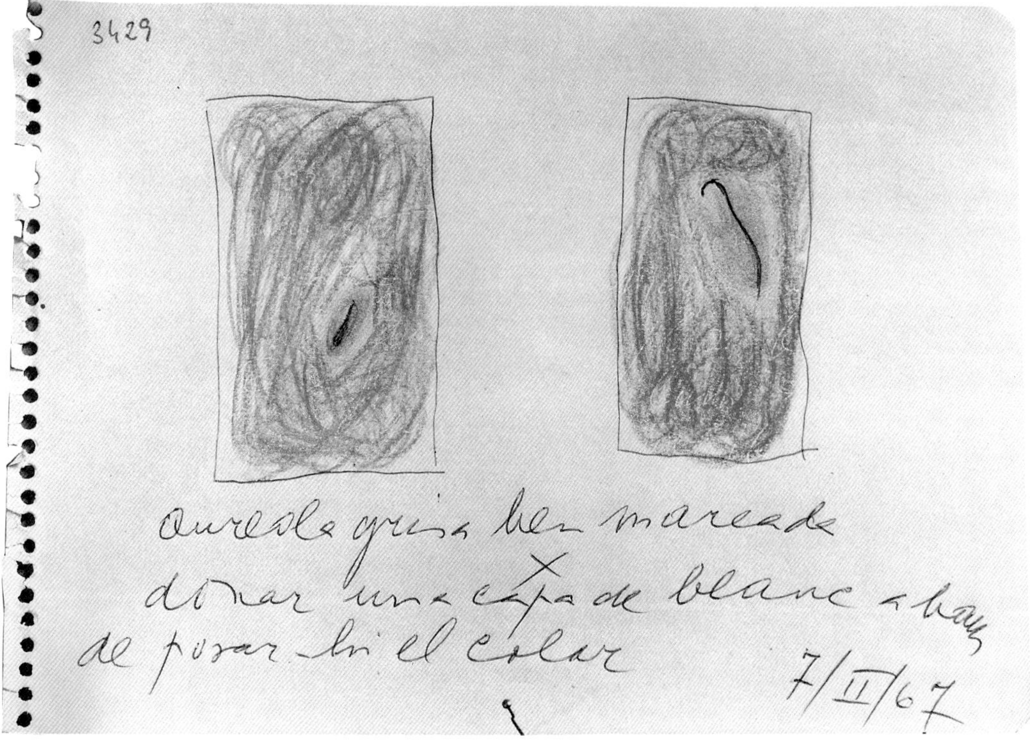

129. Studies for painting, 7 February 1967

1970s

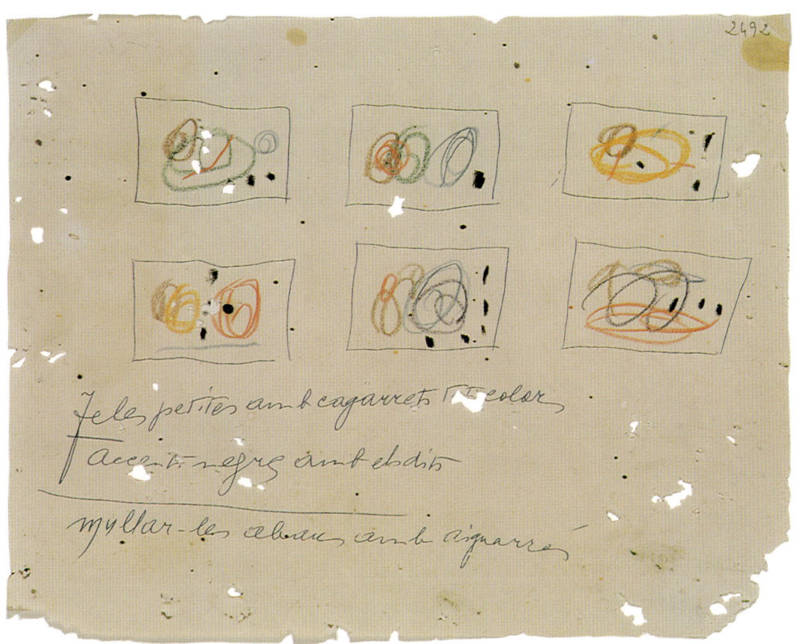

130. Studies, ca. 1971

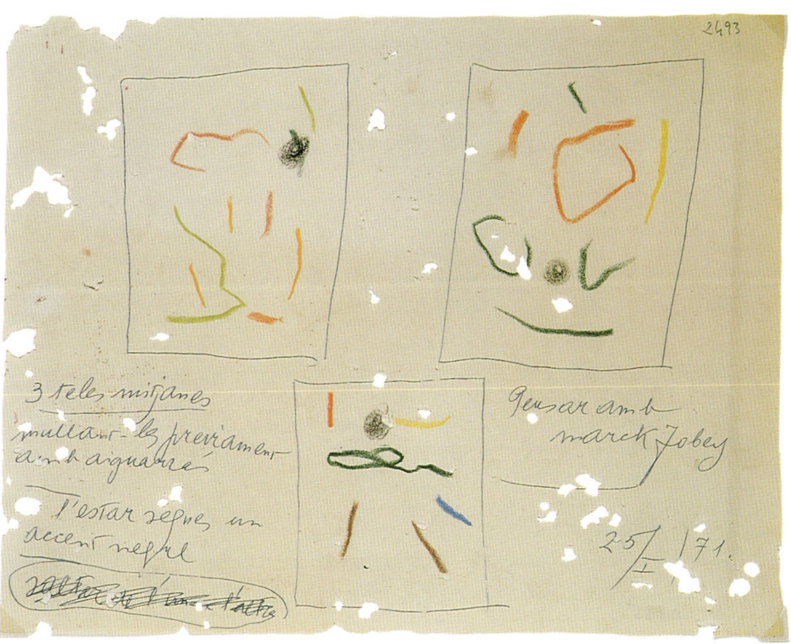

131. Studies, 25 January 1971

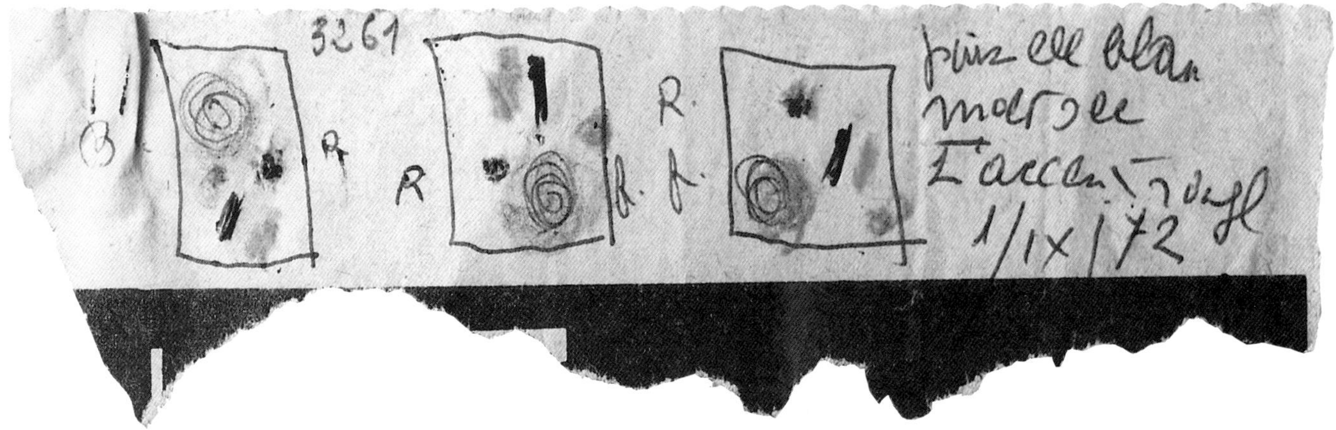

132. Study for *Red Accent*, 1 September 1972

135. *Landscape*, 1973

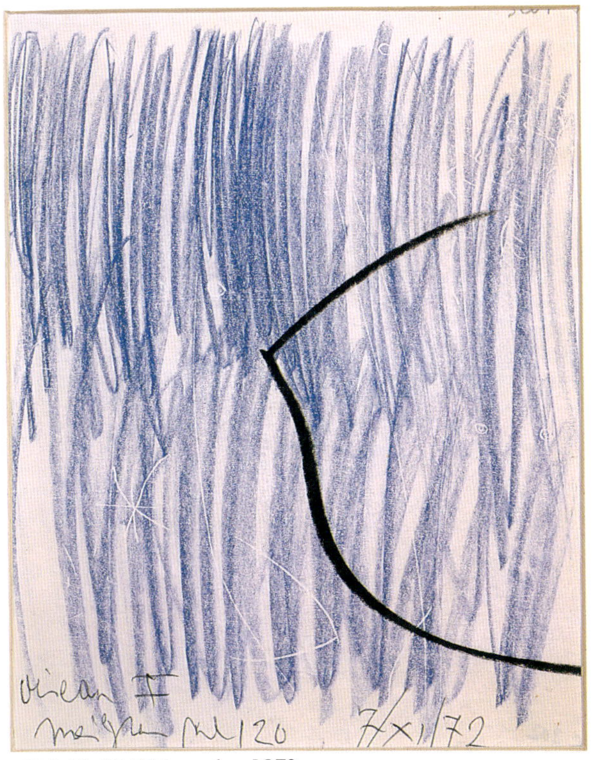

133. *Bird I*, 7 November 1972

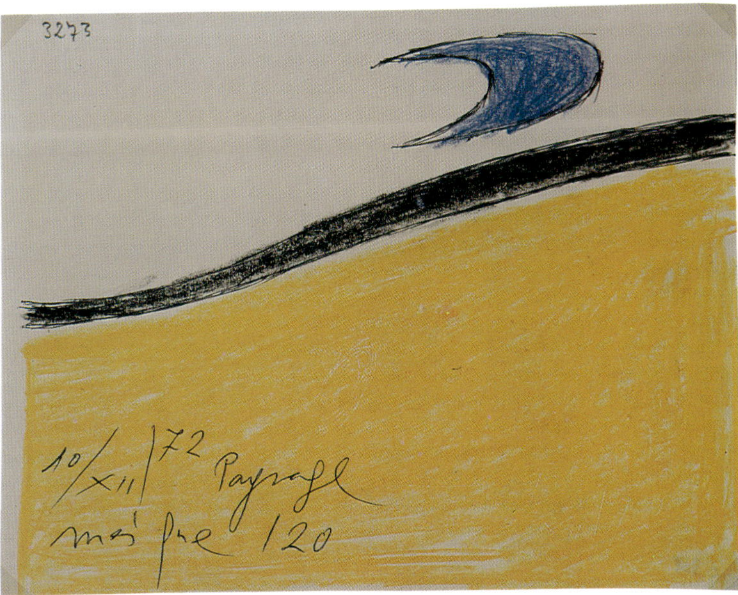

134. *Landscape*, 10 December 1972

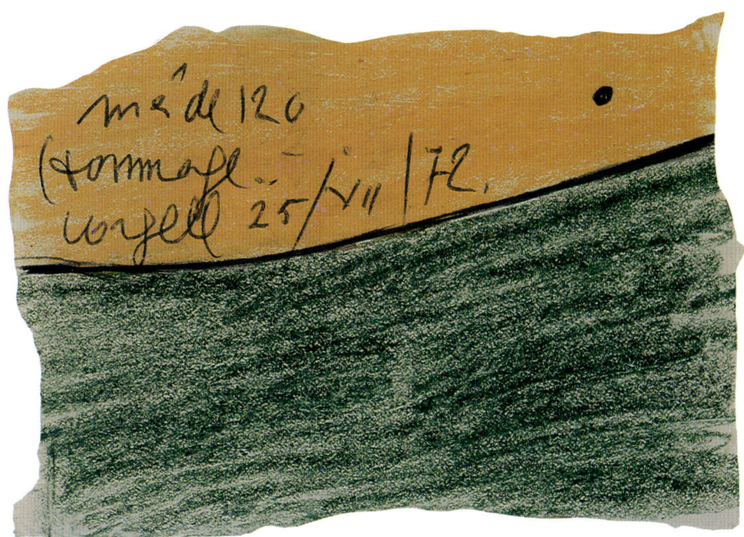

136. *Landscape: Homage to Urgell*, 25 December 1972

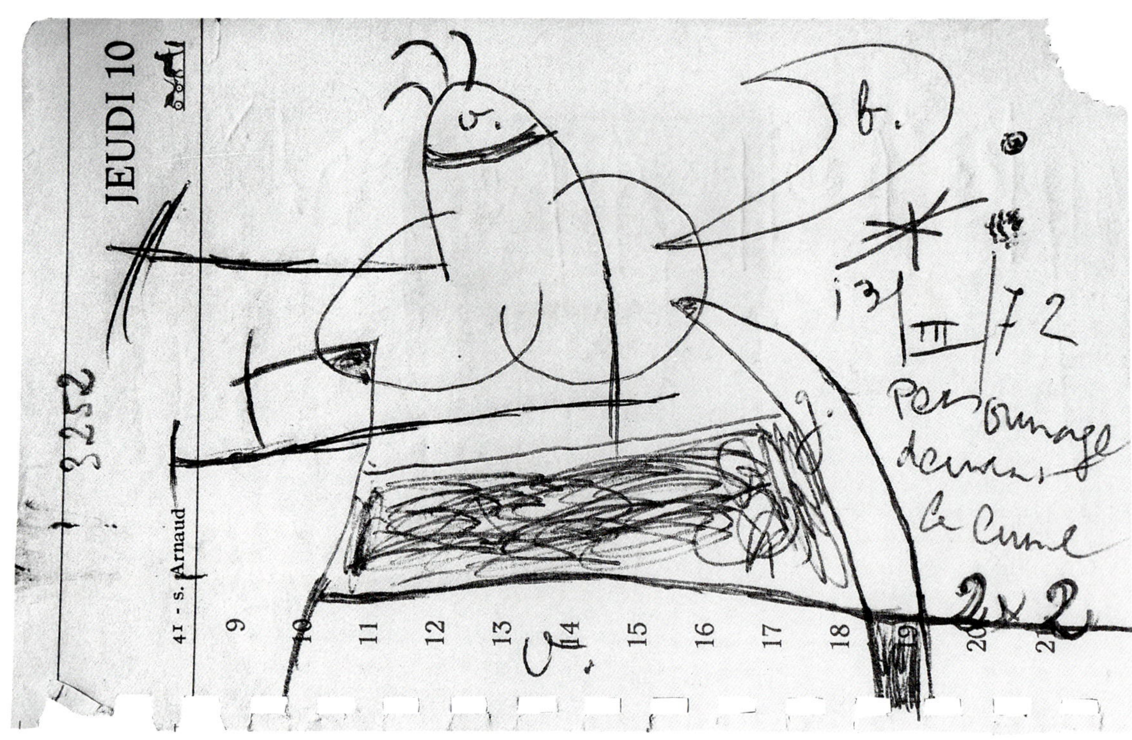

137. *Person in Front of the Moon*, 13 March 1972

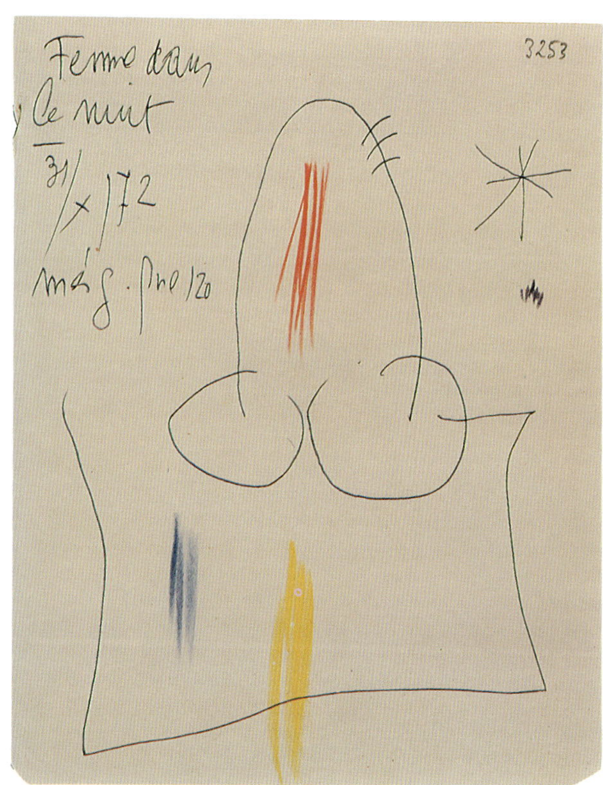

138. *Woman in the Night*, 31 October 1972

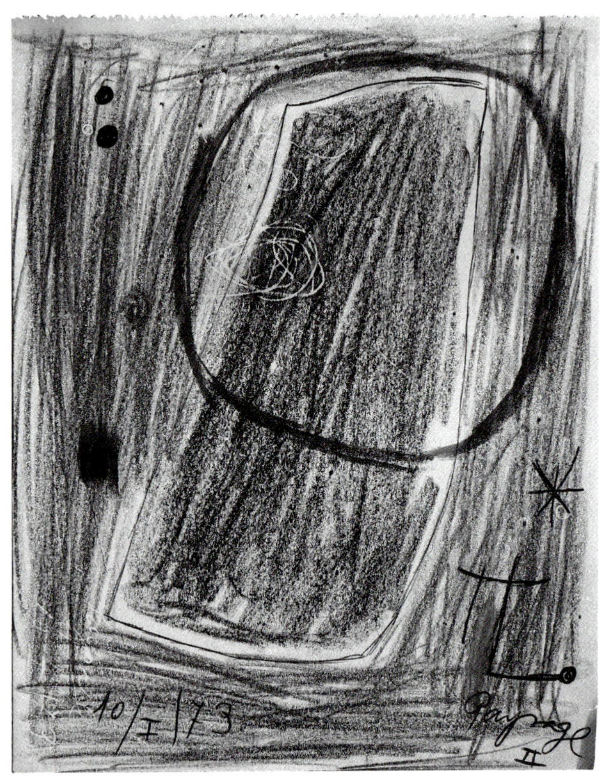

139. *Landscape II*, 10 January 1973

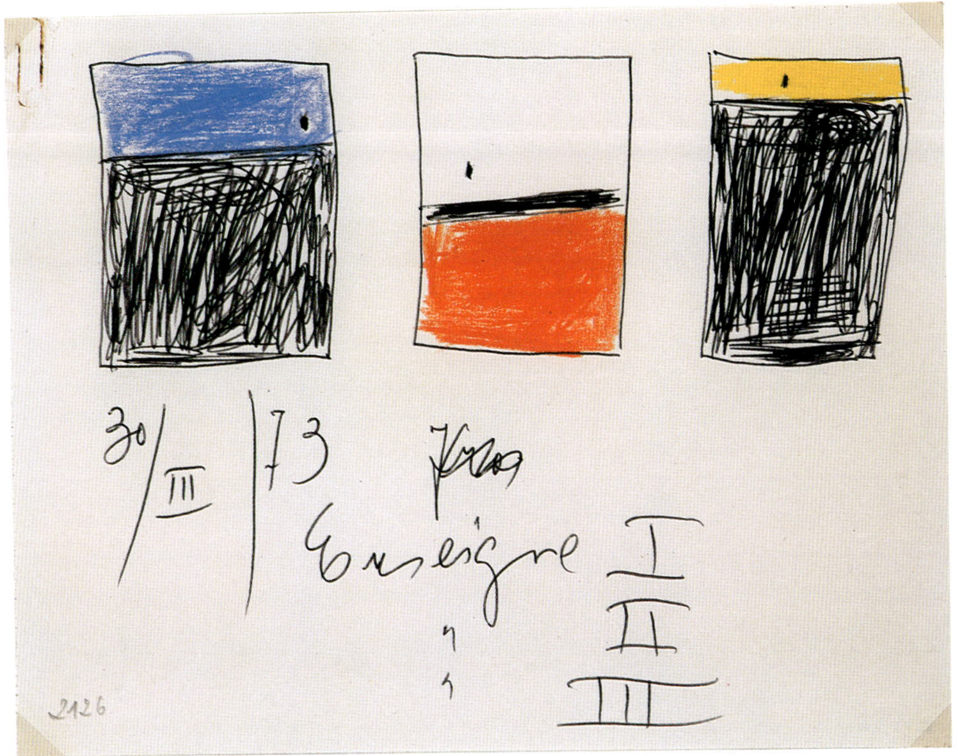

140. Studies for *Sign I, II, III*, 30 March 1973

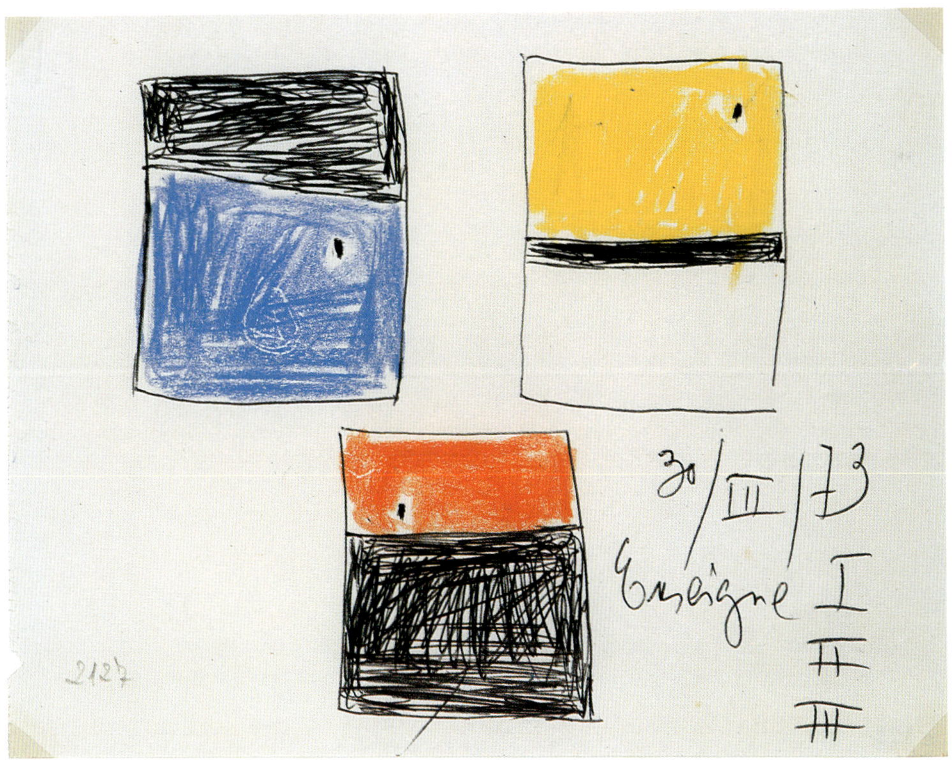

141. Studies for *Sign I, II, III*, 30 March 1973

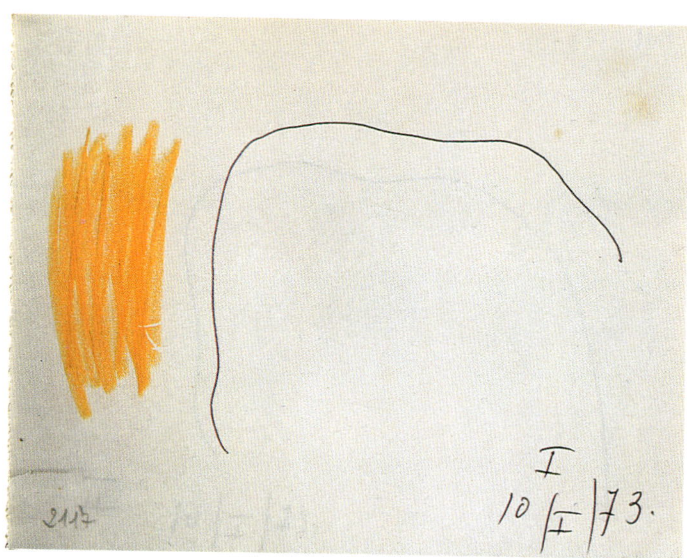

142. Study for *The Hope of the Condemned Man*, 10 January 1973

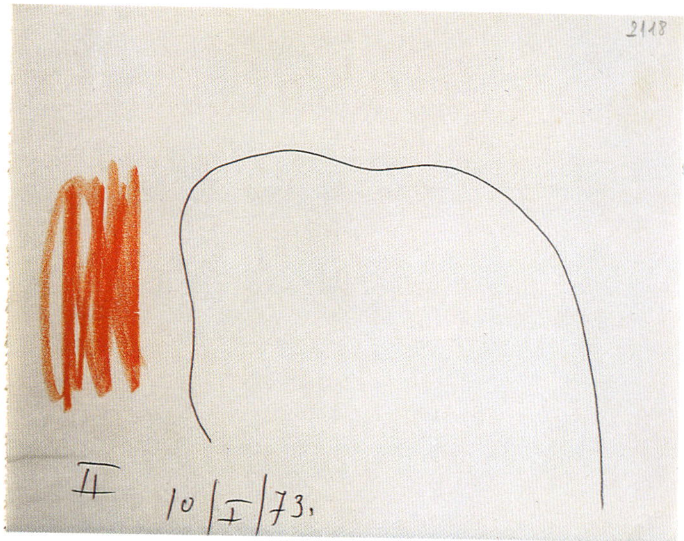

143. Study for *The Hope of the Condemned Man*, 10 January 1973

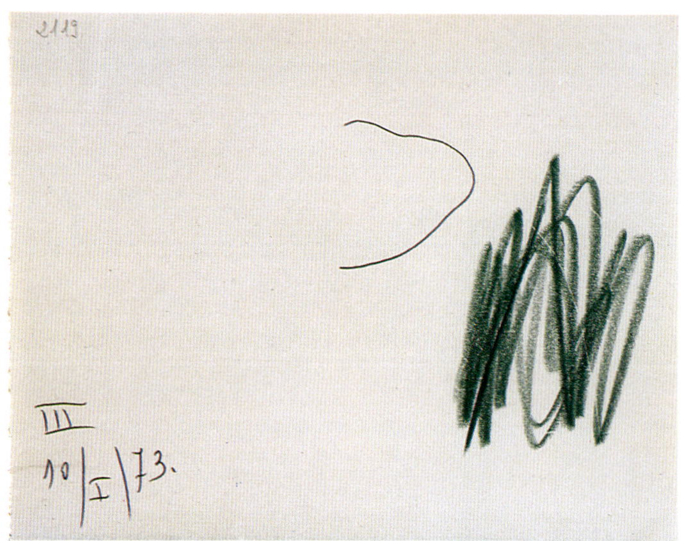

144. Study for *The Hope of the Condemned Man*, 10 January 1973

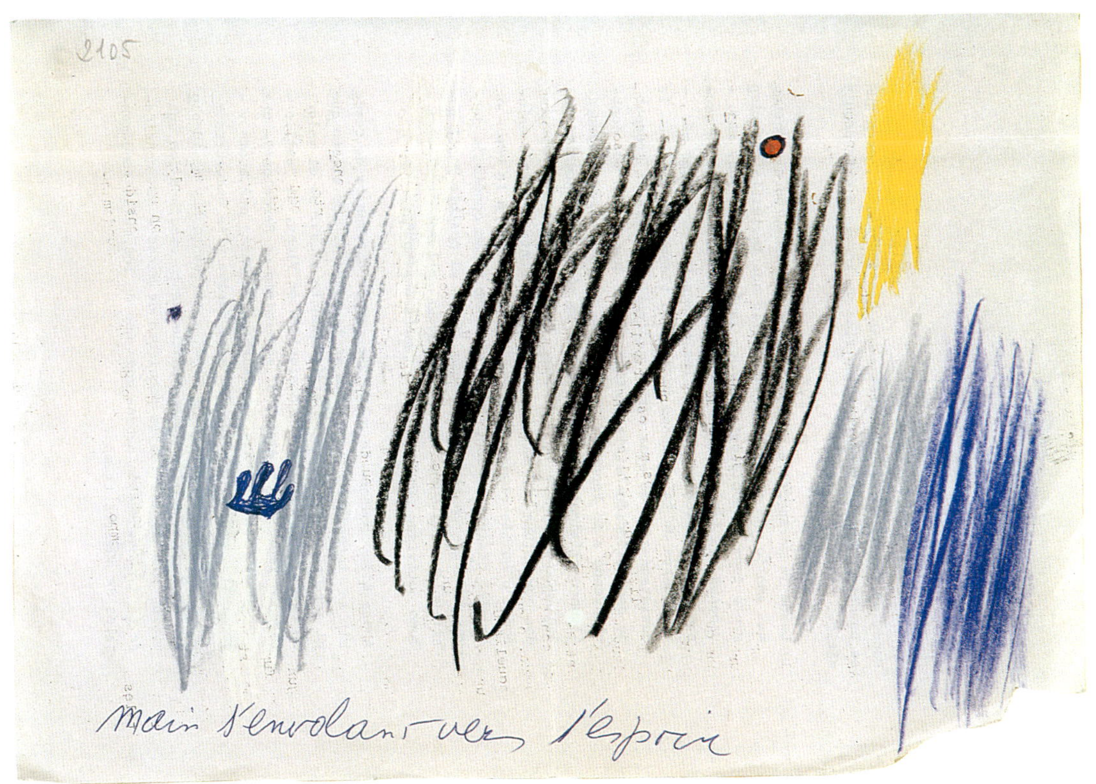

145. *Hand Flying Off Toward Hope*, n.d.

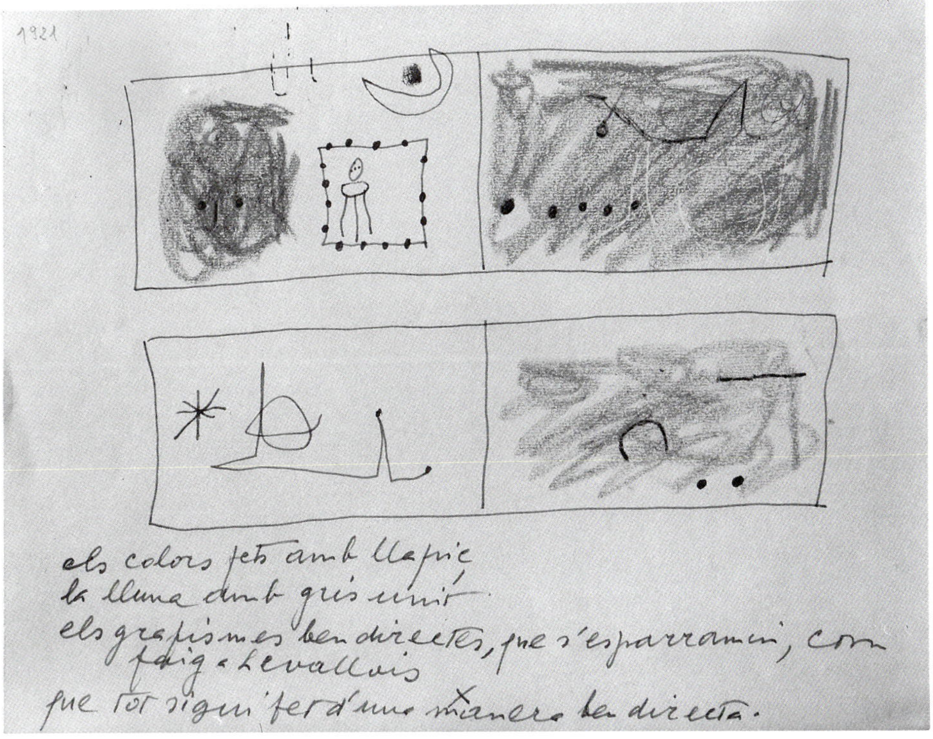

146. Studies for a series, ca. 1973

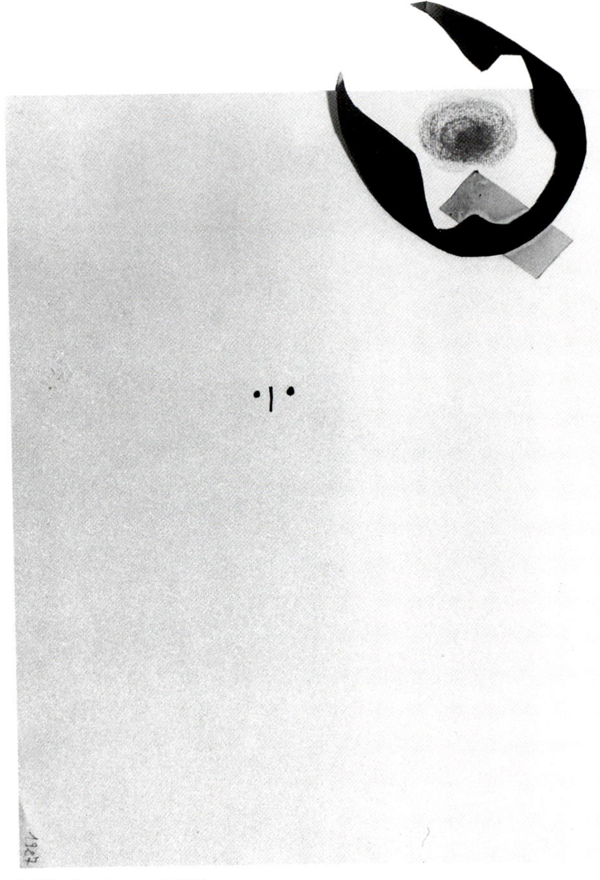

147. Study, ca. 1973

148. Study, ca. 1973

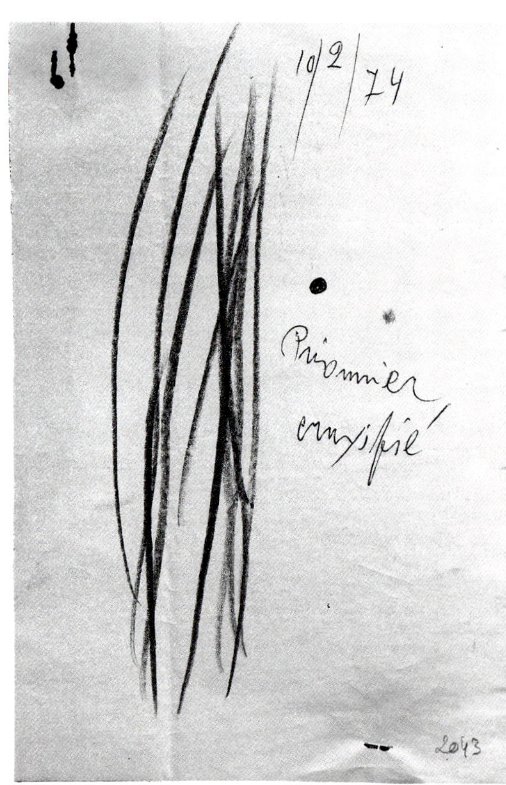

149. *The Crucified Prisoner*, 10 February 1974

Trustees

Mrs. Brooke Blake
Co-Chairman

Christian Frederiksen
Co-Chairman

Donald M. Cox
President

Roger Mandle
Chairman of the Executive Committee

Tom L. Freudenheim
Vice President

Irvin L. Levy
Vice President

Joseph F. McCann
Vice President

Marena G. Morrisey
Vice President

Mrs. Donald A. Petrie
Vice President

Thomas K. Seligman
Vice President

John W. Straus
Vice President

Dr. Evan H. Turner
Vice President

Gilbert S. Edelson
Secretary

John M. Cranor, III
Treasurer

Mrs. James W. Alsdorf
Thomas N. Armstrong
Vera Blinken
J. Carter Brown
Robert T. Buck
Mrs. Carroll L. Cartwright
George M. Cheston
Ralph T. Coe
Mrs. John D. Coffin
Mrs. Catherine G. Curran
Hugh M. Davies
Mrs. Kenneth N. Dayton
Philippe de Montebello
Professor David C. Driskell
Edward E. Elson
Arthur D. Emil
Stephanie French
John H. Hauberg
Lee Hills
Robert K. Hoffman
Eunice W. Johnson
Janet Kardon
Peter Kimmelman
Lyndel King
Gilbert H. Kinney
Richard Koshalek
Hilva Landsman
Richard S. Lane
Dr. Thomas W. Leavitt
William S. Lieberman
Mrs. Robert E. Linton
Peter C. Marzio
Mrs. Frederick R. Mayer
Cheryl McClenney-Brooker
Thomas E. McDonnell
Robert M. Meltzer
N. Richard Miller
Barbara Babcock Millhouse
Elinor Bunin Munroe
George W. Neubert
Mrs. Peter Roussel Norman
Mrs. John W. O'Boyle
Richard E. Oldenburg
Harry S. Parker, III
Earl A. Powell, III
Mrs. Joseph Pulitzer, Jr.
Mrs. Judith Rothschild
Mrs. Rudolph B. Schulhof
Alan Shestack
David M. Solinger
David W. Steadman
David P. Tunick
Mrs. George W. Ullman
James M. Walton
Mrs. Robert C. Warren
Mrs. Paul L. Wattis
Stephen E. Weil
James N. Wood
Mrs. Bagley Wright

Honorary Trustees

Mrs. Jacob M. Kaplan
President Emerita

Roy R. Neuberger
President Emeritus

John Walker

National Patrons

Mr. & Mrs. James W. Alsdorf
Mrs. Sharon Bender
Mr. & Mrs. Winslow W. Bennett
Mrs. Edwin A. Bergman
Mrs. George F. Berlinger
Mr. & Mrs. Charles M. Best
Mr. & Mrs. Van-Lear Black III
Mrs. Brooke Blake
Mr. & Mrs. Leonard Block
Mr. & Mrs. Robert H. Bloom
Mrs. Donald J. Blum
Mr. & Mrs. Duncan E. Boeckman
Mrs. Leo Brady
Mr. & Mrs. Eli Broad
Mr. & Mrs. R. E. Brooker
Mary Griggs Burke
Mr. & Mrs. Peter M. Butler
Mr. & Mrs. Carroll L. Cartwright
Mr. & Mrs. Norman U. Cohn
Mr. & Mrs. McCauley Conner
Mrs. Gardner Cowles
Mr. & Mrs. Donald M. Cox
Mr. Edwin L. Cox
Mr. & Mrs. Earle M. Craig, Jr.
Mr. & Mrs. James F. Crumpacker
Mrs. Catherine G. Curran
Mr. & Mrs. Eugene A. Davidson
Mr. David L. Davies
Dr. & Mrs. David R. Davis
Mrs. Julius E. Davis
Mr. & Mrs. Walter Davis
Mr. & Mrs. Kenneth N. Dayton
Mr. & Mrs. Robert Henry Dedman
Mrs. John deMenil
Mr. & Mrs. Charles M. Diker
Mr. & Mrs. C. Douglas Dillon
The Herbert & Junia Doan Foundation
Mr. & Mrs. W. John Driscoll
Mr. & Mrs. Gilbert S. Edelson
Mr. & Mrs. Maurits E. Edersheim
Mr. William S. Ehrlich
Mr. & Mrs. Edward E. Elson
Mr. & Mrs. Arthur D. Emil
Madeleine Feher
Mr. & Mrs. David Fogelson
Mr. Leo S. Guthman
Mr. & Mrs. John H. Hauberg
Mrs. Wellington S. Henderson
Mr. & Mrs. Henry L. Hillman, Jr.
Mr. & Mrs. A. Barry Hirschfeld
Mr. & Mrs. Theodore S. Hochstim
Ronna & Eric Hoffman
William J. Hokin
Jan & James L. Holland
Mrs. Eunice W. Johnson
Mrs. Samuel K. Ketcham
Mr. & Mrs. Peter Kimmelman
Mr. & Mrs. Gilbert H. Kinney
Mr. & Mrs. C. Calvert Knudsen
Mr. & Mrs. Robert P. Kogod
Mr. & Mrs. Oscar Kolin
Mr. & Mrs. Anthony M. Lamport
Mr. & Mrs. A. R. Landsman
Mr. & Mrs. Richard S. Lane
Natalie Ann Lansburgh
Mr. & Mrs. Leonard A. Lauder
Mr. & Mrs. Edward H. Leede
Mr. & Mrs. Albert Levinson
Mr. & Mrs. Irvin L. Levy
Ellen Liman
Mr. & Mrs. Joseph Linhart
Mr. & Mrs. Robert E. Linton
Mr. & Mrs. David B. Magee
Mr. & Mrs. James H. Manges
Mr. & Mrs. Melvin Mark, Jr.
Mr. & Mrs. Irving Mathews
Mr. & Mrs. Allan M. May
Mr. & Mrs. Frederick R. Mayer
Mrs. Robert B. Mayer
Mrs. Walter Maynard, Jr.
Roderick A. McManigal
Mr. & Mrs. Paul Mellon
Robert & Meryl Meltzer
Mr. & Mrs. William D. Miller
Mr. & Mrs. Ellison C. Morgan
Mr. & Mrs. Roy R. Neuberger
Mrs. Peter Roussel Norman
Mrs. John W. O'Boyle
Mr. & Mrs. William B. O'Boyle
Mr. & Mrs. Peter O'Donnell, Jr.
Mr. & Mrs. George O'Leary
Mr. & Mrs. Dean Papé
Mr. & Mrs. Robert L. Peterson
Mr. & Mrs. Donald A. Petrie
Mr. & Mrs. Nicholas R. Petry
Mr. & Mrs. Charles I. Petschek
Barbara Pfouts
Barbara & Max Pine
Mrs. Sue R. Pittman
Mr. & Mrs. John W. Pitts
Mr. & Mrs. Lawrence S. Pollock, Jr.

Mr. & Mrs. Peter O. Price
Mr. & Mrs. Jerome Pustilnik
Francoise & Harvey Rambach
Mr. & Mrs. Walter S. Rosenberry III
Mr. & Mrs. Milton F. Rosenthal
Selma & Lawrence Ruben
Dr. & Mrs. Raymond R. Sackler
Mr. & Mrs. Douglas R. Scheumann
Mr. & Mrs. Mort Schrader
Mr. & Mrs. Rudolph B. Schulhof
The Rev. & Mrs. Alfred R. Shands III
Mr. & Mrs. George A. Shutt
Mr. & Mrs. Herbert M. Singer
Barbara Slifka
Mrs. Lawrence M. C. Smith
Mr. & Mrs. David M. Solinger
Mr. & Mrs. Moise S. Steeg, Jr.
Ann C. Stephens
Mr. & Mrs. James G. Stevens
Mr. & Mrs. W. T. C. Stevens
Mr. & Mrs. John W. Straus
Mrs. Norman Tishman
Mrs. George W. Ullman
Mr. & Mrs. Michael J. Waldman
Mr. & Mrs. Robert C. Warren
Mr. & Mrs. John R. Watson
Mrs. Paul L. Wattis
Mrs. Nancy Brown Wellin
Dr. & Mrs. William T. Weyerhaeuser
Mr. & Mrs. Dave H. Williams
Enid Silver Winslow
Mr. & Mrs. Howard Wolf
Mr. & Mrs. Bagley Wright
Mr. & Mrs. Howard S. Wright
Mr. & Mrs. T. Evans Wyckoff

Corporate and Foundation Supporters

Alcoa Foundation
Altos Computer Systems
American Airlines
American Can Company Foundation
American Express
AT&T Foundation
Atlantic Richfield Foundation
The Bank of New York
The James H. Barry Printing Company
BellSouth Corporation
The Brown Foundation
CBS, Inc.
Champion International
Chevron U.S.A. Inc.
CIBA-GEIGY Corporation
Citicorp Industrial Credit
Club DV8, Inc.
Coca-Cola Foundation
Compton Foundation, Inc.
Consolidated Edison Company of New York
Continental Airlines
Dart & Kraft
Dayton Hudson Foundation
DeWitt Wallace Fund, Inc.
The Dillon Fund
Donaldson Lufkin & Jenrette
Drexel Burnham Lambert
Emery Worldwide
Exxon Corporation
The Eugene and Estelle Ferkauf Foundation
Ford Motor Company Fund
Greyhound Exhibitgroup, Inc.
Grow Group, Inc.
Henry J. and Drue E. Heinz Foundation
Huntington T. Block Insurance
IBM
The J.M. Kaplan Fund
Knight Foundation
Samuel H. Kress Foundation
Lannan Foundation
The Henry Luce Foundation
Lufthansa German Airlines
Manufacturers Hanover Trust Company
The Andrew W. Mellon Foundation
Mercedes-Benz of North America
Metropolitan Life Foundation
Michael Mabry Design
The Mitsui Foundation, Inc.
Mobil Foundation, Inc.
The Mabel Pew Myrin Trust
New York Telephone
The New York Times Company
North American Van Lines, Inc.
J.C. Penney Company
PepsiCo
Pepsi-Cola Company
Pfizer Foundation
Philip Morris Companies
Philips Petroleum Foundation
Profit Freight Systems
Republic National Bank of New York
Reynolds Aluminum
R.J. Reynolds Industries, Inc.
The Rouse Company
Salomon Inc.
Security Pacific Foundation
Sherman Fairchild Foundation
L.J. and Mary C. Skaggs Foundation
The Soros Foundation
Syntex Corporation
Tandy Corporation/Radio Shack
Time Inc.
Times Mirror Company
Touche Ross & Company
United Technologies
Ward Howell International
The Xerox Foundation